THE COMPLETE BOOK OF
PREDICTIONS

The Diagram Group is the world-famous team of writers, researchers, editors and designers who produced *Rules of the Game, Sports Comparisons* and several other highly acclaimed visual reference books.

THE COMPLETE BOOK OF
PREDICTIONS

by the Diagram Group

1996
INDEX

This edition printed 1996
For Index,
    Unit 1
    Garrard Way
    Kettering NN16 8TD

Copyright © Diagram Visual Information Limited 1983

ISBN 19 000 32554

Printed and bound in Finland by WSOY

THE DIAGRAM GROUP

Editor	Susan Bosanko
Contributors	Jan Dalley
	David Harding
	Ruth Midgley
Art director	Mark Evans
Artists	Neil Copleston
	Brian Hewson
	Joseph Robinson
	Graham Rosewarne
	Jerry Watkiss
Art assistant	Jenny Hoffman

Contributing consultants Alla (palmistry)
Nerys Dee (cartomancy)
Patricia Marne (graphology)
J. Maya Pilkington (astrology)
Denis Price (tarot)

The authors and publishers wish to thank:
Routledge and Kegan Paul, and Princeton University Press
for permission to quote from the Richard Wilhelm
translation of the *I Ching*;
Matt Geffin of Mysteries the Psychic Shop.

Foreword

The Complete Book of Predictions is a fascinating guide to more than 100 ways in which you can try and foretell the future. It brings together the methods of fortune tellers from past and present, east and west, and explains how and why these forms of divination have been considered worthy of serious study.

More importantly, **The Complete Book of Predictions** explains step-by-step the basic techniques and principles of the enormous variety of methods of predicting in use today. The familiar Diagram Group style, integrating hundreds of illustrations and diagrams with a clear explanatory text, makes it possible for this wealth of information to be easily assimilated and put into practice at all levels, from telling fortunes at parties to the beginning of serious studies in one of the major disciplines.

In compiling this book the writers, artists, and editors of the Diagram Group have been joined by experienced practitioners from all the major fields of character analysis and divination. **The Complete Book of Predictions** includes their sample readings and interpretations based on the lives and questions of real people – an invaluable guide to the most difficult aspect of divination, integrating the separate facets of the reading into a complete picture.

Some people take predicting the future seriously; others regard it as frivolous amusement. But even the most sceptical can be secretly susceptible, and you should remember this when making your predictions. Intuition, discretion, and sympathy are the hallmarks of good fortune tellers, plus an awareness of their own fallibility. Predictions of the future may give us an indication of future trends in our lives; it is up to us what we make of the opportunities we are offered.

Contents

IL BAGATTEL.

Part 1 FORTUNES IN YOURSELF

1 A self-portrait by the seventeenth-century Dutch painter Teniers showing the artist and his wife with a gypsy palmist.
2 An illustration from a seventeenth-century treatise on palmistry that ascribed a sign of the zodiac to each phalange of the fingers.
3 An illustration from another seventeenth-century book on palmistry shows patterns on the fingertips – this is believed to be the earliest mention of fingerprints in palmistry.
4 A chart of Napoleon's hand by his personal palmist, Marie-Anne le Normand.
5 The handprint of the famous World War 1 spy, Mata Hari.
6 A nineteenth-century phrenological chart, entitled *A Symbolical Head Illustrating the Natural Language of the Faculties*.
7 To graphologists, signatures offer the most revealing clues to character. Compare, for example, these signatures of Napoleon, George Washington, Charles Darwin, Charles Dickens, Thomas Edison, Isaac Newton, and William Shakespeare.

Palmistry 1

Palmistry is a misleading name, for a great deal more than the palm of the hand is considered in this type of prediction. The experts prefer more resonantly impressive terms like "chirognomy," "chirology," or even "chiromancy," from the Greek word *cheir*, meaning hand. But whatever you choose to call it, it remains a process rooted in the belief that you literally hold your future in your hands.

People have always been fascinated by the markings on their hands – palm prints have even been discovered in Stone Age cave paintings. Although no physical evidence exists to support their theories, some practitioners have claimed that the origins of palmistry lie far back with the ancient Egyptians, Chaldeans, Sumerians, or Babylonians. It seems likely that palmistry began in the east and spread to the west, perhaps carried by the Romany peoples. The earliest verifiable references to the art seem to be in Indian literature of the Vedic period (c.2000BC) in the east, and in the works of Aristotle (384–322BC) in the west – but both these bear witness to a rich history of oral tradition on the subject. Palmistry has had a checkered history: in the seventeenth century it was taught at the universities of Leipzig and Halle in Germany, while at

the same time it was being outlawed in England as a form of witchcraft.

But why read hands? There are thousands of nerve endings in your hands which are in direct contact with your brain, and so there is a constant two-way traffic of impulses along the nerves. Because of this traffic, the lines and marks on your hands are supposed to show a reflection of your personality, to mirror your physical and emotional condition. Palmists have always known this intuitively: today's scientists are finding evidence to support the theory, and some geneticists and psychiatrists already use hand analysis to assist them in the diagnosis of a variety of physical and mental illnesses.

The proper place to begin both the study of palmistry and any specific reading is with the whole hand. Or, in fact, both hands, since your left hand is said to indicate the potentialities that you were born with, and your right hand to reveal your individual nature as it is now, and what its future may be – unless you are left-handed, when the reverse applies. The differences can be usefully revealing of the directions the subject has taken through life, and of the effect of the years on the subject.

Handprints

There is much to be said for reading a hand from a print, rather than the hand itself. You will be in no danger of being affected by the subject's possible reactions to your comments as you build up the reading. And if you keep the prints safely, some years later you can determine for yourself whether the hands have changed in any of their details – and if so, what those changes may indicate.

The easiest way to produce a good print is with a small roller. Squeeze out some ink (water-based for easy

removal) onto a smooth surface, and pass the roller through it several times (**a**). Then use the roller to transfer a thin film of ink as evenly as possible to all the surfaces of the palm (**b**). Make the print (**c**) by pressing the subject's hand carefully but firmly onto a sheet of paper, making sure that you get a good impression of the center of the palm as well as the fingers and thumb – a rubber pad under the paper will be helpful. Lift the hand away carefully, making sure that you do not blur the print (**d**).

The cardinal rule in palmistry, as in all the major forms of fortune telling, is that an overall view is essential. You cannot hope to achieve any certain picture of your subject's character and potential from only the shape of the hand, or from any other isolated detail. You must wait until all the clues have been gathered and see then how one factor balances or compensates for another, how different elements are reinforced, others canceled out, and so on.

This paramount rule partly explains why good palmists rarely make sweeping, unequivocal statements along the lines of "you will be rich this time next year" or "you have only six months to live." There are too many factors in a subject as broad and complex as palmistry. They cannot be interpreted simply, in the way of the omens of folk belief, or the flat assertions of newspaper horoscopes. What you achieve, when all the details are collated, is a probable pattern, a set of tendencies, with very little in it of fixed, unavoidable fate. Every reading, like every human being, is a mixture of good and bad.

There are some further points you should remember when making your readings. First, be careful. Real hands seldom show marks as clearly as do the illustrations in this book, and you will need to have studied a great many hands before you can be completely confident in your recognition of detail. Second, be open-minded. Don't leap to conclusions about the nature of a hand, for there is then the temptation to ignore other details, or subconsciously to twist their meaning, when they do not conform to your too-hasty interpretation. Let your reading build slowly, and accept all the contradictions, divergences, and inconsistencies.

Third, remember to correlate all the details into a complete, balanced picture before delivering your interpretation. Most people get along through life fairly well, with plenty of ups and downs, good times and bad, in general balancing each other out. Try to find a similar kind of balance in your readings.

And finally, consider the chirognomists' assertion that destiny as revealed in the hand is not fixed and predetermined. The lines and marks can change, it is said, over a period of time, as obviously can the fleshiness of the fingers and mounts. And so good or ill omens may in fact come and go.

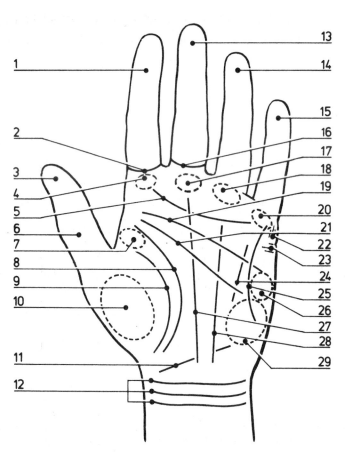

Map of the hand
1. Finger of Jupiter
2. Solomon's ring
3. Phalange of will
4. Mount of Jupiter
5. Girdle of Venus
6. Phalange of logic
7. Lower mount of Mars
8. Lifeline
9. Line of Mars
10. Mount of Venus
11. Via Lasciva
12. Rascettes
13. Finger of Saturn
14. Finger of Apollo
15. Finger of Mercury
16. Ring of Saturn
17. Mount of Saturn
18. Mount of Apollo
19. Heartline
20. Mount of Mercury
21. Headline
22. Child lines
23. Line of marriage
24. Hepatica
25. Line of intuition
26. Upper mount of Mars
27. Line of fate
28. Line of the sun
29. Mount of the moon

Palmistry 2

Traditionally, fortune tellers asserted that there were seven basic types of hand shape. And these seven revealed some equally traditional attitudes to society and its hierarchy – for at one end was the delicate, languid hand of the aristocrat, and at the other was the peasant's coarsened and work-hardened fist. But even so, there may be useful clues to be gained in your own readings from this old classification, and the seven types deserve to be briefly noted.

These days, however, palmists are more ready to admit that these seven rigid classifications are somewhat unrealistic. So modern palmists have refined their classification of hand shapes into only four basic types, which do tend more or less to occur in reality. They also keep a traditional flavor by relating them to the four elements of the ancient world – earth, fire, water, and air – which are linked in turn with corresponding character traits.

Whichever classification system you use, however, it will give you nothing more than a few initial hints, general pointers to start off your overall reading. Further pointers can be found in the size and texture of

TRADITIONAL HAND CLASSIFICATIONS

1 Elemental A thick, broad, short-fingered hand. A slow-thinker, perhaps with a crude, physical nature.

2 Square (or useful) A square palm, with broad and blunt fingers. A practical, conventional, unadaptable, unintellectual nature.

3 Spatulate A spade-shaped and straight-fingered hand. An ambitious and energetic nature, independent, erratic, not much given to intellect.

4 Philosophical Broad-palmed, with heavy joints on the fingers. A logical, cautious nature, thoughtful and introverted, analytic rather than fanciful.

5 Artistic (or conic) A long and flexible hand with tapering fingers. A sensitive, creative nature, more impulsive than methodical.

6 Idealistic (or psychic) An even longer and more delicate hand. A nature far removed from harsh reality, a dreamer, mystic, aesthete.

7 Mixed A necessary, if vague, category, since almost no-one fits precisely into just one of the foregoing six pigeonholes. Most people's hands combine two or more of the types mentioned, as do most people's natures.

your subject's hand. Someone whose hand is small in comparison to the rest of their build will think and act on a large scale, behaving decisively, and leaving the detail to others. Proportionately large hands indicate a thoughtful, patient mind and – surprising as it may seem – a skill with fine, delicate, detailed work.
A palm with a firm and elastic texture usually belongs to an optimistic, healthy person; a soft, flabby, and fleshy palm indicates sensuality and indolence; and a hard, dry, wooden palm a tense, chronic worrier.
Nearly all doctors inspect a patient's fingertips when

making an examination, as the nails give important indications of a person's state of health. And just as we usually accept that people who bite their nails tend to be tense and anxious, so the shape and color of the nails can give us hints to the character of their owner.
So, as you begin your reading, carefully consider the hand as a whole before going on to look in detail at the fingers, mounts, and lines. If you intend to work from a handprint, remember to take a good look at the whole hand as you make the print!

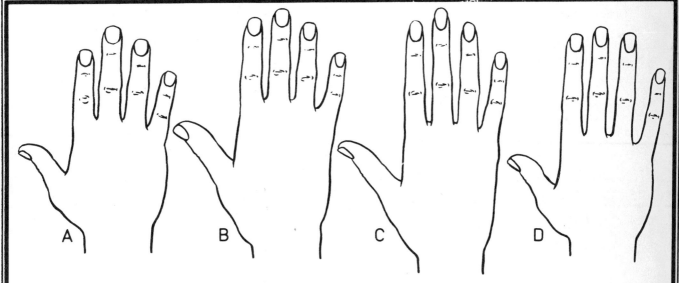

MODERN HAND CLASSIFICATIONS
A Practical A square palm with short fingers. An honest, hard-working, feet-on-the-ground person. Linked with the element of earth.
B Intuitive A long palm with short fingers. An energetic, restless, individualistic nature. Linked with the element of fire.

C Sensitive A long palm with long fingers. An imaginative, emotional nature, often moody or introverted. Linked with the element of water.
D Intellectual A square palm with long fingers. A clever, rational, articulate nature, aware and orderly (sometimes too orderly). Linked with the element of air.

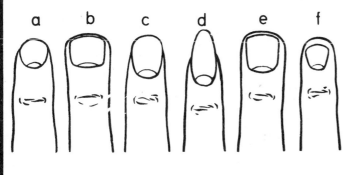

NAIL SHAPES
a   Short nails Energetic, curious, intuitive, logical.
b   Short nails, broader than they are long Critical and quick-tempered.
c   Broad, long nails, rounded at the tip A person of clear, sound judgment.
d   Long, almond-shaped nails A placid and easy-going person, a dreamer.
e   Very large, square nails Cold and selfish.
f   Wedge-shaped nails Over-sensitive.

NAIL COLOR
White Cold, conceited, and selfish.
Pale pink A warm and outgoing nature.
Red A violent temper.
Bluish Unhealthy.

Palmistry 3

Palmistry has its connections with astrology. The signs of the zodiac, for instance, divide into four groups of three that are linked with the four elements, as are the modern types of hand shapes. But the astrological connection becomes even more explicit with the names given to the fingers – names of Roman gods that are also in most cases the names of planets, and so impart some of the planetary qualities as the horoscope sees them.

The index finger is the finger of Jupiter – the king of the gods for the dominant finger. In this finger can be seen much of the person's outer, worldly tendencies – ambition, prospects for success, life energy.

The middle finger is the finger of Saturn, and if it is strong it reveals the presence of the saturnine qualities of character – a certain seriousness and melancholy. The third or ring finger is the finger of Apollo (astrologically, the sun), with which we move toward inner concerns. And the little finger is the finger of Mercury, revealing much about human relationships. Palmists look too at the shape of the fingers, their flexibility, and their position on the hand in relation to one another. They also read much into the separate segments or "phalanges." So, as always, you should remember to take the overall view. For example, in a square, smooth-jointed finger, the reflective qualities of

AREAS OF THE HAND
Palmists regard the hand as being divided into four main areas, each related to a particular facet of the personality.
A The inner active area, relating to close relationships and sexuality.
B The outer active area, relating to social attitudes and relationships with the outside world.
C The inner passive area, relating to the subconscious.
D The outer passive area, relating to energy and creative potential.

FLEXIBILITY AND BEND OF THE FINGERS
Stiff fingers A stiff person, unyielding, rigid, set in their ways, but also practically inclined.
Curved fingers, bending slightly toward the palm A prudent and acquisitive nature.
Curved and stiff fingers Fearful, cautious, narrow-minded, tenacious.
Supple fingers Attractive and unconventional, somewhat careless.
Curved fingers, bending away from the palm Someone who ignores rules and regulations, who is chatty and good company.
Backward curving and supple fingers An open mind, inquisitive, attractive.

FINGER SHAPES
Long Intelligent.
Short Impulsive, hasty, less intelligent.
Large Painstaking, slow-thinking.
Square (1) Thoughtful, cautious.
Spatulate (2) Energetic.
Waisted Considerate.
Tapered (3) Impulsive, artistic, punctilious.
Slender Introverted, an aesthetic nature.
Thick and short Selfish.
Crooked Malicious, easily irritated.
Puffy Hedonistic.
Smooth joints (4) Quick-thinking, impulsive.
Knotty joints (5) Deep-thinking, dignified.
Large joints Methodical, rational.

the square shape will balance the impulsive nature shown by the smooth joints, and indicate a person of good intuition. But in a pointed, smooth-jointed finger we have a double indication of impulsiveness – quite possibly a person who never looks before they leap. For many palmists, the thumb is almost as important to a reading as all the fingers put together. Some Hindu palmists are known to restrict their reading to the thumb alone, and to ignore the rest of the hand! The thumb bears no god's name (although it is sometimes linked with the first house of the horoscope) but it is a key indicator of the level of vitality or life energy. The larger the thumb, the more vital and powerful the

personality, especially when linked with a strong index finger.

The thumb's phalanges each have their traditional associations – the first (bearing the nail) with the will, the second with logic. Like the fingers, the thumb properly has three phalanges, but the third is the pad of flesh that frames one side of the palm. This is traditionally put together with the other similarly prominent pads on the hand, which are known as mounts.

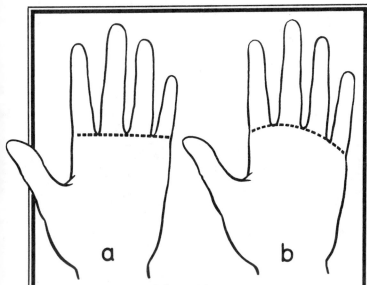

THE SET OF THE FINGERS
The second finger is never set low, but decides the level for the other fingers.
Even set (a) A person with a positive nature and plenty of common sense, one who will do well in life.
Uneven set (b) The most common set: life will be more of a battle, full of ups and downs.
Low set first finger A shy, unassertive person, who inwardly feels superior to everyone else.
Low set third finger A person frustrated in career matters, one who has had to take a job contrary to real talents and inclinations.
Low set fourth finger Nothing comes easily, and this person will have to struggle hard to succeed.

HAND SPAN
Fingers held stiffly together Cautious, suspicious, and unsociable.
Evenly spaced fingers A well-balanced mind, likely to be successful in any field.
Well-separated fingers Independent and freedom-loving.
Wide gap between all fingers Frank, open, and trusting – an almost child-like nature.
Widest space between thumb and first finger Outgoing, a generous disposition.
Widest space between first and second fingers Not easily influenced by others, independent in thought and action.
Widest space between second and third fingers Free from anxieties for the future, light-hearted.
Widest space between third and fourth fingers (I) An independent and original thinker
Fourth finger very separated from the other fingers (II) Difficulties in personal relationships, isolated and alienated.

Palmistry 4

THUMB

Long A good leader, clear-minded, willpower tempered by good judgment.

Very long Tyrannical, despotic, determined to get own way.

Short Impressionable, indecisive, with the heart ruling the head.

Large Capable and forceful.

Short and thick Obstinate.

Small and weak Lacking in energy and willpower.

Straight and stiff Reserved, loyal, reliable, cautious, stubborn.

Flexible A flexible nature, easy-going, generous, tolerant, tends to be extravagant.

Smooth joints Full of vitality.

Knotty joints Energy comes in erratic bursts.

High set Acquisitive, mean.

Low set (1) Courageous, versatile.

Lies close to palm (2) Not quite honest.

❹ THE FIRST, INDEX, OR FORE FINGER: JUPITER

Top level with bottom of nail on second finger A leader, a person with the power to govern.

Top below bottom of nail on second finger Timid, feels inferior, avoids responsibility.

Same length as, or longer than, second finger (A) A dictator, self-centered, one determined to make others obey.

Curved in a bow toward second finger Indicates acquisitiveness. This can range from collecting as a hobby if the curve is slight to hoarding and miserliness if the curve is pronounced.

Top phalange bending toward second finger Persistent, stubborn.

Normal length, but shorter than third finger (B) A good organizer, capable of taking charge, but preferring to work in partnership.

Same length as third finger Well-balanced and self-assured.

Longer than third finger Proud, ambitious, longing for power.

Long and smooth Good prospects in work, business, and in the outside world in general.

Short Lacks stamina and confidence.

Very short Self-effacing, frightened of the outside world.

Very thick Dogged and determined.

Very thin A person who will succeed in imagination but not in reality.

Crooked Unscrupulous, determined to get their own way regardless of the consequences.

Phalanges marked with deep straight vertical lines These are known as the "tired lines." They indicate overwork and fatigue.

❺ THE SECOND OR MIDDLE FINGER: SATURN

Straight, and in good proportion to the other fingers A prudent and sensible person, with good concentration and an ability to plan ahead, but who needs privacy.

Long, strong, and heavy Serious and thoughtful, likely to have a hard and difficult life.

Same length as first and third fingers (C) Irresponsible.

Slightly longer than first and third fingers Dry, cool, socially withdrawn.

Very long (D) Morbid, melancholic, pedantic.

Short Intuitive, unintellectual.

Middle phalange longest Green-fingered, loves the country.

Curved Shows the inclination to the inner or the outer side of life, depending on the direction of the curve.

Crooked Full of self pity.

Bent, hidden under fingers Unhappy and self-destructive.
Forming clear right angle to palm when outstretched A strong sense of justice.
Forming an angle greater than a right angle Too tender-hearted.

PHALANGES OF THE THUMB
Equal length (a) Well-balanced personality.
Full thumb – first and second of fairly even width (b) Blunt, outspoken.
Broad and sturdy first Plenty of stamina and well-directed energy.
First longer than second Energy uncontrolled by logic.
Very tapered first Lacks stamina and vitality.
Clubbed first (c) Violent, full of uncontrolled energy. Traditionally the "murderer's thumb."
Broad and sturdy second Logical, thoughtful, thinks before acting.
Second longer than first Inhibited, feels restricted.
Waisted second (d) Quick-thinking, tactful, impulsive, can be evasive.

⊙ THE THIRD OR RING FINGER: APOLLO
Strong and smooth Emotionally balanced.
Smooth, with smooth joints Creative.
Long Conceited, longing for fame, wanting to be in the limelight – a good sign for those with careers in show business or advertising.
Very long Introverted.
Short (E) Shy, lacks emotional control.
Third phalange longest Desires money and luxury.
Bending toward second finger Anxiety-ridden, always on the defensive.
Second and third fingers bending together (F) Secretive.
Nail phalange bending toward second finger Afflictions of the heart – these may be emotional or physical.
Bending or drooping toward palm when hand is relaxed Has difficulty in coming to terms with the inner or intuitive aspects of the personality.
Crooked or otherwise distorted, or out of proportion to the rest of the hand Emotional difficulties.

☿ THE FOURTH OR LITTLE FINGER: MERCURY
Reaching above top crease on third finger Highly intelligent, fluent, expressive, good business ability.
Reaching nail on third finger (G) Untrustworthy.
Short (H) Difficulty in making the best of oneself.
Long first phalange Knowledgeable, considerable interest in education.
First phalange very much longer than the others Tends to exaggerate or to embroider the truth.
Short or almost non-existent third phalange Degeneracy.
Bending toward third finger Shrewd, clever in business and at making money.
Bent toward palm when hand is relaxed Sexual difficulties.
Twisted or crooked Dishonest, a liar, uses questionable business practices.

Palmistry 5

The base of the thumb, its third phalange, is called the mount of Venus. And – like the goddess, or the planet in astrology – this phalange brings emotional matters to join will and logic in the thumb's overall range of reference.

As we have already seen, the areas nearer the thumb are concerned with our relationships with the outside world, and those farther away with inner matters. So on the other side of the palm is another important pad of flesh, called the mount of the moon. And it reflects both lunar folklore and astrological references in its connection with intuitive, imaginative, even mystic mental activity.

Other mounts around the palm are found at the base of

the fingers. They share the same names as the fingers (the mount of Apollo is also known as the mount of the sun), and usually either reinforce or counterbalance what the fingers reveal. Worthwhile personality clues can also come from a blurring of the boundaries between the mounts.

Mars, the god of war, does not give his name to any of the fingers, but instead to two mounts on the hand, the upper and lower mounts of Mars. The upper is linked with moral courage and resistance; the lower, roughly triangular in shape, with physical courage and aggression.

♀ MOUNT OF VENUS (1)
Broad, firm, and rounded Healthy, warmhearted, sincere, compassionate, loves children.
Flat, underdeveloped Delicate constitution, detached and self-contained nature.
Large A high degree of vitality.
Very large, overdeveloped Extremely energetic physically, hedonistic.
High and firm Highly sexed.
High and soft Excitable and fickle.
Lower part of mount more prominent Energy probably channeled into artistic concerns.
Marked with a large saltire A person who has only one great love in their life.

♂ LOWER MOUNT OF MARS (2)
Normal size Physically brave, resolute, able to keep a cool head in a crisis.
Flat, underdeveloped Cowardly, afraid of physical suffering.
Very large, overdeveloped Violent and argumentative, possibly cruel, but never afraid of taking risks.

♃ MOUNT OF JUPITER (3)
Normal size Enthusiastic, ambitious, good-tempered, friendly. Self-confident and generous. Conventional and conservative at heart, a lover of pomp and ritual.
Flat, underdeveloped Selfish, lazy, inconsiderate, lacks confidence.
Very large, overdeveloped Arrogant and overbearing, totally self-centered, driven by ambition.
Connected with the mount of Saturn Happier working in partnership than alone.

♄ MOUNT OF SATURN (4)
Normal size An introspective nature, serious-minded, studious, prudent.
Flat, underdeveloped A run-of-the-mill person with an unremarkable destiny.
Very large, overdeveloped Gloomy, withdrawn, a recluse. Possibly morbid and suicidal.
Leaning toward the mount of Jupiter A solemn person who aims high.
Leaning toward the mount of Apollo Has an intense appreciation of beauty.

☉ MOUNT OF APOLLO (MOUNT OF THE SUN) (5)
Normal size A pleasant, sunny nature, with a lucky streak. Has good taste and artistic leanings.
Flat, underdeveloped Leads a dull, aimless existence, and has no interest in the arts or any form of culture.
Very large, overdeveloped Pretentious, extravagant, and hedonistic.
Leaning toward the mount of Mercury Able to make money from the arts.
Connected with the mount of Mercury Any introvert or extravert tendencies shown in the fingers will be reinforced.

☿ MOUNT OF MERCURY (6)
Normal size Quick-thinking but subtle. Lively, persuasive, hard-working, needs variety and company.
Flat, underdeveloped Dull, gullible, and humorless. A failure.
Large A good sense of humor.
Very large, overdeveloped A sharp conman, materialistic and light-fingered, a cheat.
Marked by short, straight lines (a) The "medical stigmata." Caring, compassionate, a potential healer. Usually found in the hands of doctors and nurses.

♂ UPPER MOUNT OF MARS (7)
Normal size Morally courageous.
Flat, underdeveloped Cowardly, interested only in self-preservation.
Very large, overdeveloped Bad-tempered, sarcastic, mentally cruel.

☽ MOUNT OF THE MOON (8)
Normal size Sensitive and perceptive, romantic and imaginative, artistic, possibly with a great love of the sea.
Flat, underdeveloped Unimaginative, unsympathetic, unstable, cold, bigoted.
Very large, overdeveloped Overimaginative, introspective, probably untruthful.
High and firm Creative, with a powerful and fertile imagination.
High and soft A touchy, thin-skinned, fickle dreamer.
Reaching to the mount of Venus Extremely passionate.
Reaching toward the wrist Supposed to indicate the possession of occult powers.

Palmistry 6

The three major lines – the head, heart, and life lines – appear on nearly every hand. Although it is possible to have one or more of these lines missing, in practice it is unlikely that you will ever see such a palm.

The lifeline does not indicate how long you will live: the old wives' tale that a short lifeline indicates a short life should be forgotten. What the lifeline does show is the strength of a person's vitality, their "life energy," and so it should be read in conjunction with the thumb, the finger of Jupiter, and the mount of Venus, which are also important in this area. Similarly, the heartline, which is concerned with our emotions, should be referred to those other indicators of our feelings, the finger of Mercury and the mount of Venus.

The headline is concerned with our mental attitudes. Like all the lines in the palm, it should be related to the shape of the hand. For example, you would normally expect to find a straight headline on a practical hand: a sloping headline would be unusual. (It could indicate a person who uses their imagination in a practical way, perhaps a designer or inventor.) But a sloping headline on a sensitive hand would merely act as a confirmation of the imaginative nature you had already suspected. Unlike the major lines, the minor lines – the line of fate, the line of the sun, and so on – can be present or absent. Indeed, the lines on the palm can and do change, growing clearer or less clear, developing disruptions or losing them. So it would not be surprising to see a strong line of fate (the most changeable of all the lines) in the hand of an adult where there had not been one in the child. And in some cases, we would certainly prefer the line to be absent: the more robust your constitution, the less likely you are to have the misnamed line of health in your hand. Of the more commonly occurring lines, the line of fate relates to our destiny; the line of the sun to our good fortune, and to our creativity; the girdle of Venus to passion; the Via Lasciva to our desires – for money, sensual pleasure, and so on; and the bracelets to health, wealth, and travel. The lines of health, marriage, children, and influence have their own eponymous spheres of influence.

RARE LINES

Some lines are extremely rare. The line of intuition (a), for example, which curves from the mount of Mercury to the mount of the moon, and is only found in the hands of the strongly psychic, as is the mystic cross (b), a large cross appearing in the space between the headline and the heartline. Or the ring of Saturn (c), a semicircle on the mount of Saturn, which is held to indicate a constant striving for the impossible, leading to continual disappointment. And the ring of Jupiter (d), known as Solomon's ring, which circles the base of the index finger and is found in the hands of great leaders and those of great wisdom.

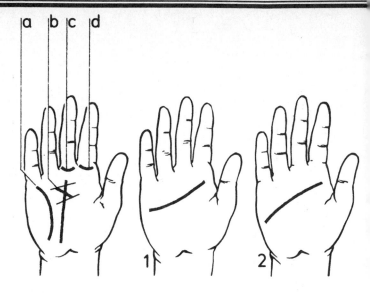

HEADLINE

Length This indicates the level of intelligence, breadth of understanding, and use made of intellectual potential. The longer the line, the greater the importance played by intellectual matters.

Straight across palm (1) Practical and realistic, down-to-earth, a good organizer.

Long and straight Shrewd, a good forward planner with a good memory.

Sloping toward mount of the moon (2) Sensitive and imaginative.

Long, reaching top part of mount of the moon (3) A talent for self-expression.

Long, reaching lower part of mount of the moon Over-imaginative.

Running toward center of wrist Out of touch with reality.

Curving up toward heartline Good business ability, good at making money.

Running close to heartline Narrow in outlook.

Weak, and some distance from lifeline A tendency to gamble.

Clear and distinct Good concentration.
Chain-like appearance Poor concentration, scatterbrained.
Break in the line. A traumatic event with a far-reaching effect on mental attitudes.
Discontinuities in the line Changes in mental attitudes, but less traumatic.
Starts just touching lifeline (4) A prudent, moderate, and balanced nature.
Starts with a small separation from lifeline (5) Independent and enterprising, in need of a definite direction in life to prevent wasting energy on trivia.
Starts with a wide separation from lifeline (6) Foolhardy and excitable.
Starts linked to lifeline for some distance (7) Very cautious. Needs encouragement, responds badly to criticism.
Starts inside lifeline on mount of Mars (8) Touchy, irritable.
Ends with a large fork that touches both the mount of the moon and the heartline (9) Able to be subsumed in another's personality, will give up everything for love.

Long, sloping, ends with a fork Clever and diplomatic, with a talent for self-expression.
Straight, ends with a small fork pointing to the mount of the moon (10) Imagination restrained by common sense.
Ends in a large fork (11) Too versatile, unable to achieve excellence in any one thing.
Ending in a three-pronged fork (12) Combines intelligence, imagination, and business ability.
Ends in mount of Mercury Very good at making money – has the Midas touch.
Branchline to mount of Jupiter (13) Ambitious and successful.
Branchline to mount of Saturn (14) Ambitious, but will have to struggle for success.
Branchline to mount of Apollo (15) Achieving success through the use of own talents.
Branchline ending between third and fourth fingers A successful scientist or inventor.
Branchline to mount of Mercury Successful in business.

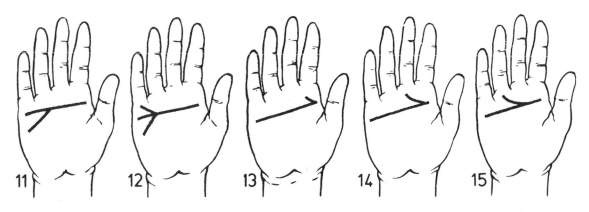

Palmistry 7

HEARTLINE

Long, generously curved, and some distance from the bases of the fingers Warmhearted, sensual, demonstrative.

Longer and stronger than headline The heart rules the head.

Straight Reserved and self-interested.

Short and faint A limited capacity for love.

Very long, deep, and close to the fingers Possessive, jealous.

Chain-like appearance A flirt.

Blurred appearance Tendency to emotional difficulties.

Many small branches (1) A vivid, dynamic personality. Each branch is supposed to represent a romantic attachment, pointing upward for those that are successful and downward for those that are not.

Broken in several places Unfaithful, lacks constancy.

Broken under second finger Jilted.

Broken under third finger A jilt.

Broken sections overlapping A temporary separation.

Starts in middle of mount of Jupiter (2) Fussy and discriminating when choosing friends and lovers, extremely loyal to those chosen. Seeks to marry well.

Starts with a fork on mount of Jupiter (3) Lovable and easy to live with, makes a good marriage partner.

Starts with a large fork, one prong on mount of Jupiter and one on mount of Saturn (4) Changeable, moody, has difficulty in living with others.

Starts between fingers of Saturn and Jupiter A relationship that involves friendship as well as love.

Starts on mount of Saturn (5) Sensual, but lacking real depth of feeling for others.

Chain-like appearance and starting on mount of Saturn Contempt for the opposite sex.

Starts at same point as headline and lifeline Extremely selfish and lacks any control over the emotions.

Branchline running to headline (6) A partner met through work, or a marriage that is a working partnership.

Running together with headline as one line Known as the "simian line." A sign of enormous internal struggle, possibly of mental handicap.

Branchline running to fateline A romance, if the branchline does not touch the fateline; a wedding if they just touch; an unhappy marriage if they cross.

LINE OF FATE

No line A smooth and uneventful life.

Straight and unbroken A successful, untroubled life.

Chain-like sections Indicate unhappy periods in life.

Wavy Argumentative, changeable, disorganized.

Break in the line Sudden change in circumstances.

Broken sections overlapping Planned major changes.

Short bar across line Setback or obstacle.

Reaching mount of Saturn Trying to exceed own powers.

Curved toward mount of Jupiter Success through effort.

Starts from headline or heartline Success late in life.

Starts from lifeline (13) Hampered by early environment and family surroundings. Point of separation of lines shows when independence was or will be achieved.

Starts from top bracelet (14) Early responsibility.

Starts from mount of the moon A varied life, much traveling.

Starts from mount of Venus, ends on mount of Saturn (15) A secure and loved childhood, supported by parents and family. Possibly success through inheritance.

Ends on headline Prone to errors of judgment, bad planning that leads to misfortune.

Ends on heartline Sacrifices necessary in the cause of love or duty.

Ends on mount of the sun Popular and talented.

Branchline to line of the sun A successful partnership. If the lines cross, the partnership will fail.

Branchline to mount of Mercury Achievement and wealth obtained through business or science.

LIFELINE

Long and clear Good vitality, a healthy constitution.

Short and checkered Lacks energy, may be physically frail.

Chain-like appearance Alternating enthusiasm and torpor, energy coming uneasily in fits and starts.

Discontinuities in the line Changes in the direction of life.

Break in the line on one hand only An illness, followed by a speedy recovery.

Break in the line on both hands A more serious illness.

Many small branches running upward Good health, prosperity.

Many small branches running downward Poor health, financial setbacks.

Starts on mount of Jupiter (7) Highly ambitious – and likely to succeed.

Starts from headline (8) Very controlled and calculating.

Starts well below headline (9) Lacks control, uninhibited.

Ends in a fork with one branch ending in mount of the moon Indicates long-distance travel.

Branchline to mount of Jupiter Self-confident and self-assured.

Two small branches from beginning of line onto headline (10) An inheritance: could be money, but more likely to have been given a good start in life by parents.

Branchline to headline from halfway down line (11) Success and recognition will come in middle age.

Branchline to mount of Saturn Life will be a struggle, must make own way without outside help.

Branchline to mount of the sun (12) Talents will be recognized and rewarded.

Branchline to mount of the moon A longing for a new stimulus, for change. Traditionally, a sea journey.

LINE OF THE SUN (LINE OF APOLLO)

No line A life of disappointments and setbacks, however talented the owner of the hand.

Clear and straight A lucky person with a charming and sunny nature.

Blurred Lacks concentration, wastes effort.

Starts close to wrist between mounts of Venus and the moon, ends in mount of the sun (16) Nothing ever goes wrong in this life.

Starts from life or fateline, ends in mount of sun Success as a result of using talents and energy.

Starts from headline (17) Success in middle age as result of own efforts.

Starts from heartline (18) Warmth, happiness, and sufficiency in old age.

Starts from mount of Venus (19) Artistically gifted.

Starts from mount of the moon (20) Strongly attractive to the opposite sex, a person idolized by the masses.

Ends in many small lines Unsettled, with many conflicting interests.

Ends in a fork with prongs on mounts of Mercury, Saturn, and Apollo (21) Lasting success on a firm base.

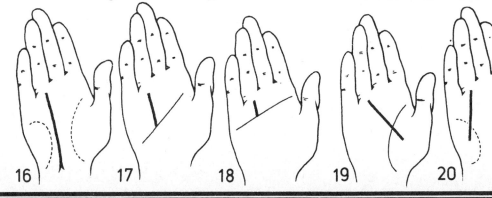

Palmistry 8

1 GIRDLE OF VENUS
No line A well-controlled, calm personality.
Well-marked Over-emotional, craves excitement and variety.
Short Keenly aware of the feelings of others.
Blurred or broken Oversensitive.
Crosses lines of fate and the sun Witty, talented.
Ends on mount of Mercury Enormous reserves of energy, but a tendency to go to extremes.
Runs off side of the hand instead of making a semicircle Vacillating, a ditherer.

2 VIA LASCIVA (MILKY WAY)
Straight Restless, easily bored.
Straight and long, reaching mount of Mercury An eloquent speaker of dubious morality.
Curved A person who is their own worst enemy.
Curved, and beginning inside mount of Venus Liable to take things to excess. Someone who could easily become addicted – to drugs, alcohol, etc.
Branchline reaching to line of the sun Potential riches if the lines do not quite touch. Financial losses as the result of a relationship (eg an expensive divorce settlement) if they cross.

3 RASCETTES (BRACELETS)
Parallel and clearly marked A healthy, wealthy, long and peaceful life.
Chain-like top bracelet Eventual happiness after a difficult life.
Top bracelet arching into the palm in a woman's hand Possible difficulties in childbirth.
Line from top bracelet to mount of Jupiter A long and profitable journey.
Line from top bracelet to mount of the sun A trip to a hot country.
Line from top bracelet to mount of Mercury Sudden wealth.
Lines from top bracelet to mount of the moon Each line represents a journey.

4 HEPATICA (LINE OF HEALTH)
No line A strong and healthy constitution.
Deeply engraved Low physical resistance.
Wavy Digestive problems.
Blurred Lack of physical stamina.
Touches lifeline Take extra care of health at that time.

5 LINE OF MARS (THE INNER LIFELINE)
When present Sustains life in time of illness or danger.

6 LINES OF MARRIAGE
Strongly marked A marriage or close relationship. The number of lines is supposed to indicate the number of such relationships.
Weakly marked Each line indicates a minor romantic attachment of little importance.
Long and straight A long and happy relationship.
Broken A divorce or separation.

Broken lines overlapping A reunion after a separation, perhaps remarriage to the same person.
Double line A relationship with two people at the same time, the relative depths of the relationships being indicated by the strength of the lines.
Curves downward Will outlive partner.
Strong curve upward to base of little finger Staying unmarried but not celibate.
Curve upward to line of the sun A marriage to a famous or wealthy person if the lines do not quite touch. If the lines cross, the marriage will be unhappy.
Starts with a fork Delay or frustration at the start of a relationship.
Ends in a fork A divorce or separation.
Crossed by a line running from base of finger of Mercury Opposition to a relationship.
Crossed by girdle of Venus An unhappy marriage, a nagging partner.

7 CHILD LINES
When present The lines run from the base of the finger of Mercury to the marriage lines. The number of lines are said to indicate the number of children, with the stronger lines representing boys, and the fainter lines girls.

INFLUENCE LINES

Starting from mount of moon and meeting line of fate (a)
A close relationship or marriage and, if the influence line is the stronger of the two, the subject's partner will also be the stronger. If the lines cross, it indicates a divorce or similar separation; if they do not quite meet, a breach in the relationship at a fairly early point, eg a broken engagement.

Starting from mount of Venus and ending on lifeline (b)
A person greatly influenced by the people they love.

Curved lines parallel to lifeline (c) Each line is said to represent a person who will have a great influence on the subject's life.

TIMESCALES

Although it is impossible to be completely accurate about when an event shown in a hand will take place, it is feasible to make a reasonably accurate guess. Here we show approximate timescales on the lifeline (**A**), line of fate (**B**), and line of the sun (**C**).

The approximate dates for romantic relationships are shown by the distance between the marriage lines and the heartline; the farther from the heartline and the closer to the base of the fingers, the later the marriage.

©DIAGRAM

27

Palmistry 9

Looking at a hand in close-up, we can see a variety of minor marks and textures and, of course, the distinctive fingerprint. All these can offer clues to the overall pattern of the hand.

Marks refer to the same area of life as the line or mount on which they appear. So, although the mark of a square always indicates protection, its meaning varies with its position. On the mount of Jupiter it protects against failure in worldly ambitions; on the mount of Mercury, against mental stress; on the heartline, from unhappiness in love; and so on.

Obviously these marks will not appear as clearly in a hand as in the illustrations, but they must be strong and distinct, however uneven in shape.

Fingerprint patterns are established about eighteen weeks after conception. Unlike the other lines on the hand, from then on they are fixed and unchanging. This, as we know, makes them very useful in the detection of criminals, but they can also be useful in the detection of personality. When more than one type of fingerprint pattern appears in a hand, their different characteristics will be blended in the personality. The number of fingers involved can give us an indication of the balance of that blend: a person with several fingers showing tented arches is likely to be considerably more stubborn than a person with just one!

Palmists also literally read between the lines. The area between the lines of head and heart should be a neat and well-defined oblong for the best possible portent of a balanced and steady progress through life – and nearly smooth, empty of all the collections of tiny lines found elsewhere. Otherwise there may be a tendency to imbalance, extremism of one kind or another, and a somewhat erratic and fitful life. And the larger the triangular area formed by the lines of head, life, and health, the better the omen.

MARKS AND TEXTURES

a Chaining Weakness, indecision, a tendency to be unlucky.

b Forked line Contradictions, divisions of interest.

c Doubled line Reinforcing and strengthening.

d Island Period of stress, weakness, breakdown.

e Break Unpleasant interruption in the progress of life.

f Bar Opposition, a barrier.

g Cross A shock or upheaval. If at the end of the line, failure.

h Star Sudden happenings, which may be triumphant or tragic. A many-starred hand indicates an exciting life.

i Square A sign of protection, good and positive qualities triumphing over the negative and bad.

j Triangle Harmony, peace, and good fortune.

k Trident Good fortune.

l Grille Confusion, lack of direction, uncertainty.

m Spot A temporary cessation.

n Circle A very rare sign. A similar effect to an island, except when found on the line of the sun or mount of Apollo. Then it is held to represent the sun and bring good fortune.

FINGERPRINTS

A Low arch Hard-hearted, insensitive, sceptical, unemotional, and materialistic.

B Tented arch Highly strung, artistic, and impulsive – but stubborn.

C Loop Mild-tempered and straightforward, with a quick, lively, and versatile mind.

D Whorl An individualist with a strong, definite personality. Potentially brilliant, best when self-employed.

E Mixed A mixed-up and muddle-headed personality. If you have any difficulty in differentiating one type of pattern from another, look for the triadus (**F**). An arch print does not have a triadus, a loop print has one, and a whorl has two.

A

B

k Ψ

a ⊃⊃⊃⊃×

g ⊬ ✕ ✕

h ✳ ✳ ✳

m · ◗ ◗

d ◗ ◗ ◗

c ⟋ ⟋

b ⟋

o ⊙ n

⌗ ▢ ⌗ i

⊬ ⟋ f

▨ ▨ l

⟋ e

▽ ◁ ⋈ j

C   D   E   F

©DIAGRAM

Palmistry 10

By looking at a brief interpretation of the hands of Ms X we can see how the meanings of the individual features can be integrated into a complete picture. The left hand (**A**) shows that X is both artistic and practical. The clearly defined headline indicates a talent for self-expression; the lines on the fingers indicate that she needs to express herself; and the long, broad first phalange of the finger of Apollo shows that she is talented with words. The straight finger of Saturn, in good proportion to the other fingers, shows a prudent and sensible nature; and the first and third fingers are the same length, showing that she is well balanced and self-assured.

The headline begins a small distance from the lifeline, showing that X is an independent and enterprising person. The clear fate line, rising in the mount of the moon, shows that she is ambitious, and will achieve success by using her imagination – although not without some struggle, as indicated by the low-set fourth finger. In X's hand, the fate line stops below the heart line, which suggests that her career may become less important to her after the age of 40; her lines of marriage suggest that this may be when she will marry. X's close relationships or marriage will only succeed if she can pursue her own independent life at the same time: her broken and branched heartline indicates a dynamic personality, and may also suggest problems in her personal relationships. The heartline is straight, showing that she has a reserved nature and is inclined to put her own best interests first. The broken girdle of Venus suggests that she may be oversensitive; the lines on the mount of Venus indicate a tendency to worry. There is little difference in the lines on the right hand between 1966 (**B**) and 1983 (**C**), indicating that there have been no major changes in the direction of X's life during this period. The area between the life, fate, and head lines is less marked in the later hand, indicating X's greater maturity and understanding of her own direction in life. As the lifeline is broken and crossed, showing a period of change, her maturity may have been developed by difficulties in her life. The clear fate line and the absence of travel lines show that there have

Ms X's handprints
A Left hand, shown at two-thirds actual size. As Ms X is right-handed, this is her birth hand.
B Right hand, shown actual size. This print was taken in 1966 when Ms X was 20 years old.
C Right hand, shown actual size. This print was taken in 1983 when Ms X was 36 years old.

A

B

1966

been no money problems, and no major changes in her environment; the difficulties may have been emotional. Changes can be precipitated by early experiences, but the unusually clear beginning to her lifeline shows that she had a very happy early childhood.

The greatest changes in X's life probably occurred before 1966, and were changes in her mental attitude – the headline has been broken and reformed. Instead of creating a wide V-shape, as on the left hand, it is now a much smaller V, suggesting that X has sacrificed part of her creative nature in order to be more practical and businesslike. The lack of flexibility in her palm and fingers shows the need for both the physical (money and home) and emotional aspects of her life to be predictable, and emphasizes the prudence and common sense already seen in the hand. The large lower mount of Mars and the stiff thumb show that she is a person who will choose her own direction in life, and that she has the strong will to see her plans through. The warm color of her hands and her spatulate fingers suggest considerable reserves of energy.

The outer areas are the stronger parts of X's hands, indicating that her energy is focused more on the outside world than on her intuition and close relationships. The prominent lower part of the mount of Venus shows that her emotions are channeled into artistic concerns. This mount is softer on the right hand than on the left, indicating a possible lack of emotional fulfillment. The presence of a mystic cross on her hand also suggests that she may be looking for some form of fulfillment not found in either her work or her personal relationships – she probably has a successful career but does not feel completely satisfied by it.

The marriage indicated on her hand will not end her problems, but will ease them – her lifeline is never completely clear, but the bars crossing it do become less frequent. As there are no travel lines or breaks in the major lines to indicate any sudden changes in her future life, it is likely that any change will be gradual, and of her own choice.

C

1983

Graphology 1

Graphology – the analysis of handwriting – is not a new science: the ancient Chinese analyzed the characteristics of their calligraphy thousands of years ago. The Romans studied character in handwriting, as did the scholar-monks of the Middle Ages. The earliest treatise on graphology that is still in existence was written in 1622 by an Italian, Camillo Baldo, who was Professor of Theoretical Medicine at the University of Bologna. In the nineteenth and twentieth centuries graphologists began to treat their subject as a science rather than as an art. Extensive research, especially by French and German graphologists, allowed them to formulate the principles of handwriting analysis that are in use today.

Psychologists like Carl Jung were among the first to realize the significance of handwriting as an aid to the study of character and personality. Today many universities in the USA, France, Germany, and Israel include graphology in their psychology and criminology courses. And in the commercial world, consultant graphologists are often employed by personnel departments to assess job applicants or existing employees.

Each person's handwriting is unique; no two handwritings are identical. They may be similar but, just as fingerprints will identify a person, so handwriting will give a very clear indication of an individual character.

Zones

Handwriting analysis is divided into three zones (**1**) – the upper zone (**a**), the middle zone (**b**), and the lower zone (**c**). The upper zone shows spiritual aspirations, dreams, hopes, and ambitions; the middle zone reveals practical attitudes toward day-to-day affairs, friends, family, and home; the lower zone shows emotional attitudes and responses to the physical aspects of life, including sex. The upper loops in the letters d, k, and l (**2**) show, according to size and height, the writer's ideals, tendency to daydream, and degree of interest in the spiritual life. If middle zones are larger than the upper or lower zone (**3**), there is sociability and a strong practical streak to the personality – a down-to-earth person. Lower loops that are inflated (**4**) indicate imagination and an exaggerated ego. If they go straight down in a simple line they show a fatalist with good concentration and an ability to get down to essentials rapidly and without fuss.

Loops that are long and rounded (**5**) indicate a romantic attitude to love and life. Triangular loops (**6**) are a sign of the domestic tyrant – male or female – or of someone who has been disappointed (usually sexually) in his or her partner.

Margins

Margins reveal educational and social qualities. A wide upper margin indicates that the writer is formal and reserved. A wide lower margin may reveal a fear of sex. A narrow lower margin often means the squirrel instinct to hoard – at the same time the writer can be over-familiar and show lack of reserve.

The left margin, if wide, indicates a good cultural background, intelligence, and an aesthetic sense. A narrow left margin is a sign of indiscriminate friendliness and often of meanness.

A wide right margin shows apprehension about the future. A narrow right margin indicates a more reserved approach to possible friends and to the world in general, and a lack of discrimination.

The only things it cannot show with certainty are the age and sex of the writer. Some people are mature at 20, some are still young in outlook at 70, and everyone has a combination of male and female traits in their psychological and biological makeup. Handwriting is a product of the brain: although the hand holds the pen it is the brain that directs the action of the hand and is responsible for the formation of the letters.

When analysing handwriting it is important to remember that no single trait can be stressed without taking note of all others. Every trait has to be taken into consideration before a complete and accurate analysis is possible. You should also remember that the same person's handwriting can vary – worry, poor health, etc can all affect it. It is not wise to over-simplify in any analysis of personality, but study of the basic rules that follow will enable you to master the essentials of graphology.

Very often signs of deeper inner psychological processes can be seen in the way certain letters or words are formed. For example, if the "motive" words – such as God, mother, father, sex – are written with heavy pressure it reveals that the writer has placed an emphasis on them from conscious or unconscious motivations. They affect the writer deeply and this shows in the handwriting.

Slant

Handwriting slanting to the right (7) is the basic clue to extraversion. This is the normal slant indicating an outward-going personality with a need and capacity for human contact, and a desire to give and receive affection.

The left-slanted script (8) is a sign of introversion. The writer is guided by the head rather than the heart. If the left slant is pronounced, the writer puts up a barrier against the world and against people, often as the result of emotional and environmental experiences in early years. This can lead to inner conflict and a tendency to retreat into self.

The more a writing slants to the right (9), the more sociable and gregarious the writer, but with less emotional control, especially under pressure. The more a writing slants to the left, the more introspective the writer.

A varied slant (10) indicates a versatile but often emotionally unstable personality, changeable and frequently moody – often pulled between impulse and control, mind and emotion.

Pressure

The pressure and thickness of the strokes reveals the strength of libido and sensual impulse.

Heavy pressure (11) indicates a sensual and energetic nature. Light pressure (12) goes with sensitivity and often with a highly critical nature. If the pressure is very light it shows a lack of vitality, which may be due to physical reasons.

Medium pressure (13) is the most general and by far the most widely seen and, as can be imagined, is that of average people with average impulses.

7 address on this letter,

8 Any way of going there

9 Many years

10 service or reference there is no care about you and your spoiled, because we both

11 go about

12 and I am not keen ondon for a week

13 if the analysis is to be done right then there is no need to accept.

Graphology 2

Size

Writing is basically classed into three sizes – large, medium, and small.

A person with a large script (1) has an expansive nature, loves being in the limelight, and needs an active social life to be happy. The writer of an over-sized script is egotistical, and may have an abrasive and overbearing personality, monopolizing conversation and dominating the social scene.

The medium-sized writing (2) of the average person shows an individual who is basically reasonable and adaptable, able to fit into most surroundings. The writer is generally polite, neither too shy nor too bold, and is usually composed in attitude.

Small writing (3) belongs to the academic who likes to rationalize everything, even emotional behavior. Scientists and researchers are found in this category as well as people who deal in ideas.

A very small script (4) which dissolves into a line shows an inferiority complex and self-effacement.

When writing varies in size (5) it indicates inconsistency, an extreme sensitivity (to the point of touchiness), and a person who is prone to fluctuating moods.

Writing that gets smaller at the ends of words shows a mature mind, and conversely that which gets larger shows varying degrees of emotional immaturity.

Baseline slope

Writing that keeps to a steady, firm, and straight baseline shows a person whose moods are kept under control. The writer is not easily swayed by other people, and is well-balanced, straightforward, and persevering. If the baseline slopes upward (6) it shows ambition and optimism; if downward (7) it shows pessimism and depression. The higher a line goes up, the more ambitious or optimistic the writer; the more it slopes downward, the more pessimism takes over.

When the lines vary, some going upward and others falling, it reveals moodiness. The writer whose writing constantly changes in pressure and slope is liable to let feeling brush aside reason, and can be impetuous and unreliable.

Spacing

The spacing between words and letters tells how generous or mean the writer is, how gregarious, and the degree of discrimination exercised in choosing friends. Narrow spacing between words (8) indicates a need for people and a full social life. Wide spaces between words (9) show reserve and caution in choosing acquaintances. Narrow spacing between lines (10) is a sign of inability to plan and of poor organizing ability. Wide spaces between the lines indicate the opposite, and the ability to look ahead objectively.

1 Give lots

2 "uncluhahle" child

3 the client represented by

4 Can you enlya

5 contact which causes

6 rising baseline

7 descending baseline

8 Her anxiety & she is told but will try and gh

9 interested in working for a few months.

10 from her magazine, the problems of her

Starting and ending strokes

Starting strokes and ending strokes on letters show fussiness and often caution. The writer with starting strokes is less receptive to new ideas or projects, often sticking to tried and tested methods because the past has a strong hold. Ending strokes show a reluctance to let go, and are found in the writing of the type of person who takes a long time to say goodbye on the telephone. Writing without starting or ending strokes to the letters indicates an ability to get down to essentials quickly without wasting time or effort.

Connecting strokes

There are four main connecting strokes in handwriting, called garland, arcade, thread, and angular.

The garland (11) is a quick way of joining letters together. It is an easy way of writing – the shallower the garland the speedier the writer's script. The positive traits it reveals are an easy-going personality, adaptability, flexibility, kindness, and sympathy. In a woman's handwriting it may indicate sentimentality and empathy. On the negative side, the writer may be lazy, easily influenced, and inclined to take the easy way out – someone with superficial feelings that are near the surface.

Arcade writers (12) have a more positive construction in their arch-like script. The positive traits of arcade writers are artistic appreciation, a sense of form and style, and a tendency to secretiveness and depth of feeling. They are often sticklers for formality. Their negative traits are a slightly mistrustful, affected pretentiousness, often accompanied by a capacity for intrigue.

Thread writers (13) are the manipulators or organizers. When the letters are joined together, linking the strokes with threadlike formation, the writer demonstrates considerable psychological skill in dealing with people. On the positive side, such writers are intelligent, versatile, highly adaptable, and can be all things to all people. On the negative side they can be elusive, hard to pin down, and sometimes deceitful. In male handwriting this style can reveal a spiteful nature.

Angular writing (14) is shown by a more disciplined movement in the linking of the letters, demonstrating strong willpower and even aggression. The writers can see things as being black or white, and can be rigid and blind to other viewpoints. Their positive traits are firmness, decisiveness, and persistence. They have a disciplined attitude to life and love, and lack adaptability. Their negative traits are an inner conflict, suspiciousness, and a domineering attitude that leads to uncompromising behavior and a lack of empathy with others.

11 another form

12 mind and one amount

13 send in specimen handwriting Here I enclose a

14 for operation thing in the in a "Bank if I want

Connected and disconnected handwriting

Connected handwriting (15) reveals logical and systematic thinking, a cooperative and reasonable approach to others, but also a lack of initiative and intuitive thinking. The writer is unlikely to be spontaneous or to give way to sudden impulses, and may lack originality.

Disconnected handwriting (16) reveals egotism, inconsistency, an obstinate streak, a person who brushes aside the ideas and opinions of others. It can also show moodiness and a dislike of social intercourse. Such writers are frequently egocentric and difficult to deal with, but may often produce original or creative ideas.

15 years ago out since my handwriting has

16 to arrive back between I hope you had

Grapholgy 3

Capitals

Capital letters reveal the writer's ego and public face. Some capitals are more graphologically significant than others, and both the size and shape must be taken into consideration.

Inflated capitals (**1**) show a desire to be admired and noticed. The writer may be a leader, or just a conceited person, or both – or may be compensating for an inferiority complex. When the letters are enrolled, or scroll-like, and full of embellishments (**2**) they reveal vulgarity.

Capital letters that are as small or smaller than the rest of the script portray an over-modest attitude, a writer who lacks self-assurance and self-confidence. Original or unique capitals are often found in the handwriting of artists or creative people. Printed capitals are frequently a sign of literary ability or familiarity with the printed word – they usually denote good taste and an ability for constructive planning.

Capital M

The capital M is important and is one of the letters that gives clues to the writer's ego, or lack of it. An M that has a higher first stroke (**3**) shows a healthy ego, but if the end stroke is higher (**4**) it shows a more cooperative or even subordinate mentality – a person who heeds public opinion.

A large loop on the beginning slope (**5**) indicates jealousy. A rounded M (**6**) is a sign of non-aggression, but an angular M (**7**) indicates forcefulness and drive, sometimes to the point of selfishness.

Capital I

The capital I is unique because it shows the writer's self-assessment and motivation. In many ways it is the most revealing of all the letters in the alphabet, and gives a clue to pride and vanity, or to modesty and unselfishness.

A capital I that is much larger than the rest of the capital letters (**8**) indicates self-interest and a demand for attention. The writer aims to appear self-confident although concealing uncertainty.

A small and poorly formed capital I (**9**) indicates a weak will and self-consciousness.

If the capital I is made in the form of a circle (**10**) it reveals introversion and a desire to protect the ego. A huge inflated round I (**11**) shows egotism and exaggerated self-importance – an irritating person who must be in the limelight.

A small letter instead of a capital I (**12**) is a sign of self-devaluation. A straight line down (**13**) indicates sophistication, a strong ego, unpretentiousness, and intelligence. A printed I (**14**) shows literary ability and good taste.

A capital I made in three parts is a sign of a fragmented personality. A capital I that slants to the left or is upright when the rest of the writing slopes to the right (**15**) reveals a guilt complex.

Small letters a and o

An open small a or o (16) indicates the talker and compulsive gossip; when these two letters are closed or knotted (17) they reveal the writer is self-contained, discreet, and able to keep a secret. The more knotted they are (18) the more likely the writer is to maintain discretion to the point of secrecy, or even deceit.

Small letters i and t

The dot over the letter i can vary considerably. It can show if the writer is sensitive or observant or even brutal. A dot that is elongated (19) reveals sensitivity and highly developed critical sense; a dot that is thick and heavy (20) shows a bad temper or worse; a dot that is light and high above the stem (21) indicates a refined character, often easily hurt. An i dot in the shape of a small arc (22) reveals an observant nature. There are many more possible variations to this letter.

Similarly the bar of the letter t is greatly varied – there are more than 60 acknowledged ways of writing this simple letter. The t bar crossing is, therefore, an important feature in graphology. One of the first things it indicates is willpower. A well-made t bar crossing slightly to the right (23) indicates firmness and self-confidence, but when it is short and timid (24) it reveals feelings of insecurity and a lack of self-assurance. A long t bar crossing going over the entire word (25) is a sign of ambition and even of a patronizing attitude. A sharpening bar (26) indicates a hasty attitude, while one that is thickening shows an even disposition. A light t bar balanced on the top of the stem (27) is a sign of the daydreamer, but if it is firmer it can show imagination and the ability to get out of a rut.

16 *and not a*

17 *to, over a*

18 *more knowledge*

19 *it is not in*

20 *i*

21 *pecimau*

22 *if*

23 *tomorrow*

24 *On that note, then, I*

25 *towards*

26 *liday*

27 *hand writing*

Ink color

The color of the ink used is of significance in handwriting analysis and is a useful guide to the graphologist. Individual preference for a color can change in the course of a lifetime.

The majority of people use blue ink, a happy color that shows a friendly attitude. Black ink is used by the more conventionally-minded, or by the coolly efficient executive who wishes to impress. Black is a more assertive color than blue, although not as assertive as red. Red ink is favored by the person who has an exaggerated ego and loves to be the center of attention, and it is also an indication of a sensual nature. Green ink is often used by young people who desire to appear different.

Figures

Written figures and numbers can also be revealing to the graphologist.

Clearly written numbers indicate a practical and open attitude toward money and material values. Small, thin figures show concentration and an awareness or involvement with monetary or financial matters – accountants, mathematicians, and executives use this script.

Overstroked figures (those written over more than once) show a neurotic attitude, and sometimes deceitfulness or deliberate falsifying. Embellished or enrolled figures show vulgarity, or an over-emphasis on money matters, often greed.

Figures written with heavy pressure may show poor taste and crass materialism. Legible figures indicate openness and honesty.

Graphology 4

Signatures

The signature is the "seal of self" and shows the facade put up to the world.

The writer whose signature is clearly written (**1**) and easily understood shows honesty and reliability.

If the signature is small, compressed, and narrow (**2**) it could reveal an inferiority complex.

If it is large and full of flourishes (**3**) it shows a lack of taste and an exaggerated ego.

Underlining a signature (**4**) shows egotism and forcefulness.

A threadlike signature (**5**) that tapers off into lines is a sign of calculating cleverness. Such a writer often possesses a talent for dealing with people, and is diplomatic and intelligent.

A circle around a signature often indicates depression, and is a cry for help. Lines going through the signature show a lack of ego, and often suggest self-doubt. Such a signature suggests an abnormal condition.

The placing of the signature on the page is very important. If it is written close to the rest of the text it reveals a need to maintain a close link with the environment. If it is a long way from the text it indicates a more independent nature.

1 *Peter Adams*

2 *Robin Doyle*

3 *Roddy*

4 *Michael Manning*

5 *angela moyling*

Alan's signature (6)

Alan has a treble underscore to his signature demonstrating that he wants to be taken for an important person. This is an ego sign and reveals a tendency to seek prestige and status. Very often his type of large capital conceals an inferiority complex.

6 *Alan*

Ann's signature (7)

Ann has a very narrow script and signature indicating a repressed personality and inhibited emotions. The squeezed letters of her name show that she is narrow-minded, lacking in ideas, but rigid and firm in her opinions.

7 *Ann*

Norman Walls' signature (8)

This signature with its copybook formation and rounded small m and n reveals immaturity and a slow, cautious mind. The slight left slant indicates the writer's introspection, while the poorly formed capitals are a sign of low self-evaluation.

8 *Norman Walls.*

Tom's signature (9)

Tom has half-circles around his signature, which in graphology indicates suicidal tendencies. He has left an opening in the circle and this is a bid for attention – a cry for help. The rest of his script with its drooping at the end of the line confirms his depression.

9

Richard Nixon's signatures (10)

These varying signatures belonging to Richard Nixon have been interpreted as evidence of mental and physical deterioration. His first signature (**a**) was written in 1959 when he was Vice President of the USA, and it has a sociable right slant. His next signature (**b**) was written in 1969 when he began his first term as President: the thread-like strokes indicate that he had learned to manipulate and deceive people. His third signature (**c**), written in 1974 just before the Watergate scandal broke, shows an awareness of future criticism of his ethics. His fourth signature (**d**) is almost illegible, showing that his manipulating powers have given way to lying and dishonesty. The weaker pressure reveals that his physical health was failing rapidly.

10a
b
c
d

Analyzing a sample of handwriting

Try to see as much of your subject's handwriting as possible – a person's script can vary. Pen and ink are more reflective of the writer than a ballpoint pen because they reveal the pressure of the strokes. Unlined paper is better than lined for getting the true baseline. Start by looking at the margins and the slant, and then go on to consider the pressure and the size of the writing. Next look at the baseline and the slope. You can now go on to study the capitals and the small letters, the individual characteristics, and the signature.

Don't aim for a long analysis at first, but begin by picking out five or six obvious traits. See how these are modified or confirmed by other indications, and go on from there to give a more perceptive and detailed analysis. Don't form your assessment too quickly – take all the details into account before forming the final picture. For example, the script may show someone who is weak-willed, but highly intelligent and intuitive: these factors would balance each other out, and the writer would thus keep on an even keel.

Specimen analysis

This small, fast, thread-like writing (**11**) shows a highly intelligent and mentally agile personality. The lightly rising lines are a sign of optimism. The straight line for the capital I indicates an ability to get down to essentials quickly and without fuss. The large spaces between words and lines show systematic thinking and social discrimination, while the lack of loops in the underlengths of letters g and y shows that the writer has channeled a lot of emotional energy into his work or career while neglecting his own emotional needs.

The thread-like strokes tapering off at the ends of words are a sign of maturity. They also indicate an ability to manipulate, and a talent for dealing with people at all levels.

The firmly made t bar crossing to the right shows self-confidence. The break between capital letters and small letters is a sign of intuition.

The rather light pressure reveals a lack of reserve energy. The writer is not a robust personality and possesses, at least physically, little real vitality. The closed small a and o indicate secretiveness and diplomacy.

11

Physiognomy 1

We are accustomed to reading people's moods from their facial expressions – from frowns, smiles, grimaces, and so on. And we generalize about weak chins, shifty eyes, sensuous mouths, and other facial features. So, in a way, we already practice physiognomy – character analysis from the physical appearance of the features. And, of course, when you are reading character in anything you are also telling fortunes, because you are perceiving potentialities and indicating the kind of life your subject can expect.

Physiognomy is an ancient art. As with palmistry, the first systematic account we have of its practice is attributed to Aristotle. But earlier sources suggest it was known and practiced by Pythagoras, Socrates, and Hippocrates, and it is obliquely referred to in a papyrus that has been dated to 1800BC. It flourished especially from the sixteenth to the eighteenth century, when the physiognomists suffered the same mixture of fates as the palmists: revered as learned scholars in some times and places, whipped and tortured as heretics and charlatans in others.

Face to face

Early physiognomists compared the faces of men and of animals, and drew curious analogies between their temperaments. A man closely resembling a ram (**A**), for example, was assumed to be impatient, courageous, of uncertain temper, and inclined to headaches. In the sixteenth century physiognomists began to consider the individual features of the face – comparing, for example, the noses of men who were peaceloving (**B**), of great intellect (**C**), vain (**D**), and lustful (**E**). Chinese physiognomists also analysed the individual features of the face, but in a very different way: in an eighteenth century work, the features are explained in terms of planets, mountains, stars, and rivers (**F**).

HOW TO READ FACES

Look at your subject full-face first, and analyze the shape of the face. Then look at your subject from the side, and consider the overall outline of the profile. Finally, analyze all the individual features of the face separately, looking at them both in profile and full face. Remember to notice which features you found particularly striking when you first saw your subject, and give them suitable weight in your overall interpretation.

FACE SHAPES

Round or oval (1) A good homemaker who loves comfort and luxury. Friendly, intuitive, with good judgment, definite values, and a strong sense of justice. Capable and hard-working in business, but able to be lazy and self-indulgent when the moment is right.

Triangular or heart-shaped (2) A quick-thinker, an intellectual with a good memory, who can be moody. Tries to make dreams come true, and can be impractical. Sensitive, introspective, and easily bored, in need of a sense of purpose.

Square or rectangular (3) A natural leader, dynamic, thorough, always needing to be active. Intelligent, practical, and mechanically skillful. Physically strong as well as strong-willed, with firm, decided opinions.

Round-triangular composite (4) Combines a good intellect with a sound commercial sense, but lacks judgment. Ingenious, optimistic, full of self-confidence but can be complacent.

Triangular-square composite Versatile, impetuous, and quick-thinking. Translates ideas into actions, and profits from the experience.

Square-round composite Very active, with a jolly, happy-go-lucky disposition. Self-interested and opinionated, but very businesslike.

PROFILES

Convex (a) Intensely enthusiastic, can be impatient, lacks concentration. A quick-thinker, practical and sharp witted. Very active, a talker, a poor listener.

Vertical (b) Always looking for the best and rarely admitting failure. Calm and reasonable, but can be stubborn and self-opinionated. An enquiring mind that sets out thoroughly and deliberately to get to the bottom of things.

Concave (c) Can appear deep-thinking and concerned with major issues while in fact being shallow and engrossed in trivia. Reserved, almost moody, but loyal and capable with a good memory.

Physiognomy 2

FOREHEAD
High Intellectual.
High and wide (1) Philosophical.
High and narrow Analytical.
Low (2) Practical, direct.
Convex Observant.
Flat (3) Deliberate, good concentration.
Concave A good listener, cautious.

EYEBROWS
Heavy (4) Intense, blunt.
Thin Fastidious, fussy.
Straight (5) Alert, active.
Curved Inquiring, curious.
Arched Imaginative.
Sloping up (6) Ambitious.
Sloping down Petulant, resigned.
Wide apart Adaptable, easily influenced.
Close together Full of nervous energy.

EYES
Round Naive, trusting.
Oval Shrewd, good-humored.
Slanting (7) Secretive, self-indulgent.
Wide open (8) Confiding, friendly.
Hooded (9) Scheming, envious.
Narrowed Keen, suspicious.
Wide apart Confident, broad-minded.
Close together Responsible, narrow-minded.
Protuberant Smooth talker, full of repartee.
Deep set (10) Slow-talking, sticks to the facts.
Neither protuberant nor deep set A convincing speaker and a good listener.

NOSE
Large Aggressive, worldly.
Small Quiet, unassuming.
Thin Nervous, irritable.
Wide Exuberant, careless.
Long (11) Careful, worried.
Short (12) Cheerful.
High-bridged, pointed (13) Vigorous, inquisitive.
Straight Steady, thorough, regimented.
Short and snub (14) Friendly, secretive, plodding.

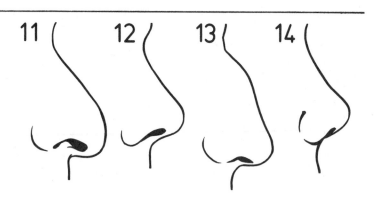

EARS

Large Intellectual.
Small Instinctive.
Longer than they are wide (15) Keen, impractical.
Wider than they are long Very practical.
Pointed Artful, conniving.
Large lobes (16) Independent, strong-minded.
Small lobes Dependent, lacks initiative.
No lobes (17) Unresponsive, lacks sense of purpose.
Set close to head Plans ahead, thrifty.
Sticking out (18) An original thinker.

MOUTH

Large Generous, extravagant.
Small Selfish, miserly.
Curving up (19) Cheerful.
Curving down Discontented.
Large lips (20) Hedonistic.
Narrow lips Unemotional.
Straight lips (21) Self-controlled.
Curved lips (22) Changeable.
Protruding upper lip Critical, tends to exaggerate.
Protruding lower lip Considerate, pleasant.
Lips even in profile Restrained, assertive, analytical.

CHIN

Long Stubborn.
Short Changeable.
Pointed (23) Enthusiastic.
Cleft Self-centered.
Double chin (24) Amiable, self-indulgent.
Receding Argumentative, impatient, trivial.
Blunt (25) Firm, almost stolid, a calm surface hiding a quick temper.
Jutting forward Deliberate, purposeful, and stubborn.

Metoposcopy

The development of metoposcopy (from the Greek *metopon,* meaning forehead) is usually credited to an Italian, Geronimo or Gerolamo Cardano (1501–1576). otherwise known as Jerome Cardan. Cardan was an eminent physician, physicist, mathematician, and astrologer; among his many achievements were the first clinical description of typhus fever, and the first systematic dissertation on the mathematics of chance and probability. To arrive at his theory that character could be read in the lines of the forehead, he combined his knowledge of astrology with his observations of several hundred faces. In 1570 he lost his right to publish his work after being imprisoned for heresy. The end of his life may have been a self-fulfilling prophecy – he is said to have starved himself to death in order to prove the validity of his own horoscope.

Cardan's faces
Jerome Cardan (**A**) illustrated his book on metoposcopy with almost 800 woodcuts showing interpretations of different combinations of lines.
1 A peaceful and successful nature.
2 A quarrelsome, murderous nature.

3 An exalted, religious nature.
4 A man destined to die by violence.
5 An infirm man.
6 A successful warrior.
7 A poisoner.
8 A man destined to be wounded in the head.

READING THE LINES

Divide the forehead into seven equidistant and parallel strips: the distance between them will vary with the size of the subject's forehead. These strips will allow you to establish which of the planetary lines are present, and to interpret them. You can then go on to examine the forehead for other lines and combinations of lines, and include them in your overall analysis.

PLANETARY LINES

1 Line of Saturn If straight and well-defined – caution, intelligence, perception, discernment.

2 Line of Jupiter If straight and well-defined – integrity, magnanimity, good fortune; if longer than the line of Saturn – riches.

3 Line of Mars If deeply etched – courage, ambition, endurance; if broken – argumentative, self-indulgent.

4 Line of the sun If straight and well-defined – ambition, worldly success; if broken – egotism, greed; if curved – malevolence; if crossed by another line – honor, acclaim, wealth.

5 Line of Venus If clear – happiness in love; if broken – a series of romances.

6 Line of Mercury If curved upward – good luck; if divided into three – humor, eloquence.

7 Line of the moon If clear – travel, imagination, intuition; if broken – temperamental; if crossed by another line – good fortune in times of war.

FOREHEAD LINES

Wavy line Travel by sea. If turning down at both ends – travel on land; if turning up at both ends – travel by air.

Straight line curved at one end Ill health.

Slightly tilted line Happiness.

One horizontal line Success in war.

One diagonal line Adventure.

Two well-spaced horizontal lines Happiness, good fortune.

Three horizontal lines placed high on forehead Gentle, peaceful, financially unstable.

Three horizontal lines placed low on forehead Aggressive.

Three well-spaced horizontal lines Intelligent, kind, good, religious.

Three horizontal lines cut by a vertical line Longevity.

Line running close to hairline If complete – intelligence; if broken – irritability.

Line over left eyebrow Imaginative.

Line over right eyebrow Ambition. If long – success; if broken – egotistic.

Vertical lines between eyebrows One line – singleminded; two lines – changeable; three lines – practical, dutiful; four lines – active mind, involved in a wide range of activities.

Phrenology

It was in Vienna in 1796 that Dr Franz Joseph Gall, a practicing physician, first announced his theory of phrenology. His researches had led him to believe that as we think, so we affect the shape of our brain, which, in turn, affects the formation of our skull, causing irregularities in its surface. Dr Gall considered that character could thus easily be evaluated by examination of these irregularities – popularly referred to as "bumps" but called "faculties" or "organs" by phrenologists. By the middle of the nineteenth century, when phrenology was at the height of its popularity, Gall's successors had classified 42 separate faculties, each corresponding with a particular facet of the personality.

Idiots, malefactors, and poets

Readers of *Heads and Faces, and How to Study Them; A Manual of Phrenology and Physiognomy for the People* (by Nelson Sizer and Dr H. S. Drayton, 1896) were encouraged to put their learning to practical use: "This knowledge will enable employers to choose wisely and will enable employees to meet the requirements of peculiar people whom they may be required to please." Employers and employees alike could learn to locate the faculties of cautiousness (**a**) and approbativeness (**b**). The various lines on other illustrations allowed them easily to distinguish between an idiot (**c**), a malefactor (**d**), and a poet (**e**), or between persons of criminal (**f**) and moral (**g**) characters.

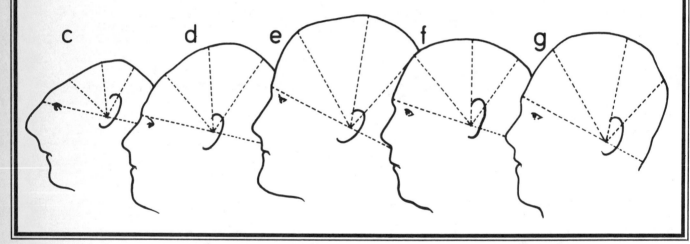

Reading a head

First consider the overall shape of the head. A rounded head is said to indicate a strong, confident, courageous, sometimes restless nature. A square head is held to reveal a solid, reliable nature, deeply thoughtful and purposeful. The wider head is said to suggest an energetic, outgoing character, while the narrower head suggests a more withdrawn, inward-looking nature. An ovoid shape belongs to an intellectual – an "egghead." Next run your fingertips over the head of your subject, pressing gently but firmly so that you can feel the contours of the skull. Work systematically, judging the individual size of each faculty and its prominence in comparison to other parts of the head. As the brain consists of two hemispheres, phrenologists believe that each faculty can be duplicated: check both sides of the skull.

A faculty that is underdeveloped in comparison to the others indicates a lack of that particular quality in the personality; one that is well developed indicates that the quality is present to a considerable degree. So, for example, a small organ of alimentiveness indicates a light and finicky eater, possibly a teetotaller; if this faculty is well developed, it indicates a person who enjoys food and wine; and if over-developed, a glutton, who may also drink to excess.

Identifying all the details of the landscape of the skull is not easy, but can be developed with practice.

Remember to take the overall view and to consider the interrelationships of all the organs before giving your final reading.

THE FACULTIES

1 Amativeness Interest in the opposite sex, sex appeal.

2 Conjugality Capacity for constant, faithful love, the desire for marriage.

3 Philoprogenitiveness Capacity for parental love, filial affection, and care of the less fortunate.

4 Adhesiveness Capacity for affection, friendship, sociability.

5 Inhabitiveness Love of one's home, patriotism.

6 Continuity The ability to concentrate, to give a subject continuous attention, to make reasoned connections.

7 Vitativeness The love of life, ability to resist ill health.

8 Combativeness Capacity for courage, assertiveness, resistance.

9 Execution Executive capabilities, the power to endure.

10 Alimentiveness The appetite, love of food.

11 Acquisitiveness The desire to accumulate, the capacity for thrift.

12 Secretiveness Capacity for reserve and discretion.

13 Cautiousness Capacity for being careful.

14 Approbativeness The desire for popularity.

15 Self-esteem Self-confidence, the desire for authority.

16 Firmness Willpower, endurance, and determination.

17 Conscientiousness Integrity and moral discrimination.

18 Hopefulness Optimism.

19 Spirituality Capacity for religious faith, intuition, psychic abilities.

20 Veneration Respect for society, its rules and institutions.

21 Benevolence Generosity and sympathy.

22 Constructiveness Mechanical and practical ability.

23 Ideality Aesthetic qualities, the love of beauty and perfection.

24 Sublimity The love of the grand concept and the great creation in both nature and art.

25 Imitativeness Capacity for mimicry, drama, social skills.

26 Mirthfulness Cheerfulness, sense of humor.

27 Causality Thinking and reasoning ability, capacity for planning and deduction.

28 Comparison Ability to form analytical judgments.

29 Humanity Ability to judge people's characters and motives.

30 Agreeableness Capacity for persuasiveness and verbal dexterity.

31 Eventuality Memory for facts, events, and experiences.

32 Time Capacity for judging rhythm, tempo, and timing, for punctuality, for remembering dates.

33 Tune The "ear for music."

34 Language Ability to learn foreign languages, capacity for eloquence in writing and speaking.

35 Individuality The inquisitive mind, the ability to be discriminating and to apply what has been observed.

36 Form Visual skills and memory.

37 Size Ability to judge proportions, sizes, and measurements.

38 Weight Good balance, judgment of weights.

39 Color Skill in blending and using colors.

40 Order The ability to be organized, systematic, and tidy.

41 Calculation Mathematical ability.

42 Locality Sense of place and direction, enjoyment of travel.

Moleoscopy

Most people have a few of the benign blemishes on the body that we call moles. Because we are born with these marks, and because they can alter in appearance during our lifetime, they have been considered since the time of the ancient Greeks to be significant indicators of our character and fortune.

Moleoscopy reached the height of its popularity in the sixteenth and seventeenth centuries, when elaborate treatises linked the relative position of moles on the body with the horoscope, in a complex analysis of the nature and destiny of their owner. (As each part of the body was considered to be ruled by a specific sign of the zodiac and each part of the face by a specific planet, the position of each mole was considered of great astrological significance.) Today the process has been considerably simplified, but it is still said that you can learn much about yourself and your future from the appearance and position of your moles.

MOLES ON THE FACE

A Middle of forehead Bad tempered, can be cruel. Should guard against accidents in middle age.

B Left temple Spendthrift, headstrong. Should try to live a quiet life.

C Right temple Exceptionally able. Should guard against illness in later life.

D Eyebrow Persevering, happy in marriage. Should beware of lightning and food poisoning.

E Outside corner of eye Honest, forthright, needs to be loved.

F Ear Wealth, fame, and recklessness.

G Left cheek Serious, studious, struggling.

H Right cheek Successful life.

I One on each cheek Success after a hard struggle.

J Bridge of nose Lust, extravagance.

K Left side of nose Changeable, untrustworthy, but lucky. Should beware of falls.

L Right side of nose Great traveler, needs an outdoor occupation involving plenty of movement.

M Tip of nose A sincere friend.

N Nostrils A rover.

O Lips Greedy but benevolent.

P Lower lip Quiet and studious, more fortunate in later life.

Q Chin Conscientious, has common sense and artistic ability. Makes the best of any opportunities, and improves with age.

R Left lower jaw Critical, should beware of ill health.

S Right lower jaw Should beware of danger from fire or water.

MOLES ON THE BODY

1 Throat An artistic temperament, successful.

2 Chest Lazy, unsteady, quarrelsome, financially unsound.

3 Right breast Indolent, intemperate.

4 Left breast Active, energetic.

5 Nipple Fickle and unfaithful.

6 Right ribs Insensitive, cowardly.

7 Left ribs Lazy, humorous.

8 Navel Great good fortune.

9 Abdomen Voracious, intemperate, and self-indulgent. Should marry someone placid.

10 Hips Resourceful, valiant, over-amorous.

11 Loins Mendacious.

12 Right groin Ill health, prosperity.

13 Left groin Frail.

14 Right thigh Wealth, a happy marriage.

15 Left thigh A warm temperament.

16 Right knee A friendly disposition, a happy marriage.

17 Left knee Rash, extravagant, ill-tempered, with a good business sense.

18 Right leg Energetic and persevering.

19 Left leg Lazy.

20 Ankle A sharing nature, a sense of humor.

21 Heel Mentally and physically active. Should beware of making enemies.

22 Right foot Loves traveling.

23 Left foot Thoughtful, gloomy, prefers a sedentary life.

24 Instep Athletic, quarrelsome.

25 Neck Many ups and downs. Should be frugal.

26 Shoulder blades Restrictions, unhappiness.

27 Left shoulder Satisfied with anything.

28 Right shoulder Prudent, discreet, faithful, restless.

29 Left armpit Good fortune won by hard work.

30 Right armpit Heavy struggles against heavy odds.

31 Right arm Adversity in early life, contentment in old age

32 Left arm Courteous, industrious.

33 Elbow Great talent, great desire to travel.

34 Right wrist or hand Frugal, successful in business.

35 Left wrist or hand Ingenious, artistic disposition.

36 Finger Dishonest, prone to exaggerate, unable to face reality.

37 Back Frank, with an enquiring mind. Should be cautious.

38 Buttocks Total lack of ambition.

CHARACTERISTICS OF MOLES

Honey-colored Good fortune.

Red Fortunate.

Black Trouble and disappointment.

Becoming lighter Luck improving.

Becoming darker Trouble and disappointment.

Major changes in moles, eg bleeding Possible ill health: consult your doctor.

Round Implies a good character.

Angular Implies a bad character.

Oval Bad luck.

Oblong Great prosperity.

Raised Great good fortune.

Two moles close together Two marriages or serious love affairs.

Two moles on opposite sides of the body balancing each other A dual nature, one side of the character fighting the other.

©DIAGRAM

49

Biorhythms

The modern study of biorhythms is based on the fact that human life, like any other form of life, is dependent on the intake and output of energy. This intake and output should be measurable, and may be found to be less at some times, more at others. Believers in biorhythms assert that the ups and downs occur in a regular, cyclical manner. A great deal in nature is cyclical – the waxing and waning of the moon, the seasons, the menstrual cycle, etc – so it is feasible that the rise and fall of our inner energies should follow a similar pattern. Biorhythms set out to plot the rise and fall of three interrelated cycles – physical, emotional, and intellectual – enabling you to predict your peak days, when particular activities can be carried out with the greatest chance of success, and your critical days, when you will need to take extra care.

The three biorhythm cycles were discovered at the beginning of this century – the physical and the emotional cycles first, the intellectual cycle somewhat later. The physical cycle affects such things as resistance to disease, strength, coordination, physiology, and athletic prowess; the emotional cycle affects creativity, sensitivity, mental health, emotional mood, etc; and the intellectual cycle, mental alertness, memory, logic, the power of analysis, and so on.

All three cycles begin together on the day of birth, starting from a common baseline. Each cycle then rises and falls in its own regular rhythm, forming a wave-like pattern called a sine curve. When a cycle is above the base line, it is said to be in a positive phase, and the energies and abilities associated with it are high – highest of all on the peak day or days. Below the base line it is in the negative phase, and the energies and capabilities are somewhat diminished – a time for recuperation, for recharging the batteries. The critical days are those that occur when the cycle changes from the positive to the negative phase, or vice versa, and so crosses the baseline – and these are the days when we are at our weakest and most vulnerable.

Because the three cycles are of different lengths, they rarely coincide, and so throughout our lives we are usually affected by mixed rhythms. One rhythm or another may be more important in your life, and so may be dominant in the mixture. For example, if you were a top-class athlete, you could expect your physical cycle to be dominant, and might try to plan your major competitions for the positive half of that cycle. But biorhythms can only give you an insight into predispositions – if you have no reason to exert yourself physically during the peak of your physical cycle, you will never know if your physical performance would have been at its best at that point.

Books of charts, personal calculators, slide rules, home computer programs, and so on are all available to give you readouts of your three cycles over periods of years. But it is quite simple to calculate your own – all you need is your date of birth and some simple arithmetic.

1 Physical cycle

Length	23 days
Peak days	5, 6
Critical days	11, 23
Lowest day	17

2 Emotional cycle

Length	28 days
Peak day	7
Critical days	14, 28
Lowest day	21

3 Intellectual cycle

Length	33 days
Peak day	8
Critical days	16, 33
Lowest days	24, 25

Calculating biorhythms

First work out how many days it has been since you were born – not forgetting to include the extra day in each leap year! For example, if you were born on April 16, 1958, and wanted to know your biorhythms for February 3, 1983, you would have been alive for 8906 days.

Divide this number by 23, the number of days in the physical cycle. The remainder from this calculation tells you how many days you are into your current physical cycle on your chosen date. In our example, 8906÷23=387, remainder 5. So on February 3, 1983, the subject is 5 days into the physical cycle.

Now repeat for the emotional cycle, by dividing by 28, and for the intellectual cycle, by dividing by 33. 8906÷28=318, remainder 2; 8906÷33=269, remainder 29. So the subject is 2 days into the emotional cycle, and 29 days into the intellectual cycle.

You can repeat the calculation for any day on which you wish to know your biorhythms, or you can use it as a starting point for drawing your own biorhythm charts. If you were born very late in the day, ie close to midnight, you may find that you obtain more characteristic and accurate biorhythms by using the day after your birthday as the basis for your calculations.

4 Biorhythms at birth

Biorhythms are assumed to begin at the moment that a baby begins to function as an autonomous human being, ie when it takes its first breath. All the cycles begin together from the common baseline; they next coincide and rise from the line together 58.6 years later.

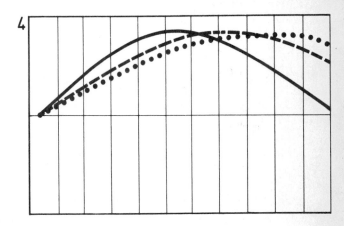

5 Triple critical

A triple critical occurs when all three cycles cross the baseline on the same day, even though they are not in the same phase. Such a day occurs once a year. Biorhythm theory suggests that it is a day that requires extra prudence, and that you should avoid it when planning any strenuous or demanding activities.

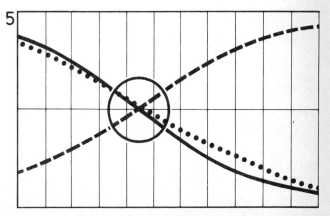

Oneiromancy 1

Everyone dreams, but not all dreams foretell the future. Long before Freud and other psychoanalysts showed us just how many of our dreams come from our subconscious and unconscious minds, Aristotle had argued that precognitive dreams were impossible. But history is full of well-attested precognitive dreams (Abraham Lincoln's dream of his own assassination is perhaps the most famous), and so their existence cannot be dismissed out of hand.

Oneiromancy – divination by dreams – is known everywhere in the world. No-one knows when it began, but records of prophetic dreams and their interpretations survive from the most ancient cultures. The oldest surviving comprehensive book of dreams and their meanings was compiled by Artemidorus of Ephesus in the second century: it was translated into English in the seventeenth century, reprinted 32 times before 1800, used by Freud in his researches, and still influences the dream dictionaries available today.

Dream interpretation

The more clearly you remember a dream, the greater is said to be its significance. But dream images fade rapidly from the conscious memory; keeping a pencil and paper beside your bed and writing down your dreams as soon as you wake up will prevent you forgetting any important details.

If you think a dream may be precognitive, break it down into its separate elements and consider them individually. Ignore any that relate to your everyday life: for example, if you commute to work by train each morning, a train appearing in your dream will have no significance. Ask yourself if any events in your recent past or in your earlier life or childhood could have caused a particular image: if so, ignore that element of your dream as well.

Use a dream dictionary to interpret the elements of your dream that remain. Begin with the most important – the image that you recall most vividly – but include all the details, however minor or contradictory, in your final overall interpretation.

Which dreams?

Precognitive dreams usually occur between 3.00 am and 7.00 am, when digestion has been completed, and the mind and the body are both relaxed. Dreams that do not foretell the future and have no prophetic value include those:

a occurring during the early part of the night;
b caused by indigestion or illness;
c with a reasonable outside cause – noise, temperature, sleeping position, etc;
d caused by a disturbing book, television program, etc;
e concerning the events of the previous day.

Egyptian dreams

1 One of the earliest written records of dreams and their interpretations is a papyrus of c.1250BC, which records some 200 dreams and their interpretations according to the priests of the falcon-headed god Horus.

2 According to the book of Genesis, the Pharaoh's precognitive dream of seven fat kine and seven lean kine was correctly interpreted by Joseph as prophesying seven fat years and seven lean years for Egypt. This dream was a popular subject with medieval artists, as for example in this illustration from a thirteenth-century French psalter.

Dream images classified

a) Any sharp-edged object – eg knife, scissors, sword, etc – tells of bad news to come.

b) Clean, shiny objects are omens of good fortune; dirty, dull objects are omens of ill fortune.

c) Ascending in any way – eg up ladders, stairs, ropes, escalators, etc – is always a sign of success. Descending or falling indicates reverses or failures. The higher you ascend, the greater your success; the farther you fall, the greater the setbacks.

d) Dreams of being entertained can indicate either good or ill fortune. I˝ you dreamed that you enjoyed a radio or television program, a movie, or a play at a theater, the omens are good; if you were bored, or the performance was canceled, or you disliked what you saw, the omens are bad.

e) Depending on their appearance and/or their contents, some images can indicate either a favorable or an unfavorable future. For example, a full cupboard indicates plenty, an empty cupboard want. Similarly, calm water indicates good fortune, rough water difficulties, and murky water ill luck. Other images with comparable variations of interpretation include the following:

air	cellar	grass	plants
bank	clouds	hamper	roads
barn	cup	harvest	sky
bowl	drink	landscape	smells
bridge	farm	letters	straw
broom	field	market	vine
cage	garden	pantry	warehouse
canal	glass	paths	wind

f) Obstacles in dreams indicate the severity of the difficulties facing you. For example, a door that opens easily suggests minor difficulties, while one that will not open at all suggests insurmountable obstacles. Other obstacle dreams include the following:

abyss	embankment	island	struggling
barefoot	envelope	jumping	tower
bolts	examinations	labyrinth	traffic
canyon	fence	locks	valley
cave	floods	mountain	walking
cavern	gate	prison	wall
cliffs	gravel	questions	window
crutches	hedge	rivalry	zipper
ditch	hills	rocks	
drawer	hunting	sewing	

g) Some dreams are considered to be "dreams of contrary," ie their meaning is the opposite of the image. For example, a dream of misery and crying is considered an omen of happiness. Other dreams of contrary include the following:

ambition/setbacks	inferiority/superiority
calm/disturbance	losses/gains
criticism/appreciation	luxury/poverty
encouragement/discouragement	quarrels/affection
fear/courage	rejoicing/regrets

2

©DIAGRAM

Oneiromancy 2

A

Abandoning Being abandoned – troubles will end; abandoning another – trouble coming.

Abbey Seen in daylight – good luck; seen at night – temporary sadness.

Abdomen Pain in abdomen – good health; abdomen exposed – treachery.

Abroad If you go – change, upheaval; if others go – enemies will be overcome.

Absence Of a friend or lover – emotional difficulties.

Accident Be on your guard.

Accountant, accounts Take greater care of your money.

Acid Broken promises.

Acorn Good fortune, happiness.

Acrobat Beware of accidents, especially when traveling.

Acting If you are acting – temporary troubles; if others are acting – travel.

Admiral Successful social life.

Adultery If you commit it – betrayal by friends; if you resist it – happiness.

Adventure Good fortune.

Advertisement Placing an advertisement – avoid speculation; reading an advertisement – plans will work out.

Aerial, antenna Extra money.

Age Yourself in old age – illness; other old people – good luck.

Agony Great joy.

Airplane Good news, financial benefit.

Alarm Exciting, profitable times.

Alcohol In moderation – success; in excess – embarrassment.

Alien New friends, major changes.

Alligator, crocodile Beware enemies.

Almond, almond tree Good fortune. Bitter almonds – a warning.

Alphabet Good news coming.

Altar Release from worry.

Ambulance Important hopes fulfilled.

Amputation Performed on you – a useful gain; performed on others – setbacks coming.

Ancestors Unexpected honors.

Anchor Economize.

Angel Protection, success, happiness.

Anger Achievement, useful assistance.

Animals If calm – business success; if hostile – business reverses.

Ankles Your own – success after a struggle; belonging to someone of the same sex – a problem solved; belonging to someone of the opposite sex – an unwise affair.

Antiques Looking at antiques – happiness at home; buying them – an eventual inheritance; selling them – don't lend or borrow money.

Ants Beneficial changes are coming. Infesting house – hard work and frustration ahead; on food – happiness.

Anvil Great good fortune.

Ape A mischief maker.

Apron Financial improvement.

Arch If whole – present efforts will be successful; if broken – change of direction needed.

Arm Pleasant company.

Army Obstacles ahead.

Arrow Wounded by arrow – betrayal; broken arrow – a broken relationship.

Artist Time is being wasted.

Ashes Setbacks. From a cremation – an unexpected inheritance; emptying ashes – financial difficulties.

Atlas Travel.

Attic Casual promiscuity.

Author Widening interests, but don't lend money.

Avalanche Seeing one – serious obstacles ahead; buried by one – good luck; others being buried – change of surroundings.

Award Good fortune.

B

Baby Attractive baby – good friends; ugly – treacherous friends; helpless – difficulties ahead; walking – sudden independence; several babies – satisfaction.

Back If bare – loss of status; your own back – problems will disappear.

Badge Security.

Bag Paper – money troubles; cloth – financial improvement; leather – travel.

Baking Improving fortunes.

Baldness Your own – ill health; of others – betrayal.

Ball games Good news, good friendship.

Balloon Setbacks and misfortunes.

Bandage New influences.

Banquet Good fortune.

Barbecue Imposed on by relatives.

Barber Success after difficulties.

Bath Empty – keep your temper; taking a bath – sorrow.

Battles Serious quarrels.

Beans Difficulties ahead. Cooking beans – increasing income.

Beard A good omen, the fuller the better.

Bed A strange bed – improved circumstances; your own bed – security; making a bed – unexpected visitors.

Beer Success. Flat beer – failure.

Bees Good news and financial success. Killing bees – ruin; beeswax – love affair; empty beehive – financial difficulties.

Beetles Beware enemies. Killing beetles – temporary difficulties.

Beggar Help coming.

Bell One bell – bad news; several bells – good news; church bells – opposition; high belfry – good news.

Belt Happy future.

Bench Important business news.

Bereavement Happiness.

Berries Well-being and achievement.

Bicycle Unexpected help.
Birds Good fortune. Dead birds – bad times coming.
Birth Achievement.
Bishop Unpleasant news.
Black Any black object is an ill omen.
Blemish On neck, chest, or arms – success in love; on body or legs – scandal.
Blindness Beware of deceit.
Blood Your own – avoid hostility in the family; blood of others – beware of enemies.
Boat A symbol for your life. The omen corresponds with what the boat is doing – smooth sailing, becalmed, etc.
Bones Human – unexpected income; animal – financial setbacks; fish – illness; animal eating bones – ruin.
Books Happiness and contentment.
Bottle Full – prosperity; empty – loss; spilled – domestic quarrels; bottle of wine – bad temper; bottle of perfume – happiness; bottle of brandy – good news.
Bread Fresh – good fortune; stale – family troubles; buying bread – success.
Breakfast Misfortune.
Bricks Sudden, unfavorable change.
Bride Good fortune.
Bridegroom Unexpected delays.
Bruise Avoid high living.
Bubbles Difficulties will be short lived. Blowing bubbles – beware of extravagance.
Burglar Improved finances.
Burial A birth or a wedding.
Burning Increased prosperity.
Butterfly Social success.
Button New and shiny – good fortune; lost – beware overspending.

C

Cake Happy times, achievement.
Calendar Worries disappearing gradually.
Call Your own name – important news; another's name – disruption ahead.
Camera Deceit and troubles.
Camp Good fortune.
Candle Lit – good fortune; unlit – domestic disappointment; guttering – new opportunities; candlestick – social activity.
Cannon Achievement.
Cap End of troubles. Worn and dirty cap – minor reverses.
Carpentry Enjoyment, security, love, leisure.
Carpet Good luck.
Carrots A legacy.
Castle In good repair – good fortune; in ruins – curb your temper.

Peddling dreams
a This eighteenth-century English engraving shows a street peddler selling dream books.
b Until Freud published his work on dreams, most dream books – such as this English version published in 1874 – were still based on the interpretations listed by Artemidorus c.200AD.

THE DREAMER'S TRUE FRIEND.

CONTAINING NEARLY
1,000 DREAMS,
Wherein is explained all the phenomena of spiritual imagination in Drams, &c

B. MARCH, 1, Woodbridge Street, Clerkenwell, London, E.C.

©DIAGRAM

Oneiromancy 3

Cat Treachery and deceit.
Catastrophe Complete change of lifestyle.
Cattle Peace and prosperity.
Cemetery Good fortune.
Chains Worries soon over.
Chair Comfort, unexpected news. Rocking chair – legacy.
Cheese Eating cheese – luck in love and money; strong smelling cheese – embarrassment; processed cheese – need for change; grated cheese – money coming; making cheese – business success.
Children Business success.
Chimney Very high – unusual achievement; average size – favorable times ahead; smoking – good news; on fire – avoid antagonizing others; in bad repair – trouble; collapsed – a celebration.
Chips Wood chips – irritations; gaming chips – successful speculation; potato chips – change for the better.
Church Seen from outside – good fortune; seen from inside – trouble ahead.
Circus Financial good fortune.
Cleaning Beware being drawn into something illegal.
Clock Don't waste time.
Clothing Plenty of clothes – ill luck; lack of clothes – prosperity.
Coffee Good news, happiness. If bitter – a broken

friendship; if spilled – small disappointments.
Coins Unexpected income: the smaller the coin, the greater the gain. If counterfeit – minor illness.
Comet Setbacks and opposition.
Committee An upheaval.
Cooking Good fortune, material well-being. If cooking soup – a rise to a position of power.
Corn Great good fortune.
Cough Danger from fire, flood, or pestilence.
Court Financial setbacks.
Crash Important achievement.
Crime If seen – beneficial changes; if you commit it – success on the way; if you are caught in the act – curb your tongue.
Crockery Domestic happiness. Broken crockery – an unwanted change.
Cross Adversity followed by good fortune.
Crowd Happiness. Angry mob – danger.
Cuckoo Upsetting news.
Curtains Unknown enemies are about.
Cushions Economies.

D

Dagger Beware treachery.
Dam Beware impulsive actions.
Dancing New friends, social success.

Kekulé's dream
In the early nineteenth century, scientists recognized an important group of chemicals, all of which were derived from benzene. The structure of benzene was unknown until 1865, when the eminent German chemist Freidrich August Kekulé (**A**) dreamed of a snake whirling in space while biting its own tail – a traditional image of the alchemists, as shown in this illustration from a fourteenth-century Venetian manuscript (**B**). This dream enabled Kekulé to postulate a formula for benzene (**C**) that is still in use today in a modified form (**D**).

Dawn New opportunities, improved conditions.
Death Your own – a change for the better; someone else's – a birth, unexpected good news.
Devil Resist temptation, beware hidden enemies.
Directory A good time for flirtation and gambling.
Dirt Illness.
Dish Full – good luck; empty – static period; broken – domestic difficulties.
Dizziness Passionate attraction.
Doctor Good fortune.
Dog Good omen if friendly, the larger the better.
Doll Domestic happiness.
Dragon Assistance from a powerful person.
Drill Stop wasting time.
Drowning Business reverse.
Drugs Warning against unwise decisions.
Drunkenness Your own – beware of dissipation; someone else's – a loss.
Dust Minor setbacks.

E

Ears Surprising news. Painful ears – treachery; pierced ears – domestic loss; earrings – avoid gossip.
Earth Profits.
Eggs Contentment, prosperity.
Elastic Your capabilities will be tested.
Election Short-term success. Casting your vote – a wish coming true; ballot box – you need a change of lifestyle.
Elephant Good fortune.
Eloping A romantic disappointment.
Embarrassment Success, well-being.
Embezzlement Seek professional advice.
Enemies Aid coming from loyal friends.
Engagement Romantic troubles.
Escaping Heading for success.
Evening Increasing contentment in later life.
Evergreens Success with money.
Execution Your own – good health; someone else's – setbacks ahead.
Extravagance Domestic happiness.
Eyes Strange eyes – a beneficial change; painful eyes – beware deceit; attractive eyes – lucky in love; eyelids – someone else's troubles; false eyelashes – discovering secrets.

F

Faces Pleasant – happiness, prosperity; unpleasant – loss; strangers' faces – a change of place; washing your face – troubles you have caused yourself.
Factory Success after a struggle.
Fear Difficulties will be overcome.
Feathers Good luck, social popularity.
Feet Large, bare feet – good luck; painful feet – trouble; itchy feet – travel.
Fever An end to worries.
Fighting Major changes, upheaval.
Fire To see one – trouble; to make one – a new romance; to be burned – bad luck; a fireplace – contentment; a fire engine – money luck.
Fish Catching them – prosperity; dead fish – disappointment; tropical fish – ephemeral pleasures.
Flag Good times, financial improvement.
Flies Petty annoyances.
Floating Success, prosperity.
Floor Profitable business activities.
Flowers Bright and fresh – personal happiness; dead – beware of overconfidence; wild – an exciting adventure; artificial – don't act against your conscience.
Flying Ambition achieved.
Food Preparing fresh food – good fortune; lack of food – reverses; selling food – money luck; buying food – a celebration; tasting food – loss of property.
Footprints Difficulties.
Footsteps Learning something to your advantage.
Forest Release from worries.
Fork Decision to be made.
Fountain Fulfillment.
Friends Happy times, good news.
Fruit Ripe – good luck; unripe, sour – bad luck.
Furniture In good condition – good luck; in poor condition – bad luck.

G

Gallows Good luck.
Gambling Losing – financial success; winning – losses.
Gangway A period of transition.
Garage Improvements.
Garlic Protection.
Ghost Good fortune. Frightened by a ghost – beware ill considered ventures.
Giant Obstacles and enemies overcome.
Giggling Financial embarrassment but social success.
Gloves Your own – emotional security; new – financial security; lost – rely on your own resources; found – unexpected help; dirty – disappointments.
Goat Avoid gambling and anything illegal.
Gold Guard your possessions. Gold objects – financial luck.
Gondola Romantic boredom.
Gong Excitement.
Grain Prosperity.
Grave Loss and sadness.
Greenhouse Love, success.
Gun You will be wronged in some way.
Gypsy Uncertainty, travel.

H

Hammer Achievement, good luck.
Hand Clean and well-kept – good fortune; injured – misfortune.
Handcuffs Your worries are over.
Handkerchief Quarrels, hostility.
Hangover Family worries solved.
Harem Busy social life, gossip.

Oneiromancy 4

Hay Dry and sunlit – money troubles; wet or in a stack – money luck.

Hearse Seeing a hearse – responsibilities lightening; riding in a hearse – responsibilities increasing.

Heat Keep your temper.

Helmet Problems caused by lack of organization.

Hiding If you are hiding – beware ill-considered actions; if an object is hidden – take others' advice.

Hinge Family difficulties, gossip.

Hole Digging one – travel; being in one – false friends; holes in clothes – financial benefits.

Holiday Hard work coming before any respite possible.

Honey General good fortune.

Hood Deception.

Horn Good news, improved social life.

Horse Good luck, success. Horse being shod – money; falling off a horse – misfortune.

Hospital As a patient – do not overtax yourself; as a visitor – good news.

Hotel Lucky in love.

House Security and well-being. Derelict house – grief; buying a house – a love affair; selling a house – release from responsibilities; large house – wealth; small house – money troubles.

Hunger Good times coming.

I

Ice Success after adversity. Slipping on ice – difficulties ahead.

Iceberg Hidden opposition.

Illness Temptation, a dilemma.

Income Large – financial failure; small – financial success.

Inheritance A legacy or inheritance.

Injury Recognition.

Ink A problem solved.

Insects Trivial difficulties.

Insult A rise in status, loyalty, esteem.

Invalid Delayed success.

Invisibility Beneficial changes coming.

Invitations Financial gains.

Island New developments.

Itching Stop worrying.

Ivy Wealth and happiness.

J

Jail Hardship ahead.

Jealousy A series of problems, hostility.

Jewelry Valuable jewelry – good fortune; costume jewelry – vanity; giving or receiving jewelry – lucky in love.

Job Looking for a job or being fired – good luck.

Journey Changes. Boat journey – friendship; airplane journey – quarrels.

Judge Setbacks and hardships.

Jug New and good friends.

Juggler Easy profits.

Jungle Avoid risky financial or emotional entanglements.

K

Kettle Boiling – good luck; boiled dry – unexpected expenses.

Keys In a lock – pleasurable love affair; finding, giving, or receiving keys – good luck; losing keys – bad luck; broken – lost opportunity; keyhole – treachery.

Killing Human killed – avoid emotional upheaval; animal killed – help is on the way.

Kiss Pleasure and contentment. Avoiding a kiss – a minor illness; kissing babies – success in a difficult task.

Knife Ill fortune.

Knight Protection.

Knitting Peace of mind.

Knots Anxiety.

L

Lamp If lit – success; if you light it – benefit from past efforts; if you put it out – a rest or holiday.

Lateness Trouble, deception.

Laughter Ill luck in love and friendship.

Lava Exciting social life.

Lawyer Business worries.

Dropping off

Winsor McCay's famous American comic strip *Little Nemo in Slumberland* told of Little Nemo's dream adventures. In this extract *right* from a 1905 strip Little Nemo is seen falling through space. Dreams of falling from a great height are common, and are said to indicate future reverses or failures in your life. Like Little Nemo, most people wake up before they reach the end of their fall.

I WONDER WHAT THE OOMP WILL SAY, OH!

Leaves Green and growing – health and happiness; falling – a parting.
Light Good fortune.
Lion Social and financial advancement.
Lizard Beware false friends.
Log Good luck and happiness.
Love Happiness and contentment.

M

Machinery Running and well-tended – success; idle or derelict – employment problems.
Man Family prosperity. Several men – nervous strain.
Map Change, travel.
Mask Deceit.
Meat Business prosperity.
Mending Unexpected windfall.
Messenger A lucrative offer.
Milk Fresh milk – good health; sour or spilled milk – illness.
Mirror Dishonesty and disloyalty.
Money Good fortune.
Moon Waxing – a change for the better; waning – a change for the worse.
Mouth Keep silent.
Music Pleasant music – good fortune, happiness; discordant – ill fortune; playing an instrument – sudden changes.

N

Neck Good luck financially. Broken neck – money mismanagement.
Needle Bad luck. Threading a needle with ease – good luck.
Newspaper Good fortune, happy times.
Night Obstacles, delays.
Nose Sore or injured – trouble, opposition; blowing your nose – the end of a bad time.
Nudity Your own – financial and social success; of others – beware deceit.
Nurse Family unity.
Nuts Good fortune. Cracking nuts – health, success.

O

Office Changes ahead in personal relationships.
Oil Finances improving.
Operation Major changes ahead.
Orchard Achievement and satisfaction.
Orders Obeying them – better times ahead; giving them – domestic discord.
Ornaments Personal ornaments – improved prospects; household ornaments – setbacks; broken ornaments – good luck.
Oven Cold – regrets; warm or hot – fruitful efforts.
Owl Setbacks and disappointments.

P

Painting A house – beware ill-considered actions; a picture – circumstances improving.
Paper Effort and opportunity.
Paralysis Internal conflict.
Parents Happiness and achievement. Becoming a parent – unexpected news.
Park A new and happy love affair.
Party Social pleasure.
Pearls Prosperity through hard work.
Pebbles Gossip, depression.
Pendulum Unexpected changes.
Perfume Used by a woman – a new love affair; used by a man – misunderstanding.
Photographs Happy friendships.
Pictures Treachery.
Pigs Troubles at home but progress at work.
Pins Finding one – good luck; being pricked by one – trouble; in use on clothing – trouble; full pincushion – achievement.
Politics Success, responsibilities.
Power The greater the power, the greater your achievement.
Prize Success and achievement.
Publicity Be diplomatic.
Puppets Fear of being manipulated.
Pyramid Success, enjoyable change, and travel.

Oneiromancy 5

Q

Quarrel Peace and happiness in personal relationships.
Quilt Prosperity, domestic bliss.

R

Rabbits Satisfying changes, prosperity.
Race Success, advancement.
Raft Enforced travel.
Rain Good fortune and prosperity, unless you are already wealthy in which case it means bad luck.
Rainbow Troubles ending.
Rats Ill fortune, hidden enemies.
Razor Control yourself.
Refrigerator Prosperity, unexpected guests.
Relatives Freedom from worry, help when needed.
Restaurant Cheap – improved finances; modest – social happiness; expensive – setbacks.
Ring Financial and romantic success.
Roof In good repair – good luck; repairing one – finances improving; leaky roof – unhappiness in love; roof on fire – stop worrying; falling off roof – temporary success.
Rope Success, beneficial changes.
Ruins Improving conditions.
Running Toward something – fulfillment; away from something – trouble, hardship; unable to run – lack of self-confidence.

S

Sacrifice Rejoicing.

Salt Great good fortune.
Sand Beware of new acquaintances.
Scandal Examine your conscience.
Scarf Happiness in love.
School Seeing a school – financial gain; being at school – difficulties, setbacks; leaving school – temporary financial gain.
Screaming Hearing a scream – bad news; screaming yourself – good luck.
Secrets Beware deceit and malice.
Sex Enjoyable and satisfying – good fortune; being a different sex – a change for the better.
Shadow Your own – improved finances; someone else's – dangers ahead.
Shells Unusual events, strange news.
Signature Good luck, security.
Silver Coins – improved finances; objects – beware too much concern with money.
Snake Ill luck.
Snow Happiness and prosperity after temporary setbacks.
Spider Good luck, success.
Spies Impulsive behavior.
Spoons Domestic bliss. Lost or stolen – unwise investments.
Stains Scandals, laziness.
Star Fulfillment, happiness.
Storms Discontentment.
Strangers Happy reunion.
Sun Success, happiness. Sunrise or sunset – beneficial changes.
Swamps Threats to finances and to emotional life.
Swimming Good fortune.

Creative dreaming
Charles Dickens said that many of the characters and plots of his novels first came to him while he was dreaming – as he is depicted in the nineteenth-century illustration *right*.

T

Table Improving fortunes. Kitchen table – hard work ahead.
Tea Social success.
Teeth Aching or damaged teeth – ill luck; teeth in good condition, or false teeth – good luck.
Telephone Rivalry, sad news.
Thorns Malicious associates.
Thunder Loud – good luck; distant, rumbling – treachery.
Towel Clean – health, material prosperity; wet – frustration; paper – recession.
Toys Whole – good luck; broken – stop behaving childishly.
Trial Be cautious.
Tunnel Changes bringing risks.

U

Umbrella Achievement, security. Broken – reverses; inside out – achievement after hardship.
Undressing Misplaced confidence and affections.
Uniform Security, happiness, and advancement.

V

Vampire Anxiety.
Vegetables Growing or cooking them – good times coming; eating them – troubles ahead; rotten vegetables – ill luck.
Visitor Being a visitor – beware false friends; being visited – beware actions that will harm others.
Volcano Disagreements, dishonesty.

W

Walking Obstacles will disappear.
Washing Yourself – new friends; objects – upheavals.
Watch Advancement through positive action.
Wheels Progress. The speed of progress increases with the speed at which the wheels turn.
Whispering Think before you speak or act.
Whistling Setbacks, difficulties, criticism.
Wine Health, happiness.
Woman Increasing prosperity and security.
Worms Alive – illness; killing worms or using them as bait – good fortune.
Writing Your writing – beware making trouble for yourself; someone else's writing – beware bad advice.

X

X-rays Good health.

Y

Yawn Setbacks of your own making.
Yoke Being dominated.

Z

Zoo Unexpected but enjoyable travel.

Goya's dream *right*
An engraving by the eighteenth-century Spanish artist Goya shows the sleeper haunted by a dream of owls – a symbol of setbacks and disappointments.

Clairvoyance

Clairvoyants have no need of the apparatus and symbolism required by other fortune tellers: their foreknowledge comes in the form of waking visions that can be actively and consciously summoned when they are wanted.

Shamans, soothsayers, witch doctors, seers, oracles, and prophets throughout the world have always relied on their clairvoyant talents. And while many of history's most famous clairvoyants are now more or less legendary figures (like Cassandra, who was given the gift of sight by Apollo, who also ordained that her prophecies should never be believed), there are still a great many people alive today whose foreseeings have often proved startlingly accurate. The best-known modern clairvoyant is probably the American, Jeane Dixon, who predicted the assassination of President Kennedy. Although she has quite a high failure rate, she has been correct in her predictions often enough to take her statistically beyond the level of mere chance.

Developing clairvoyance

It is generally assumed that either you have the gift of clairvoyance or you do not. Some people seem to have clairvoyant powers instantly at their command, while the rest of us seem to have no insight into the future at all.

But many authorities now believe that clairvoyant ability is a widespread human potential. They place it in the same mental area as intuition, and suggest that everyone has it to some extent, even if it is latent and lying undiscovered. They remind us of the many well-attested cases of ordinary people with no previous history of psychic ability who have had precognitive experiences at moments of unusual stress.

Many clairvoyants assert that these latent abilities can be activated. They suggest deep forms of meditation to relax the mind, to shed the restrictions of rationalist and materialist thinking, and to put you in touch with the deeper levels of your psyche. Some suggest that if

Things to come?
Present-day clairvoyants have predicted that the following events will take place before the end of this century.
A total ban on all cigarettes (**1**).
A ban on private cars in cities.
Motorists with a record of convictions for dangerous driving will be required to drive marked cars.
The police will use psychic powers to enforce the law.
A new ice age will begin (**2**).
There will be a manned landing on Mars (**3**).
Life will be discovered on planets outside the solar system (**4**).
The remains of Atlantis will be discovered (**5**).

your rational inhibitions are very strong a course of hypnosis may be beneficial, because it can sometimes be the entrance into a semi-trance state that clears away the barriers that are repressing the intuitive, paranormal mental areas. They also recommend that you use any form of device or tool that you find useful to concentrate these non-rational mental areas, and to activate and focus the extrasensory gifts.

Extrasensory perceptions

Clairaudience Literally, "clear hearing." Divination by hearing the future ahead of time.

Clairvoyance Literally, "clear seeing." Divination by seeing the future ahead of time.

Metagnomy Divination by sights of future events seen when in a hypnotic trance.

Precognition Inner paranormal knowledge of the future.

Psychometry Clairvoyant divination about a specific person through holding an object belonging to them.

Clairvoyance in focus

It has been said that all forms of predicting the future are ultimately dependent on clairvoyance, and that cards, tea-leaves, crystal balls and so on are merely a point of focus for a clairvoyant talent. Forms of predicting which might help you develop any latent clairvoyant talent, and where you would certainly find such a talent useful, include:

a reading the tarot;
b palmistry;
c tasseography;
d radiesthesia;
e captoptromancy;
f crystallomancy.

New York City will no longer exist (**6**).
Japan will merge with China (**7**).
Britain will become a republic after the death of Queen Elizabeth II.
The USA will be run by a five-member executive committee, instead of a president.
The papacy will cease to exist.

Russia will become a Christian country (**8**).
A single currency will be in use throughout the world (**9**).
A vaccine against cancer will be discovered (**10**).

Dowsing 1

Most people think of dowsing as a technique used for finding water in arid areas. But it can be used to find almost anything under the earth: to locate mineral deposits (metals, coal, oil, etc); to trace underground pipes, tunnels, and cables; to find hidden treasure, lost property, and archeological sites; and even to discover dead bodies.

Dowsing would appear to date back to at least 6000BC – a cave painting of that period found in the northern Sahara shows a man holding a forked stick just as a modern diviner would do. Certainly dowsers appear in early Egyptian, Chinese, and Peruvian carvings. From the fifteenth to the seventeenth century, dowsers searched mainly for metal, and were often attached to the staff of prospecting and mining expeditions. In the eighteenth and nineteenth centuries, they usually looked for water. And today's dowsers are often employed by public corporations or in industry to pinpoint unmapped cables, pipelines, and so on.

In the past it was probably in the professional dowser's own best interests to let people believe that his gift was extremely rare. But today's experts think it is much more likely that over 80% of us have the ability lying latent, and could – with practice – become competent dowsers. The equipment needed is minimal: you can choose between the traditional forked twig, or the more sensitive divining rods. At first the reactions you obtain may be weak, but they should become stronger with practice. With experience, it should be possible to tell from the strength and nature of the reaction exactly what you have found and how deep it is buried.

A

Making metal divining rods
Cut through a wire coat hanger in two places as shown (**1**), and then bend the smooth piece of wire to a right angle (**2**). Repeat with a second coat hanger. The rods can be held in the hand as they are (**3**), or you can make secondary sleeves that slide over the rods and allow them to move freely (**4**). A very good sleeve can be made by removing the refill and stopper from an old ballpoint pen.

Dowsing outdoors

If you are using metal divining rods, hold them in your loosely clenched fists, with your thumbs resting over your forefingers. Your forearms and the arms of the rods should be horizontal and parallel to each other, and your elbows should be well tucked in (**A**).

If you are using a dowsing twig, hold it firmly with your palms pointing upward and your thumbs pointing outward. The twig and your forearms should be in the same horizontal plane, and your elbows should again be well tucked in (**B**). Move your fists apart until the twig is tensed but balanced.

Concentrate your mind on the substance you are looking for: some dowsers find it helpful to carry a sample with them. The sample should be small enough to carry comfortably, but large enough to be in contact with both your skin and the rod (liquids can be carried in a small bottle). A sample is not usually needed when searching for water, as its influence is so powerful.

Walk slowly and steadily over your search area, taking fairly short strides. Cover the area methodically, and use markers to indicate the places where your rods or twigs reacted. The rods will react by crossing (**C**) or by swinging apart; the twig may turn up (**D**) or down, or even revolve completely.

Choosing a dowsing twig

Choose a supple, pliable twig of young (but not green) wood. Hazel is the most popular, but beech, apple, birch, willow, and privet can all be used. Do not choose a brittle wood that breaks easily.

Look for an undamaged, Y-shaped twig, with a strong joint at the Y. It should be about ⅜in (1cm) in diameter, and as even as possible. Cut it from the branch as shown (**5**). Use a sharp knife to trim the twig, but leave the bark on (**6**).

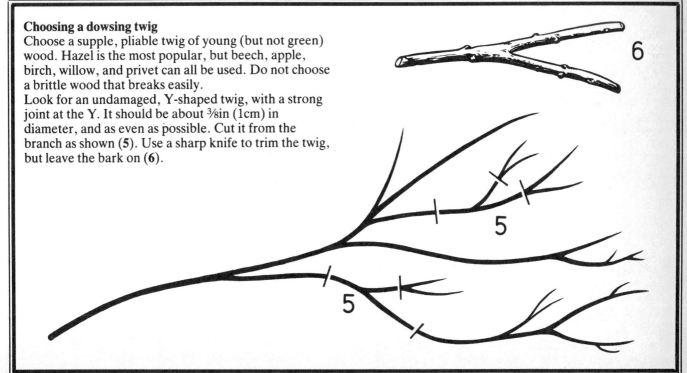

Dowsing 2

Instead of working outdoors on the site, some dowsers prefer to remain indoors and to search for their sources by running their rods over a large-scale map of the area. For this type of work many dowsers prefer a more accurate pointer in the form of a pendulum. Using a pendulum for divination is known as radiesthesia.
The earliest form of radiesthesia seems to have been coscinomancy, or divination by sieve. The suspended sieve was held in the air in a pair of tongs, which were kept closed by two people's fingertips. The sieve was then said to answer questions or to indicate the name of a guilty person by the way in which it rotated. Other forms of the art included divination with a suspended key (cleidomancy) or a suspended ring (dactylomancy) – methods that are still in use today.
Some radiesthesists practice forms of medical divination. The pendulum is held over various parts of the afflicted person's body, and the radiesthesist reads in its movements the location and diagnosis of the ailment. The pendulum is even said to be able to predict the onset of illness, and so to advise in preventive medicine. And it can apparently work without the presence of the patient: the medical radiesthesist may hold the pendulum over a sample of blood or urine, or perhaps merely over a photograph of the sufferer. But probably the commonest use of radiesthesia on the human body is in attempting to detect the sex of an unborn child.

Using the pendulum *below*
The pendulum should normally be held in your dominant hand. Hold the cord between your thumb and forefinger, allowing them to form a circle, and spread out your other fingers so that they are facing down. The arm should be firmly braced, but without tension. Cover your search area methodically, working very slowly across the map or photograph, and marking any reactions you obtain.
The pendulum can also be used outdoors instead of a divining rod or twig, but it is very susceptible to wind, and so can only be used on a calm day.

Choosing a pendulum

Many dowsers prefer their pendulums to be made of natural materials, especially wood; an average size pendulum would be about 1–2in (2–5cm) in diameter, and 1–2in (2–5cm) long. A cavity pendulum (**1**) can be used to hold a sample of any specific substance you are searching for.
But pendulums can be made in any material, and in any size and shape. You can choose from those commercially available (**2, 3, 4, 5**), or you could use a pendant or medallion (**6**), a large needle on a thread (**7**), a key tied to a piece of thin string (**8**), or a carved crystal on a gold chain (**9**). A woman who wishes to discover the sex of her unborn child traditionally uses a pendulum made from her wedding ring suspended on a hair from her head (**10**).
As long as the pendulum can swing freely and easily, the string or cord can be of any length from a few inches to about 2ft (60cm); a typical length is 5–6in (12–15cm).

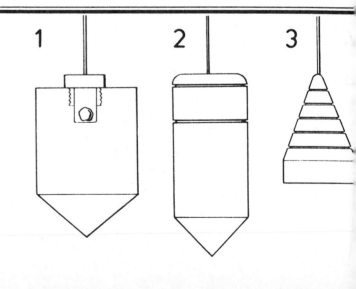

The pendulum's reactions

The pendulum is unusual in divination in that its movements are apparently sex-related (one of its traditional uses is in detecting the sex of an unborn child). With most operators, the pendulum will swing backward and forward (**A**) to indicate a man or a boy, and around in a circle (**B**) to indicate a girl or a woman. But with other operators these actions may be reversed – just as some people are right-handed and others left-handed.

Sex-determined movements apart, the pendulum's reactions seem to be particular to every individual dowser or radiesthesist. It is worth looking for known substances at first so that you can assess just how your pendulum reacts – it may oscillate a different number of times or in a different direction for different substances, or you may need to lengthen or shorten the cord to get a clear reaction. And although not everyone has the full range of radiesthesic talents, you may find that you are able to use your pendulum to answer specific questions (getting one reaction for "yes" and another for "no"), to act like a compass in directing you, or to tell you the time. By recording all the details of the gyrations of your pendulum under known conditions, you will be able to prepare your personal calibration chart for future reference.

Necromancy

In the past, necromancy was an unpleasant process that involved reanimating a dead body and forcing it to answer the questions of the living. Today, spiritualists believe that the dead will voluntarily answer questions put to them about the future, transmitting the replies either through a medium at a séance, through automatic writing, or through the mechanical methods of the planchette and the ouija board.

If you wish to try automatic writing, sit quietly in a dim light, and let the pen you are holding rest on a sheet of paper. Relax, and empty your mind completely. Your hand may – or may not – begin to write of its own accord; it may even produce legible writing, although most people find that only meaningless scribbles are left on the paper.

The planchette, which was apparently known to the ancient Chinese, allows several participants to combine their psychic talents in another approach to automatic writing. But those who find that the messages are still incomprehensible may prefer to try the ouija board, where the messages are spelled out slowly but readably using the letters of the alphabet. The board was invented in the late nineteeth century by an American,

William Fuld, and named from the French and German words for yes (*oui* and *ja*).

Obviously the scope for abuse with either the planchette or the ouija board is considerable. One of the participating fingers could take conscious control and direct the messages that are produced, perhaps including insulting or obscene messages, or practical jokes of various degrees of cruelty. It is claimed that such control can be detected and so be prevented. But it is advisable that the person asking the question does not speak it aloud, but concentrates on it in their mind, while the other participants sit in silence and clear their minds of thoughts.

Even assuming that everyone is behaving themselves, and that the planchette is moving spontaneously, there can still be problems. A great many manipulators of the board have learned, unpleasantly, that the messages can often be embarrassing, frightening, and deeply disturbing. Practicing mediums, psychologists, and researchers into the paranormal all consider that these techniques are not suitable for party games, and are best left in the hands of the experts or practiced only under controlled conditions.

Planchette

A planchette (**A**) is a small board, often triangular or heart-shaped, and usually less than six inches long. It is mounted on small wheels, castors, or felt pads which raise it about an inch off the table and allow it to move around freely. A small hole in the board can hold either a pencil or a pointer (for use on a ouija board) in a vertical position.

Use a planchette for automatic writing by placing it on a large sheet of paper, and adjusting the pencil so that its point is touching the paper. The participants should each let a finger rest very lightly on the board of the planchette, which should then seem to move of its own accord, skimming around the paper and writing out its messages.

Ouija board

The ouija board (**B**) is made of smooth, polished wood, with the letters of the alphabet, the numbers 1–9, and words like "yes" and "no" arranged either around its circumference or, more commonly, in an arc along one side. A planchette fitted with a pointer is used to spell out the messages.

You can make a simple equivalent of a ouija board by writing the letters, numbers, and words on separate pieces of paper, and arranging them in a circle on a table (**C**). A drinking glass is turned upside down in the middle of the table, and the participants each rest a finger on it, as with the planchette. The glass should move from letter to letter, forming the words of the message: the table must, of course, be smooth enough for it to slide around easily.

B

A B C D E F G H I J K L
M N O P Q R S T U V W X Y Z
0 1 2 3 4 5 6 7 8 9

YES   GOODBYE   NO

C

Part 2
FORTUNES
AT RANDOM

1 A fifteenth-century French woodcut showing a tarot reading in progress.
2 The Wheel of Fortune from an early French deck of tarot cards.
3 A nineteenth-century engraving showing a fortune teller reading a standard deck of playing cards.
4 The ace of spades, sometimes known as the "death card," is always the most elaborate card in the deck.
5 An illustration from a seventeenth-century Chinese work on the I Ching showing yarrow stalks being used to "cast" a hexagram.
6 The 64 hexagrams of the I Ching are made up from the eight trigrams of King Wen, shown here in an early eighteenth-century Chinese illustration.

③

⑤

4

6

Tarot 1

The exotically decorated cards of the tarot have always carried with them an overlay of slightly sinister mystery. For centuries, practitioners of the occult and students of the esoteric arts have been insisting that the tarot is a special kind of repository for a vast amount of ancient, secret lore, all compressed into codes and symbols that only the fully initiated, and the very learned, can begin to unravel.

Part of this mysterious reputation comes from the fact that no-one can be sure where or when the tarot first came into existence. The puzzle of its origin has led some occultists to claim that it goes all the way back to the sorcery-steeped priests of ancient Egypt, or ancient Babylon, or ancient Tibet – or even, some have said, ancient and lost Atlantis. But other people have been in no doubt about the tarot's inspiration, if not its origin, when they have labeled it "the devil's picture-book."

Devils and mysteries aside, what is certain about the tarot is that it made its first recorded appearance in medieval France, in about 1390. And it is possible that the cards evolved as part of the secret folklore of the Romany peoples (gypsies) and came to Europe with them during their westward migrations centuries ago.

Nor did it stop evolving, even after its use spread beyond the Romanies. The ordinary deck of cards that we use today for bridge or poker grew out of the tarot, and many modern occultists have redesigned the tarot cards, omitting some and changing the basic nature of others, to create more up-to-date or more personalized sets. But the traditional tarot of Europe, which became more or less fixed and standardized by the eighteenth century, remains the most impressively decorative, and the most richly furnished with shadowy symbolism.

It is not difficult to acquire tarot cards. If the place where you live does not have a shop that specializes in such esoteric merchandise, you can probably get them by mail order through an advertisement in one of the more popular occult or fortune-telling magazines. It is considerably more difficult, however, to acquire the ability to use the tarot. Each card has, of course, its own essential "meaning," its basic area of symbolic reference, explained on the following pages. But knowing those basics is like knowing how to move the pieces on a chess board: you can participate, but there is much more to know before you can become accomplished.

Each one of the tarot cards brings with it a long, dark

Tarot for you
Many different styles of
tarot cards are available.
Choose a deck that you
respond to intuitively.

train of symbolism, of subtle hints and echoes,
references and connections, which resonate far into the
depths of the occult tradition, and should also resonate
into the intuition of the skilled fortune teller. So you
are advised, by the experts, to take the tarot seriously –
to go on in your reading beyond the basics, and to
become familiar with those resonances. You are also
advised to handle your own tarot cards as much as you
can, to study the cards, think about them, attune them
to your own intuitive awareness. And you are advised
to treat them with respect. The tarot, it is said, will not
be mocked. If you approach it light-heartedly, using it
to answer frivolous questions and the like, the tradition
says that you may receive answers you would rather not
have had.

But if all this sounds a little ominous, it should be
added that in medieval times people used tarot cards to
play quite ordinary, and presumably frivolous, card
games – often for money. And history does not record
that they suffered any ill effects.

In any case, whether you intend to devote your life to
mastering the tarot, or merely wish to add it to your
collection of techniques for occasional fortune telling,
you must start at the same place – with an overall look
at the cards themselves.

There are 78 tarot cards, of which 56 divide into the
sequential cards of the four suits. The suits are cups,
swords, pentacles, and wands, which respectively are
the ancestors of our modern hearts, spades, diamonds,
and clubs. (The ancestry is even more obvious in
modern European card decks: hearts in Spain are
copas, cups; spades in France are *piques,* pikes; and so
on.) Obviously there must be 14 cards in each suit: the
intruder is an extra court card, called the knight, which
was not retained in the modern deck.

The 56 cards of the four suits are known as the minor
arcana (from "arcane" – secret), and they have their
special meanings and symbolisms, and their own uses in
fortune telling. But the main concern of the fortune
teller is with the remaining 22 cards, the major arcana,
sometimes known as the greater trumps. And with
them we enter a positive labyrinth of rich, dark, and
resonant symbolism.

Tarot 2

The 22 greater trumps form the secret heart of the tarot. The most decorated of the 78 cards, the most densely packed with occult significance, they will serve on their own, without the other cards, for enough varieties of fortune-telling practice to keep you busy for years. Especially when, as the specialists would warn, you could spend those years merely finding your way through the labyrinth of mystic symbolism, before ever beginning to deal them out for a reading.

But, because not everyone has the time or inclination to become a fully fledged occultist, these pages are offered as a simplified, preliminary map through the main routes of that labyrinth, so that – without too much effort – you can begin fairly promptly to make some use of the major arcana.

Traditionally the 22 cards are numbered and named (or at least 21 of them are numbered, as will be seen). Because scholarly experts like to disagree with one another, there has always been some argument about their proper order, and their true names. But we can cut through the argument by democratically following the majority view over the centuries. In the same way the meanings of each of the 22 cards that are given here, in capsule form, are attempts at synthesizing the most widely accepted areas of symbolic reference attached to each card.

Aside from their individual meanings, the cards are said to fall into some neat groupings that can offer useful guidelines to the fortune teller. Most important, all 22 of them can be seen to represent stages in the individual's progress through life, from the Fool (ie the innocent newborn) through to the "completion" symbol of the World, with the Wheel of Fortune at midpoint. The first 11, the first half of life, tend to be outward-looking, oriented toward the world of positive action and development. The second 11 bring the individual to a more inward-looking time, meditative and quiet, focused on inner development.

Tarot cards are of course not double-headed, and so will sometimes be laid upside down during a reading. Most experts have believed that being reversed in this way alters their meaning. Some modern fortune tellers, however, have chosen to discount this extra complication, but to dismiss a substantial part of the tradition in that way seems a trifle high-handed. So the following capsule definitions of the major arcana include abbreviated notes on the reversed meanings – which are often just the direct opposite of the card's essential implications, but can sometimes carry more subtle overtones.

Cards of the major arcana
Alternative names used in different decks are given in brackets.

  0 (or unnumbered) Fool
  1 Magician (Juggler)
  2 High Priestess (Juno, Papess, Female Pope)
  3 Empress
  4 Emperor
  5 High Priest (Jupiter, Pope, Heirophant)
  6 Lovers
  7 Chariot
  8 Justice
  9 Hermit
10 Wheel of Fortune
11 Strength
12 Hanged Man
13 Death
14 Temperance
15 Devil
16 Tower (Falling Tower)
17 Star
18 Moon
19 Sun
20 Judgment (The Last Judgment)
21 World
(In some sets, card 8 is Strength, and card 11 is Justice.)

Tarot 3

1 Magician
Only a step away from the Fool (as jester) and so relating more to a stage magician, an entertainer, than to a master of high magical lore. A fortunate card, suggesting progress in outward, worldly understanding, and progress also toward success. Its appearance suggests decisions to be made, with confidence.
Reversed Warns against hesitation, or against an unwillingness to confront the real world.

2 High Priestess
Injects an element of intuition, special knowledge, creativity, the non-rational, natural side of wisdom and understanding (including the psychic sort). Indicates a female influence, and the prospect of light being shed on a secret or problem.
Reversed Warns against over-emotionalism, irrationality, insufficient use of rational thought.

0 The Fool
Unnumbered, and has been placed at number 22. The most complex and most human of the cards – "holy innocent," wise man, and trickster, with all of humanity's contradictions (male/ female, good/evil, angel/ devil, etc). Symbol of potentiality, new beginnings, fresh challenges. Often used as the significator , to represent the person who is the subject of a reading.
Reversed Beware of foolish lack of forethought.

3 Empress
Expresses the fertility principle, the bountiful, caring, loving, enriching symbol of the Earth Mother. Another fortunate card, indicating a solid stability and also a natural growth and creativity (perhaps a new baby, material prosperity or just general well- being).
Reversed Domestic trouble and insecurity – perhaps sexual difficulties, or career setbacks.

4 Emperor

Male symbol who is the father figure to the Empress's mother. Indicates worldly success, authority and power, the triumph of rationality, outward energy, and strength of will. A fortunate card for men; for women, it can mean a dominating male influence, or achievement of ambition through forcefulness and controlled aggression.
Reversed Warns against weakness, submission.

5 High Priest

Spiritual rather than worldly power and authority – and the male counterpart of the High Priestess, offering rational knowledge, wisdom, creative intelligence, inspiring perceptions. Indicates the gaining of insight and understanding, not necessarily religious, always profound yet sensible. Can refer to the influence of an important teacher or advisor.
Reversed Beware of lies, misleading advice.

6 Lovers

Has to do with love relationships, obviously, and contains all the conflicts – choices to be made between the attractions of the flesh and of the spirit. A card that suggests a rewarding relationship or a good marriage, and extends to indicate generally positive decisions.
Reversed A wrong choice will be made, perhaps involving sexual infidelity. Also warns of sexual difficulties.

7 Chariot

Symbol of movement, indicating travel and, more generally, progress and achievement. (Some of this is also contained within the "lucky" number of the card.) Signifies an important stage has been reached in the outward advance through worldly life, with obstacles overcome and success gained through personal dynamism.
Reversed Beware of too much dynamism leading to ruthlessness.

8 Justice

A useful balance to the preceding success card, the Chariot. A reminder of the need for balance and sound judgment, awareness that a complete person needs more than material triumphs – that heart and spirit must also be served. The card also means that the person is to be judged – which can be positive unless the subject is found wanting.
Reversed Injustice, harsh or unfair judgment by others.

9 Hermit

Like Justice, a card that shows the tarot moving away from outward advance toward less worldly and material considerations. Suggests a need for revaluation, inner growth and development, perhaps for counsel about the future.
Reversed Warns against imprudence and stubbornness, a refusal to stop and think things out or to take wise advice.

Tarot 4

10 Wheel of Fortune
Another clear sign of a new stage or beginning. Change must come, or life will stagnate, and luck will play a part in decisions to be made. A fortunate card, implying that destiny will work itself out positively. Alludes to the mystic idea of karma, individual inner growth toward wholeness and harmony (symbolized by the circular mandala).
Reversed Ill luck, decline, adversity, changes for the worse.

13 Death
Not at all ominous, despite the name, number, and image. It takes the preceding card a step farther: for true inner development, a kind of death of the worldly self is required, so that an inner, spiritual, psychic rebirth can be achieved. Also implies that every setback or failure can bring new understanding, and therefore new hope.
Reversed Foreshadows destruction without renewal.

11 Strength
Indicates the need to face new developments with courage, fortitude, moral fiber. Implies setbacks and difficulties, yet the card is fortunate, for it suggests that inner resources will overcome these adversities. (Some experts prefer to transpose the positions of this card and Justice, but our ordering is as valid.)
Reversed Obstacles will not be overcome, due to lack of moral or spiritual strength.

14 Temperance
Another of the tarot's virtuous abstractions, emphasizing the need for moderation, and reminding us that a truly complete life exhibits a harmony between the material and spiritual sides of things. In short, don't go too far "inward." A fortunate card for all enterprises demanding the balancing of many complex factors.
Reversed Difficulty and setbacks caused by lack of harmony.

12 Hanged Man
When this card is right side up, the figure is upside down. Implies risk or sacrifice, perhaps a decision to abandon worldly values, and to plunge into the depths of the self, to seek the inner reality needed to become whole. From that sacrifice comes enlightenment, and renewal.
Reversed Beware a rigid refusal to accept that there is more to life than the practical, rational world.

15 Devil
A distinctly ominous card, reflecting what can happen if we let some of our "inward" qualities – such as sexual impulses, selfishness, the urge to wield power – get out of control or out of balance. Yet, controlled, the strength of those drives can be positive, an energy source for more admirable development.
Reversed Warns against giving way to base impulses, the dark side of our nature.

16 Tower

Another unfortunate card, a clear picture of ruin and destruction, of hopes and ambitions being shattered. But there is a positive side: out of destruction can come rebuilding, out of suffering can come understanding – once the lessons are learned, and the painfully acquired perceptions have been assimilated.
Reversed Ruin and calamity needlessly brought upon oneself.

19 Sun

Beyond the moonlit passage of darkness, a burst of sunlit success and and happiness. The goal is visible: illumination in every sense, adversity overcome, wholeness and harmony achieved (another circular mandala). The card signifies the triumphant reward for coming through hardships.
Reversed Failure, the collapse of hopes, or at best a superficial, dubious success.

17 Star

A fortunate card, also indicating the hope of renewal after calamity. It promises new and rich horizons, perhaps in previously unforeseen directions – once one has been tempered and enlarged by having come through the bad times. A card of enlightenment and enhanced awareness.
Reversed Warns against spiritual blindness that prevents seeing or taking advantage of new horizons.

20 Judgment

Not to be confused with Justice, this card concerns a day of judgment – when you pause to weigh up what you have done, and what you have become, in your passage through life. A fortunate card, indicating that you have achieved worthy goals, have attained inner development, and are now entering a time of serenity and happiness, a time of new beginnings.
Reversed Regrets, remorse, recriminations.

18 Moon

All the irrational, supernatural associations of the moon can make this an unfortunate card for the rational person, because it indicates a time when only intuition, the non-rational side, can overcome obstacles. Yet the non-rational must be used with care, for it can lead toward a dangerous fantasy world.
Reversed Warns against fearing the non-rational and settling for a life of stagnation and sterility.

21 World

The final stage, the ultimate circular mandala symbolizing completion, triumph, fulfillment. And because the major arcana can be seen as a circle, a closed cyclical system, you can see it moving on to the Fool again, beginning a new cycle – but perhaps on a higher plane, with greater goals.
Reversed Ultimate failure rather than ultimate fulfillment, a bleak immobility, the inability to progress on and up.

Tarot 5

As the name minor arcana indicates, the remaining 56 tarot cards have far less range and richness of meaning for fortune telling. So you may feel inclined to leave this section aside for a while, until you feel more at home with the mysteries and meanings of the 22 great cards that have just been described.

But a time may come when you want to expand your fortune-telling horizons and aspire to the use of the whole tarot. So the following pages provide capsule introductions to the spheres of influence where the minor arcana has relevance.

Once again, if the card is dealt upside down, its meaning is reversed – but usually in an even more explicitly opposing or extreme manner than with the major arcana. So these fairly obvious reversed meanings have not been included here.

In a reading using the lesser cards, you can choose a significator – a card that represents the person who is the subject of the reading – from among the court cards. It should usually correspond with the subject in sex, complexion, and (where possible) personality.

Spheres of influence

Each tarot suit has its own symbolic sphere of influence and relevance. Cups (**a**) relate to emotional matters, love, sex, marriage, fertility, and creativity. Pentacles (**b**) have to do with wealth, finance, commerce, prosperity, and economic security. Swords (**c**) concern activity and progress, opposition and conflict, the need to impose order on chaos. Wands (**d**) relate to the mind, the world of ideas and deep thought, intellectual strength, range, and purposefulness.

Choosing the significator
For a reading for a fair-haired young woman, use the queen of cups.
For a fair, mature woman (especially if well-to-do), use the queen of pentacles.
For a dark and perhaps dangerous woman, use the queen of wands.
For a dark and sad woman, use the queen of swords.
For a fair young man, or any young man in love, use the knight of cups.
For a wealthy young man, use the knight of pentacles.
For a dark young man, use the knight of wands.
For a dangerous young man, use the knave of wands.
For a fair-haired mature man, use the king of cups.
For a wealthy mature man, use the king of pentacles.
For a mature man in a position of power, use the king of swords.
For a dark and/or dangerous mature man, use the king of wands.

SUIT OF CUPS

1 **Ace of cups** Fertility, love, abundance.
2 **Two of cups** Love, friendship, harmonious connections.
3 **Three of cups** Happiness and joy from love.
4 **Four of cups** Emotional joy (but beware of excess).
5 **Five of cups** Joy turned sour, loss, reassessment.
6 **Six of cups** Happy memories, the past reawakened.
7 **Seven of cups** Ambition, hope (with forethought).
8 **Eight of cups** Disappointment, search for new paths.
9 **Nine of cups** Peace, contentment, fulfillment.
10 **Ten of cups** Peace again, happiness, achievement.
11 **Knave of cups** A thoughtful, helpful youth.
12 **Knight of cups** A bright, cheery youth, a lover.
13 **Queen of cups** A fair, loving, creative woman.
14 **King of cups** An intelligent, successful, worldly man.

Tarot 6

SUIT OF SWORDS

1 Ace of swords Success, attainment of goals.
2 Two of swords Good fortune out of adversity.
3 Three of swords Benefits from paths being cleared.
4 Four of swords Serenity, calm, respite from struggle.
5 Five of swords Further struggle, possible defeat.
6 Six of swords Difficulties surmounted, travel, good news.
7 Seven of swords Difficulties – be brave and careful.
8 Eight of swords Difficulties – be patient.
9 Nine of swords Disaster and failure – be steadfast.
10 Ten of swords Disaster, the darkest hour before dawn.
11 Knave of swords A clever, even guileful, young man.
12 Knight of swords A soldier, a dark, strong youth.
13 Queen of swords A dark, clever woman, a widow.
14 King of swords A dark, authoritative man.

SUIT OF PENTACLES

15 Ace of pentacles Material prosperity.
16 Two of pentacles Disruptions in material matters.
17 Three of pentacles Achievement in business.
18 Four of pentacles Wealth, pinnacles of success.
19 Five of pentacles Ruin, financial collapse.
20 Six of pentacles Financial aid, stability.
21 Seven of pentacles Material progress, but be wary.
22 Eight of pentacles Rewards for care and effort.
23 Nine of pentacles Riches, achievement.
24 Ten of pentacles Wealth, an inheritance.
25 Knave of pentacles A careful, sensible youth.
26 Knight of pentacles A good, honorable young man.
27 Queen of pentacles A sensible, generous, wealthy woman.
28 King of pentacles A careful, practical, successful man.

SUIT OF WANDS

29 Ace of wands Inspiration and new beginnings.
30 Two of wands Good fortune, well deserved.
31 Three of wands Gains from brave initiatives.
32 Four of wands Success and popularity.
33 Five of wands Setbacks and obstacles – be determined
34 Six of wands Achievement, encouraging news.
35 Seven of wands Troubles, but promising prospects.
36 Eight of wands Forward progress – be confident.
37 Nine of wands Opposition – be unyielding.
38 Ten of wands Obstacles and struggles.
39 Knave of wands A dark, lively youth, an employee.
40 Knight of wands A dark, energetic man, a journey.
41 Queen of wands A practical, dominant woman.
42 King of wands A powerful, determined man.

Tarot 7

Reading the tarot
Both you, as the reader of the cards, and the querant should concentrate fully while you are shuffling, dealing, and reading the tarot. First place the deck in order, with every card the right way up. Select the significator if one is needed for your chosen spread. Shuffle the cards thoroughly, turning some from top to bottom to ensure that there is a good chance of reversed cards appearing in the spread. Ask the querant to repeat the shuffle. Take back the cards, deal the spread (preferably onto a silk cloth) and begin your reading.

Dealing the spread
The cards should be dealt in the order shown by the numbers on each spread diagram. Additional notes – for example, whether the cards should be dealt face up or face down – are given before the interpretation for each spread.

Horseshoe spread
This is the most straightforward of the tarot spreads. It is particularly useful for answering specific questions, and is generally used with the major arcana alone. The first seven cards are dealt face upward in the order shown. A significator is not required.

Interpretation
The spread *below* was laid out in response to the question "Should I change my occupation?" Past influences are represented by the reversed Hermit (**1**), implying that a poor choice was made initially – one incompatible with the querant's best interests and personal inclinations. Representing present influences, the Fool (**2**) is more favorable. He represents potential, suggesting that the present is a very suitable time for a new start. The Emperor (**3**) is also favorable, implying a satisfying fulfillment of the querant's ambitions. Death (**4**) reinforces the Hermit and the Fool, showing that a complete change would be beneficial. The reversed Empress (**5**) shows that people around the querant may be concerned or anxious at the proposed change. The reversed Star (**6**) indicates that the only obstacle confronting the querant is his own timidity. The World (**7**) reaffirms the theme of the first four cards in the spread, and shows that the only possible outcome is success and, in particular, personal satisfaction.

Positions on the horseshoe spread
1 Past influences.
2 Present circumstances.
3 General future prospects.
4 Best course of action.
5 The attitudes of others.
6 Possible obstacles.
7 Final outcome.

21 card spread

This is a very useful, in-depth, and easily interpreted tarot spread. Each individual aspect of the reading is allocated three cards, giving a more detailed picture of each area than the simple interpretation allowed by the single card on the horseshoe spread.

Deal the 21 cards face down in the order shown, and place the significator face up at the right. Turn the cards over and interpret them in columns of three.

Interpretation

The spread *below* was laid out in response to a query from a young man who wished to know if he would succeed in his new career, music. His significator (**S**) was the knight of wands.

Column A gives a very favorable impression of his character. Ambition and determination can be seen in the five of wands (**1**) and the two of swords (**8**), as can a refusal to be put off or discouraged by setbacks. The four of swords (**15**) tempers this audacity with calm and presence of mind.

Column B reflects his career to date. The ace of pentacles (**9**) indicates just and deserved rewards for past efforts; the eight of pentacles (**2**) that he has also had good luck; the seven of pentacles (**16**) that he is concerned about the possible loss of this success.

Column C – the three of wands (**3**), Sun (**10**), and Tower (**17**) – shows that his hopes and ambitions are compatible with his character: he realizes the rewards he can gain from personal enterprise, is fully aware of the risks involved, and has a stoic resistance to setbacks.

Column D shows that he aims high, especially for material gains, but the nine of cups (**18**) indicates that he also expects to find personal fulfillment.

Column E reveals some more ominous possibilities. Crushing disappointment in the eight of cups (**5**), endurance and optimism tested to the limit by disaster and failure, and emotional and physical excesses.

In column F, however, the querant's prospects for the immediate future are better. The nine of wands (**6**) shows success won through sheer force of character, and the seven of wands (**20**) indicates success through adversity.

Because of the preceding cards, column G is very promising for the querant's long-term future. We can see a powerful, determined man, one who has gained worldly success through personal dynamism and, perhaps more importantly, in the ace of cups (**14**) there exists satisfaction, fulfillment, and happiness.

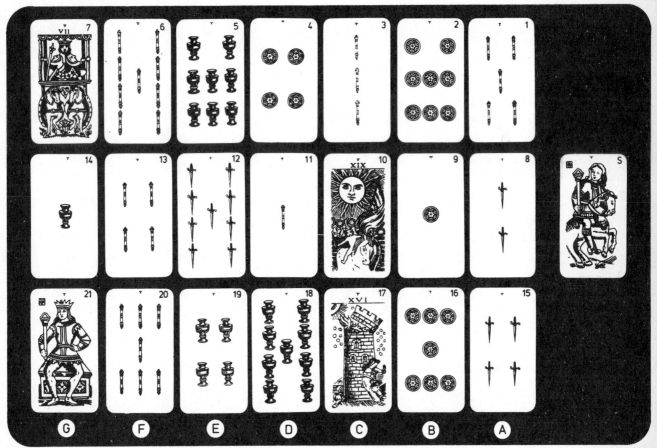

Columns of the 21 card spread
A Present circumstances.

B Domestic situation.
C Hopes and ambitions.
D Expectations.

E Unexpected events.
F Immediate future.
G Long-term future.

Tarot 8

Seven-pointed star
This spread can be used on any day of the week to predict events for the next seven days. The first seven cards are dealt face down in the order shown, and the significator is placed face up in the center. The cards are then turned up in order and interpreted.

Interpretation
The querant's significator is the queen of pentacles, and the reading took place on a Sunday.

Monday's card is Death (1), representing an upheaval, a radical departure from normal practice at the very start of the week. It indicates a new beginning, perhaps a message, an offer, some totally unexpected development or news. It is not without an optimistic note.

If Death represented a surprise, the Star (5) on Tuesday implies that the querant will realize the fortunate side of Monday's developments. On Wednesday Judgment (2) implies that the querant will have to take or, more likely, will choose a particular course of action as a result of Monday's developments and the fortunate light in which these appeared on Tuesday.

Thursday brings the Emperor (6), indicating material success as a result of wise and careful decisions, not impulses or emotions. It represents an opportunity successfully seized and acted upon. On Friday the Moon (3) brings an unrealistic although not unfortunate aspect to the week. It implies deception, self-deception, and fantasy, an elation that takes the querant away from reality. This is natural in the light of the eventful nature of the week.

The weekend has a more reflective tone. On Saturday the High Priest (7) shows that constructive advice and a rational point of view can be gained from a trustworthy friend or relative. On Sunday the High Priestess (4) shows a satisfactory end to the week because of the advice received on Saturday. The High Priestess represents awareness, realization, and a problem seen in perspective.

Positions on the seven-pointed star
S Significator.
1 Monday.
2 Wednesday.
3 Friday.
4 Sunday.
5 Tuesday.
6 Thursday.
7 Saturday.

Circular spread

This spread gives a general impression of the coming year, based on 12 months from the date of the reading. The first 13 cards are dealt face down in the order shown. A significator is not required. The first card refers to the coming month, the second card to the second month, and so on around the circle. The thirteenth card gives the main emphasis of the reading, and is interpreted first. Cards 1–12 are then interpreted in order. Cards whose tops point toward the center of the circle are considered upright; all others are reversed.

Interpretation

The seven of cups (**13**) indicates that the emphasis for the whole year is on personal hopes and ambitions. The implications are favorable for personal enterprises as opposed to material acquisitions. This is complemented by the Hanged Man (**1**), which represents the abandonment of material aims and favors the querant's personal ambitions. The Tower (**2**) represents an unforeseen catastrophe in the querant's material affairs, and a discouraging blow to his hopes. Provided that he does not waver in his aims, the six of wands (**3**) in the next month brings encouraging news about or from a woman. The Chariot (**4**) is an auspicious card of expectation and anticipation, and especially of success

as a result of a journey. It is a card of self-confidence, which will have been bolstered by the six of wands. The ace of cups (**5**) is a singularly fortunate and happy card for the fifth month. It shows perfect love, and implies that the querant will meet a woman with whom he will be perfectly compatible. His happiness continues into the next month with the three of cups (**6**). The emphasis here is on the pleasures of the senses, joy, and happiness through love. The next three cards confirm the suggestion of the seven of cups that the main events of the year will be of a personal or emotional nature. The High Priestess (**7**) shows a growing female influence on the querant, which increases in the eighth month with the queen of wands (**8**), representing a practical, dominant woman. The two of cups (**9**) is a natural progression from the ace of cups, and suggests harmonious love, friendship, marriage, or a longstanding relationship. In this context the eight of cups (**10**) cannot represent disappointment, but instead a person whose life is for the moment completely devoted to its new direction. This is confirmed by the four of cups (**11**) representing emotional joy. The king of cups (**12**) represents an intelligent, successful, worldly-wise man who is spiritually and emotionally fulfilled.

Tarot 9

Celtic cross

This is probably the most useful and versatile of all the tarot spreads. It can be used to answer specific or general questions, or to give a picture of the year ahead. The whole tarot deck can be used, or the major arcana can be used alone. It is, in fact, suitable for any combination of cards, question, querant, and reader.

Laying out the spread

Place the significator (**S**) face up. Deal out the first 10 cards face down in the order shown, saying as you set them out:

for card **1** (representing the querant's present situation or state of mind), "This covers you";

for card **2** (referring to events or influences in the very near future), "This crosses you";

for card **3** (showing the querant's best course of action and the results of ignoring it), "This crowns you";

for card **4** (an event or matter in the past relevant to the querant's present situation), "This is beneath you";

for card **5** (a more recent relevant event), "This is behind you";

for card **6** (the likely state of the querant's affairs in about six months' time), "This is before you";

for card **7** (influences or events in the querant's main sphere of life or work), "This is yourself";

for card **8** (influences or events in the querant's home and social life), "This is your house";

for card **9** (reflecting the querant's feelings and influencing the likely outcome of events), "Your hopes and fears";

for card **10** (the accumulative statement of the whole spread, the final outcome), "This is what will come."

Turn up the cards one by one, and interpret them in order.

Interpretation

Here we compare two celtic cross readings for the same querant. The first spread uses the full tarot deck, the second uses the major arcana alone.

The querant is dissatisfied with her present way of life. She plans to move abroad, where she has met several people she likes, and one young man in particular. She wishes to know if it would be a wise course of action. Her significator (**S**) is the queen of swords.

The Empress (**A, a**) shows a capable and affluent woman but, when qualified by the significator, one who is also very insecure. The Fool (**B, b**) refers to her plans to move abroad, indicating that they are ill-omened and based on foolishness rather than forethought. The Wheel of Fortune (**C, c**) confirms her need for change, but shows that because her plans are based on an impetuous decision, their success will depend largely on chance.

The Emperor (**D, d**), representing the young man she met abroad, reveals one of the main factors prompting her. The ace of cups (**E**) in the full deck spread and the Lovers (**e**) in the major arcana spread both show a recent infatuation overshadowing reality and common sense – a tendency to see this young man in a rosy light. The High Priest (**F, f**) indicates some form of partnership with him in the future. However, taken with the significator it implies that this will not necessarily be in or for the querant's best interests. In the major arcana spread the Devil (**g**) shows that the querant channels her career efforts in the wrong direction, and also indicates physical excess. In the full tarot deck spread the king of swords (**G**) is more specific, suggesting that she is being influenced by a man who is really working toward his own ends. The Moon (**h**) in the major arcana spread shows her living in a fantasy world, divorced from reality. The three of cups (**H**) in the full deck spread is more specific – she is looking for solace and refuge in the face of social, physical, and emotional excess.

The ten of swords (**I**) and the Tower (**i**) both represent desolation, disaster, and despair. On the basis of the preceding cards, this seems the most likely outcome. The Chariot (**J, j**) must also be judged in the light of the earlier cards. It suggests an ill-omened journey, then more travel – possibly the querant's return home. Normally fortunate, this card shows the querant's enterprise ending in quarrels, and her realization that her drastic measures were not an appropriate solution to her problems.

When we compare the two spreads, we can see that the full deck gives more precise details than the major arcana used alone. The frequency with which major arcana cards appear in a full deck spread is important. The more often major arcana cards occur, the more the outcome depends on the querant; minor arcana cards represent more external influences.

Tarot 10

Tree of life

The tree of life spread is most often used for assessing a querant's character, potential, shortcomings, and capacity for the various aspects of human existence. It can also be used to give a very detailed reading of a querant's life if it is laid out and read three times – once for the past, a second time for the present, and the third time for the future.

The cards should be dealt face down in packs of seven in the order shown. A significator is not required. The eight cards remaining are left face down to one side; they are only used if additional clarification is needed when the main reading has been completed. The piles of cards in the spread are turned over and read, both separately and in conjunction.

The pillars and triangles

The tree of life is sometimes likened to a human being. The upper triangle represents qualities attributed to the head – idealism, wisdom, and knowledge. The central triangle represents qualities attributed to the breast, heart, and arms – charity, severity, and sacrifice. The lower triangle is associated with the legs and genitals, and represents triumph, fame, and stability. The outside pillars of love and discipline are built of the extremes and opposites of these characteristics, while the central pillar represents a harmonious amalgamation of the two.

Positions on the tree of life
Pack 1 Idealism.
Pack 2 Wisdom.
Pack 3 Knowledge.
Pack 4 Charity.
Pack 5 Severity.
Pack 6 Sacrifice.
Pack 7 Triumph.
Pack 8 Fame.
Pack 9 Stability.
Pack 10 Realization.
Pack 11 Discards.
Packs 3, 5, 8 Pillar of discipline.
Packs 1, 6, 9 Pillar of harmony.
Packs 2, 4, 7 Pillar of love.
Packs 1, 2, 3 Intellectual triangle.
Packs 4, 5, 6 Spiritual triangle.
Packs 7, 8, 9 Intuitional triangle.

Interpretation

Interpreting a complete tree of life spread is a lengthy and complex business, but we can illustrate the principles of its interpretation by considering just the upper triangle. This triangle, the intellectual or cerebral triangle, is associated with mental qualities, abilities, and aspirations.

The cards first show that the querant is well-intentioned but totally single-minded – a person who is passionately devoted to furthering a particular cause, whether it be political, social, or religious. Two cards immediately seem to be out of place: the Hanged Man, representing sacrifice (among other things), ideally belongs in the pillar of harmony rather than in the pillar of discipline; the Sun, representing triumph, more properly belongs in the pillar of love rather than in the pillar of harmony. Both cards are ill-aspected in their present positions. The querant's sphere of knowledge contains mainly compatible readings indicating, for example, success,

rationality, and strength of will, but there is an implication of bitterness in the five of cups that could lead the querant to abandon worldly values. The sphere of idealism is even more striking, with the eight of cups echoing the meaning of the five of cups in the sphere of knowledge. Death shows a desire for radical change, and the Sun indicates success – but the four of cups shows that this will be for the personal gratification of the querant, and not in the interests of the cause he purports to serve. His aims are not necessarily evil, but their causes and foundations are imperfect, especially with respect to the sphere of wisdom. The knight of pentacles confirms the querant's good intentions and honorable status, but ambition, hope, and optimism are spoiled by the reversed Fool and the reversed nine of pentacles (indicating foolishness and badly made plans) and by the fantasy of the Moon on top of the pillar of harmony.

Cards in the intellectual triangle

Pack 1
Moon
Two of wands
Death
Sun
World
Eight of cups
Four of cups

Pack 2
Fool (reversed)
Star
Judgment (reversed)
Nine of pentacles (reversed)
Seven of cups
Four of pentacles
Knight of pentacles

Pack 3
Emperor
Five of cups
Devil
Six of wands
Three of pentacles
King of pentacles
Hanged Man

Cartomancy 1

As modern playing cards evolved from the tarot deck, it is not surprising that they are used to predict the future. The 52 cards in a standard deck are derived from the tarot's minor arcana; four court cards – the knights – have been dropped. The only trace remaining of the 22 cards of the major arcana of the tarot is the Fool, who has become the joker of the modern deck. The current standard deck in use around the world is of French origin, and probably originated in the late fifteenth century. Cards were then painted by hand or printed with woodblocks; they were not mass-manufactured until 1832. They were originally made to be viewed from one direction only (as tarot cards still are) – the double-headed playing card was not introduced until the late nineteenth century.

The interpretations of the individual cards in predicting the future probably also derive from the tarot. Until comparatively recently, the interpretations were preserved only in the oral tradition, and so can vary from source to source, or perhaps appear confusing or contradictory. The interpretations given here are those that are most generally accepted today.

52 or 32?

You can use the full deck of 52 playing cards when you are trying to read the future – or, if you prefer, you can discard all the twos, threes, fours, fives, and sixes, and use only the remaining 32-card deck. Both decks will give you equally good results. Use whichever you prefer, but make sure not to confuse the two: the meanings of the individual cards in the 52-card deck are not the same as those in the 32-card deck, and the methods of laying out the cards also vary. But the areas of influence of the four suits do not change whichever deck is used, nor does the choice of client card or your general preparation before laying out the cards.

The influence of the suits

When you are laying out the cards for a reading, you may find that one suit is more strongly represented than the others. As each suit is said to have its own particular area of influence, you must take this into account in your reading, and allow the atmosphere conveyed by the prominent suit to modify your interpretation of the other cards.

Hearts are considered lucky. Your emotions and your domestic life – love, affection, friendship, marriage, the family – are all said to be under their influence. They also stand for ambitions successfully realized.

Clubs are the cards of success and are connected with money, business, and loyalty. But they can also be associated with failure, betrayal, and financial worries.

Diamonds influence your life outside your home. They also suggest that ambitions can only be realized and money made through hard work.

Spades warn of dangers ahead. Your misfortunes – loss, suffering, enemies, treachery, failure – are all said to be under their influence.

Client card

The "client card" is a king or queen selected to represent the person who is the subject of the reading. As far as possible, choose a card that corresponds with your subject's age, sex, and hair color.

For a fair-, gray-, or auburn-haired older man, use the king of diamonds.

For a fair-, gray-, or auburn-haired older woman, use the queen of diamonds.

For a fair- or auburn-haired younger man, use the king of hearts.

For a fair- or auburn-haired younger woman, use the queen of hearts.

For a dark-haired older man, use the king of spades.

For a dark-haired older woman, use the queen of spades.

For a dark-haired younger man, use the king of clubs.

For a dark-haired younger woman, use the queen of clubs.

Preparing to read the cards

Choose the client card for your subject, and place it in the center of the table. Ask your subject to shuffle the cards thoroughly, and then cut them with the left hand; you should both concentrate fully on the cards, clearing your minds of all other thoughts. Arrange the cards around the client card in your chosen layout, and begin the reading.

You may wish to have a general indication of your subject's fortunes before you begin a complete reading. After shuffling, your subject should cut the deck into three with the left hand. Read the bottom cards of each of these three small decks, first separately, and then in combination. These cards will show whether the reading to come will be propitious – or otherwise. Ask your subject to shuffle and cut the cards again before you lay them out for the full reading.

It is traditionally considered unlucky to read your own future in the cards, or to read the cards when you are alone. It is also said that you should not read the cards for a particular subject more than once a week, or the cards will lose their power. But each complete reading may include repeated deals of the cards, providing that these extra deals are only used to clarify confusing indications in the original layout.

Tarot suits and modern suits

The traditional symbols used on playing cards in different countries of the world are all derived from the symbols of the four suits of the tarot, as shown in the table *below*. Cards from the tarot's suit of wands and its derivatives are illustrated *right*.

Deck	Suits			
Tarot	cups	wands(a)*	pentacles**	swords
English	hearts	clubs(b)	diamonds	spades
French	hearts	trefoils(c)	squares	pikes
German	hearts	acorns(d)	bells	leaves
Italian	cups	rods(e)	money	swords
Spanish	cups	sticks(f)	gold	swords

*Also known as the suit of batons
**Also known as the suit of coins

©DIAGRAM

Cartomancy 2

DIVINATION WITH THE 52-CARD DECK

When you use a full deck of 52 cards for divination, you need make no attempt to establish whether a card is upright or reversed: its meaning will be the same in both cases.

HEARTS

Ace The home. Love, friendship, and happiness.
King A good-natured, impetuous, fair-haired man.
Queen A trustworthy, affectionate, fair-haired woman.
Jack A close friend.
Ten Good fortune and happiness.
Nine "The wish card" that makes dreams come true. Wealth, status, and good luck.
Eight Invitations and festivities.
Seven False hopes and broken promises, an unreliable person.
Six An overgenerous disposition, unexpected good fortune.
Five Jealousy, indecisiveness.
Four Changes, delays, and postponements (especially of marriages).
Three Warns of a need for caution.
Two Success and prosperity.

CLUBS

Ace Wealth, health, love, and happiness.
King An honest, generous, dark-haired man.
Queen An attractive, self-confident, dark-haired woman.
Jack A reliable friend.
Tén Unexpected money, good luck.
Nine Friends being stubborn.
Eight Opposition, disappointment, the taking of reckless chances.
Seven Prosperity – providing a member of the opposite sex does not interfere.
Six Business success.
Five A new friend or a successful marriage.
Four Fortunes changing for the worse.
Three Marriage bringing money. May indicate several marriages.
Two Opposition and disappointments.

SPECIAL COMBINATIONS

Some combinations of cards have special meanings when the deck of 52 cards is used. These meanings apply only when the cards are immediately next to one another in the layout.

Ace of hearts next to any other heart Friendship.
Ace of hearts with another heart on each side Love affair.
Ace of hearts with a diamond on each side Money.
Ace of hearts with a spade on each side Quarrels.

Ace of diamonds/eight of clubs A business proposal.
Ace of spades/king of clubs A politician.
Ace of spades/ten of spades A serious undertaking.
Ace of spades/four of hearts A new baby.
Ten of hearts Cancels adjacent cards of ill fortune; reinforces adjacent cards of good fortune.
Ten of diamonds/two of hearts Marriage bringing money.
Ten of spades Cancels adjacent cards of good fortune; reinforces adjacent cards of ill fortune.

DIAMONDS

Ace Money, a letter, or a ring.
King A stubborn, quick-tempered, fair-haired man.
Queen A flirtatious, sophisticated, fair-haired woman.
Jack A relative, not altogether reliable.
Ten Marriage or money, a journey, changes.
Nine Restlessness. A surprise connected with money.
Eight A marriage late in life. A journey leading to a new relationship.
Seven Heavy losses.
Six A warning against a second marriage.
Five Prosperity, good news, a happy family.
Four An inheritance, changes, troubles.
Three Legal or domestic disputes.
Two A serious love affair.

SPADES

Ace Emotional conflict, an unfortunate love affair. Sometimes regarded as the "death card."
King An ambitious dark-haired man.
Queen An unscrupulous dark-haired woman.
Jack A well-meaning but lazy acquaintance.
Ten Misfortune and worry.
Nine Bad luck in all things.
Eight Trouble and disappointment ahead.
Seven Sorrow, loss of friendship.
Six Some improvement in circumstances.
Five Reverses and anxieties, but eventual success.
Four Jealousy, illness, business worries.
Three Faithlessness and partings.
Two Separation, scandal, deceit.

Ten of spades next to any club Business troubles.
Ten of spades with a club on each side Theft, forgery, grave business losses.
Nine of hearts next to any card of ill fortune Quarrels, temporary obstacles.
Nine of hearts/five of spades Loss of status.
Nine of clubs/eight of hearts Gaiety.
Nine of diamonds next to any court card Lack of success, an inability to concentrate.
Nine of diamonds/eight of spades A bitter quarrel.

Nine of spades/seven of diamonds Loss of money.
Eight of hearts/eight of diamonds A trousseau.
Eight of hearts/five of hearts A present of jewelry.
Eight of diamonds/five of hearts A present of money.
Eight of spades on the immediate right of the client card Abandon your current plans.
Four of hearts next to any court card Many love affairs.
Four of clubs next to any court card A loss, injustice.
Two of clubs/two of diamonds An unexpected message.

Cartomancy 3

Seven triplets

This spread, also known as the seven packs, is used to give a general picture of the client's future. Use the full 52-card deck, and place the client card face up in the middle of the table. After shuffling, deal the first 21 cards face down in the order shown by the numbers on the diagram *below*. Beginning on the left, turn up each pack of three cards and interpret them.

Interpretation

The client is a dark-haired young woman; her client card is the queen of clubs (**C**).

The personality cards (**1**, **2**, **3**) reflect her over-generous nature, but this will bring her satisfactory rewards as she will reap the goodness she has sown. She tends to worry too much over her marriage and over money, and finds it very difficult to change.

Her present family circumstances (cards **4**, **5**, **6**) are shared with a reliable partner, and together they face life's inevitable setbacks. Her friends may appear stubborn in many ways, and they should neither be relied on nor taken for granted.

The cards showing her desires (**7**, **8**, **9**) reveal that she wants both money and worldly goods; she may well have these in the future. She is warned to be extremely cautious when writing letters, especially if she is disclosing any personal confidences.

Her expectations and hopes (cards **10**, **11**, **12**) could be frustrated by a relative who is not entirely reliable. Social events that have been planned will not be as enjoyable as she hopes: they will be overshadowed by the break-up of a long-standing relationship.

The cards revealing the unexpected (**13**, **14**, **15**) show that news about a close friend may bring shock and scandal, perhaps involving a separation or divorce. Any advice the client gives her friend will be met with strong opposition. The client will feel reckless, but should be warned that taking chances will not pay off.

In the immediate future (cards **16**, **17**, **18**) the client is due to receive an inheritance, but this could be whittled away almost before it is received. A change is likely, and trouble could result unless she is allowed to manage things entirely in her own way. She is warned against a meddlesome man.

The cards of the distant future (**19**, **20**, **21**) show that in the long term the client's life holds great promise, and the possibility of success and prosperity. Her money worries will decrease, but indecision and jealousy may cause other problems. For her future peace of mind, she must develop a positive attitude to life.

Positions on the seven triplets spread
Pack **a** Personality and state of mind.
Pack **b** Family and home.
Pack **c** Present desires.

Pack **d** Hopes and expectations.
Pack **e** The unexpected.
Pack **f** The immediate future.
Pack **g** The more distant future.

Lucky 13

This spread can be used to give a general picture of the future, or to answer a question about a specific area of the client's life. The full 52-card deck is used, and the client card is always the joker. Place the joker face up in the center, and deal the first 12 cards of the deck face down in the order shown (**1a**, **1b**, **2a**, **2b**, etc). Turn the cards face up in pairs (**1a** and **1b**, **2a** and **2b**, etc) and interpret them.

Interpretation

This spread was read for a client considering a second marriage. The good fortune and happiness indicated by the ten of hearts (**1a**) seems in direct contrast to the scandal suggested by the two of spades (**1b**), but as the ten of hearts cancels all adjacent cards of ill fortune, any threat of separation or deceit should be regarded as mere suspicion. The nine of diamonds (**2a**) and queen of hearts (**2b**) suggest that restlessness and doubt connected with a fair-haired woman could prove frustrating. A romantic relationship will soon enter a worrying phase, but the affection and trustworthiness of the lady in question should not be forgotten. Unfortunately, the combination of these two cards introduce a disturbing influence that will make success difficult.

The six of diamonds (**3a**) and eight of spades (**3b**) warn against a hasty second marriage, which would only bring disappointment at the present time. The client should review the situation before making a final commitment. The queen of spades (**4a**) and four of hearts (**4b**) in combination always indicate love affairs. In this case a delay or change of plan can be expected in connection with a love affair or wedding. An unscrupulous woman may attempt to interfere, but with foresight this can be avoided.

The six of spades (**5a**) and two of diamonds (**5b**) suggest an improvement in the client's romantic life, providing that the advice offered by the previous cards is taken. A serious love affair is indicated, and the client can look forward to happiness and harmony in the relationship. The nine of clubs (**6a**) and ace of clubs (**6b**) suggest that friends who have shared past confidences may now appear unhelpful, and it would be wise for the client not to trust them in personal matters. The final outcome cannot be bettered, however, as the ace of clubs shows that the client can expect health, wealth, love, and happiness.

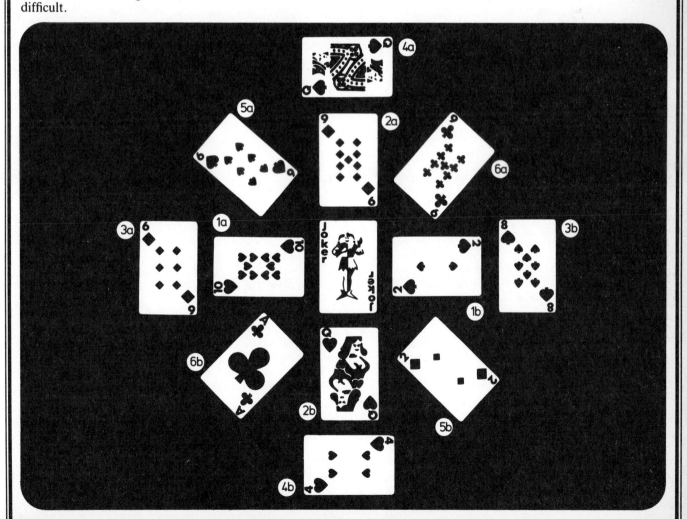

©DIAGRAM

Cartomancy 4

DIVINATION WITH THE 32-CARD DECK
The 32-card deck is formed by discarding the twos, threes, fours, fives, and sixes from a standard 52-card deck. You will need to mark the top of each card in a 32-card deck: the meanings of the individual cards differ depending on whether they are upright or reversed.

HEARTS
Ace Good news, love, domestic happiness.
Reversed A move, changes, short-lived happiness.
King An affectionate, generous, fair-haired man.
Reversed A deceitful person.
Queen An affectionate, dependable, fair-haired woman.
Reversed A widow, divorcee, or woman unhappy in love.
Jack A friend or lover.
Reversed An untrustworthy lover.
Ten Good fortune and happiness.
Reversed A surprise, a birth.
Nine The "wish" card that makes dreams come true.
Reversed Temporary troubles.
Eight An invitation, a journey, a wedding.
Reversed Unrequited love.
Seven Contentment.
Reversed Boredom.

CLUBS
Ace Good luck, good news, financial letters or papers.
Reversed Unpleasant letters, short-lived happiness.
King A friendly, honest, dark-haired man.
Reversed Minor worries and troubles.
Queen An affectionate, helpful, dark-haired woman.
Reversed An unreliable woman.
Jack An amusing, dark-haired lover.
Reversed An insincere lover.
Ten Luck, luxury, prosperity.
Reversed Business troubles, a journey.
Nine Unexpected money.
Reversed A small gift, or a slight problem.
Eight Joy and good fortune, brought by a dark-haired person.
Reversed An unhappy love affair, a legal dispute, a divorce.
Seven Minor money matters.
Reversed Financial problems.

SPECIAL COMBINATIONS
Some combinations of cards have special meanings when the deck of 32 cards is used. These meanings apply only when the cards are immediately next to one another in the layout.
Ace of clubs with a diamond on each side Money coming.
Ace of clubs/nine of diamonds Legal affairs.
Ace of diamonds/eight of clubs Unexpected money.
Ace of diamonds with a diamond on each side Financial prosperity.
Ace of diamonds/seven of diamonds Quarrels.
Ace of diamonds/seven of diamonds/jack of diamonds A cable or telegram.
Ace of diamonds/nine of spades Illness.
Ace of spades/queen of clubs A tiresome journey.
Ace of spades/nine of spades Business failure.
Ace of spades/eight of spades Betrayal.
King of hearts/nine of hearts A happy love affair.
King of clubs/ten of clubs A proposal of marriage.
King of diamonds/eight of spades An unexpected journey.
King of spades/seven of clubs Be cautious with your investments.
Queen of hearts/seven of diamonds Unexpected delights.
Queen of hearts/ten of spades Danger, adventure.
Queen of clubs/seven of diamonds An uncertain future.

Queen of diamonds/seven of hearts Happiness tainted by jealousy.
Queen of diamonds/seven of spades Success in the village rather than in the city.
Queen of spades/jack of spades Great evil.
Jack of hearts/seven of clubs A lover motivated by greed.
Jack of clubs/jack of spades Business difficulties, financial losses.
Jack of diamonds/nine of spades Beware of bad advice.
Ten of hearts/nine of clubs Show business.
Ten of hearts/ten of diamonds A wedding.
Ten of clubs next to any ace Large sums of money.
Ten of diamonds/eight of clubs A honeymoon.
Ten of diamonds/seven of spades A delay.
Ten of spades/seven of clubs An unfortunate future.
Nine of hearts/nine of clubs A fortunate legacy.
Nine of clubs/eight of hearts Celebrations, festivities.
Nine of diamonds/eight of hearts Long-distance travel.
Eight of hearts/eight of diamonds New and important work.
Eight of clubs/eight of diamonds True love.
Eight of diamonds next to any club A prolonged journey.
Eight of spades/seven of diamonds Help needed.
Seven of diamonds next to any club Money problems.
Seven of spades/king, queen, or jack of spades A traitor.

DIAMONDS

Ace A letter, money, or a ring.
Reversed Bad news.
King A powerful fair-haired or gray-haired man.
Reversed Treachery, deception
Queen A spiteful, talkative, fair-haired woman.
Reversed Malice.
Jack A messenger, employee, or person in uniform.
Reversed A trouble-maker.
Ten Moving house, a journey, a major change.
Reversed Changes for the worse.
Nine News, surprises, anxieties.
Reversed Domestic disputes, lovers' quarrels.
Eight A love affair, a short journey.
Reversed A separation, affections ignored.
Seven Teasing, criticism, a small gift.
Reversed Minor scandal, gossip.

SPADES

Ace Emotional satisfaction, business propositions.
Reversed Bad news, disappointments, death.
King An untrustworthy dark-haired man, possibly a lawyer.
Reversed An enemy.
Queen An older dark-haired woman, probably a widow or a divorcee.
Reversed A cunning, treacherous woman.
Jack An ill-mannered young person, possibly connected with medicine or law.
Reversed A traitor.
Ten Grief, a long journey, confinement.
Reversed Minor illness.
Nine Loss, failure, misfortune.
Reversed Unhappiness for a close friend.
Eight Bad news, impending disappointments.
Reversed Quarrels, sorrow, separation, divorce.
Seven New resolutions, a change of plan.
Reversed Bad advice, faulty planning.

QUARTETS, TRIPLETS, AND PAIRS

It is considered to be very significant when two, three, or four cards of the same value are immediately next to one another in the layout. These groups should be interpreted first, as they have an influence on the layout as a whole.

Four aces Separation from friends or from money. The more aces reversed, the greater the separation.
Three aces Flirtations, foolishness, and temporary anxieties. The more aces reversed, the greater the folly and anxiety.
Two aces A marriage. Two red aces – a happy marriage; a red ace and a black ace – an unhappy marriage; one ace reversed – potential marriage breakdown; both aces reversed – divorce.
Four kings Good fortune, which lessens with each king reversed.
Three kings A new venture. The more kings reversed, the less successful it will be.
Two kings A business partnership. One king reversed – partially successful partnership; both kings reversed – partnership will fail.
Four queens A party or some other social gathering. The more queens reversed, the less successful it will be.
Three queens Visitors and conversation. The more queens reversed, the greater the degree of scandal and gossip attached to the visit.
Two queens Friendship. One queen reversed – rivalry; both queens reversed – betrayal.
Four jacks Quarrels. The more jacks reversed, the more violent the quarrel.

Three jacks Family disagreements. The more jacks reversed, the greater the disagreement.
Two jacks Loss or theft, with each jack reversed bringing it nearer.
Four tens Unexpected good fortune, which lessens with each ten reversed.
Three tens Financial and legal problems, which lessen with each ten reversed.
Two tens Changes at work bringing good fortune. Each ten reversed delays them.
Four nines A pleasant surprise. The more nines reversed, the sooner it will happen.
Three nines Health, wealth, and happiness. The more nines reversed, the longer they will be delayed.
Two nines Small financial gains. Each nine reversed delays and lessens the gain.
Four eights Success and failure mixed. The more eights reversed, the higher the proportion of failure.
Three eights Love and marriage. The more eights reversed, the less the degree of commitment.
Two eights A brief love affair. One eight reversed – a flirtation; both eights reversed – a misunderstanding.
Four sevens Enemies, mischief-makers. The more sevens reversed, the less successful they will be.
Three sevens A new enterprise, or a new baby. Each seven reversed delays it.
Two sevens A new and happy love affair. One seven reversed – deceived in love; both sevens reversed – regrets in love.

Cartomancy 5

The fan

This spread is used to give a general reading of the client's future. Shuffle the 32-card deck and spread it out face down on a table. Ask your client to choose any 18 cards and to set them out face up in the order shown. If the client card is not among cards 1–13, look for the seven of the same suit, which is an acceptable substitute; if neither card is there, the reading should be left to another day.

Cards 1–13 are read first. Considering the client card as the first card, count five cards to the right and interpret the fifth card. Use that card as the first card of the next set of five, and continue reading every fifth card until you have returned to the client card. Then read cards 14–18: interpret cards 14 and 18 together, then cards 15 and 17, and finally card 16. Summarize all your interpretations into a coherent reading.

Interpretation

The client card is the king of spades. The appropriate order for interpreting the cards in this spread is thus: **11** nine of hearts; **2** jack of spades; **6** seven of clubs; **10** queen of spades (reversed); **1** ace of spades; **5** king of diamonds (reversed); **9** seven of diamonds (reversed); **13** ten of clubs (reversed); **4** ten of diamonds; **8** nine of spades; **12** queen of hearts; **3** ten of hearts (reversed) **7** king of spades (client card); **14**, **18** ace of hearts, nine of clubs (reversed); **15**, **17** seven of spades (reversed), jack of clubs; **16** eight of diamonds.

As always, cards appearing in special combinations should also be interpreted – in this case the reversed ten of hearts (**3**) next to the ten of diamonds (**4**), and the king of spades (**7**) next to the seven of clubs (**6**).

Summarizing the interpretations, we learn that there is a dark cloud hanging over the client's career at present, but it should soon lift. These business worries will tend to get worse before they improve. The client should heed the warning to expect deception, gossip, and underhand disloyalty from colleagues at work, but can also expect the constant support and affection of a woman partner. Things will soon come to a head, bringing major changes, journeys, and a move. After this a steady improvement will be noticeable although small problems will still arise. The client's social and romantic life will continue to be happy.

The temple of fortune

This spread dates from the middle of the eighteenth century, when it was developed by a famous French cartomancer called Etteilla. It gives a complete reading of the client's life – past, present, and future.

The 32-card deck is used; a client card is not required. After shuffling, the cards are laid out face up in the order shown. Cards 1–6 and 13–16 represent the past; cards 17–21 and 26–32 represent the present; cards 7–12 and 22–25 represent the future. In each case the outer row of cards gives the primary indications of the reading, which are then modified by the inner row. Some cartomancers also consider that the outer rows refer to events in the client's outer, worldly life, while the inner rows refer to the inner, mental, and spiritual life.

Interpretation

There are five special combinations of cards that should be noted as part of the interpretation: the seven of hearts (1) next to the reversed seven of diamonds (2); the jack of diamonds (19) next to the jack of hearts (20); the king of clubs (8), reversed king of spades (9), and king of hearts (10) together; the reversed seven of diamonds (2) next to a card from the suit of clubs; and the eight of diamonds (32) next to a card from the suit of clubs. The cards representing the past show that the client's outlook on life has been greatly influenced by his childhood with his authoritative father and loving mother. When very young he lived in comparative luxury and security, but later his parents parted and he

was surrounded by domestic upheaval. Gossip and scandal brought anxiety, uncertainty, and loss of contentment. As a young man he met a dark-haired girl who brought him considerable happiness, but money problems caused them to part. These experiences have left him over-cautious, suspicious, and insecure.

The cards representing the present suggest that the client is now someone who appears both rude and arrogant on the surface. Although emotionally immature, he has gained professional status through his own efforts, but still feels that he has been robbed of happiness. He makes new resolutions but the loss of one of his parents brings setbacks. A major change follows this loss, and several journeys have to be made. A brief love affair brings him temporary joy and happiness. He has thoughts of joining the armed forces but a good friend helps him stabilize his life again. There will be more changes before he finds true contentment.

The cards representing the future suggest that the client's career will bring him into contact with a reliable, generous person who will help restore his faith in life. An old antagonist will reappear, but will make little impact because of the client's new, reliable friends. The client will meet a woman who will make him happy, and may marry her. An older, dark-haired woman will try to stir up the past, and a temporary setback must be anticipated. He can, however, expect success and contentment in the not too distant future.

Cartomancy 6

Grand star

The popular star spreads are found in a number of traditional forms. Of these, the grand star is probably the most useful for a general reading.

The 32-card deck is used. Place the client card (**C**) face up in the center, and deal the first 21 cards of the shuffled deck face down around it in the order shown. Turn up and interpret the cards in pairs, in the order **13**, **15**; **20**,**18**; **14**, **16**; **19**, **17**; **9**, **5**; **11**, **8**; **10**, **6**; **12**, **7**; **3**, **1**; **4**, **2**. Read the final card, **21**, on its own. Cards above the client card represent success and achievements to come; those below refer to the past, and to things already accomplished. Cards to the left of the client card represent obstacles and opposition; those to the right refer to the future, and to help and assistance to come.

Interpretation

The client card is the king of hearts (**C**). The special combination that should be noted for interpretation is the jack of diamonds (**13**) in conjunction with the nine of spades (**15**).

There is a strong warning of a troublemaker who could bring loss, misfortune, and failure to the client, and a spiteful woman will also be a threat and a danger. Many changes will bring criticism and loneliness: these appear inevitable. A dark-haired, reliable man will offer support, and will help the client avoid certain events and disappointments. The client should listen to this man and take his advice. An affectionate dark-haired woman will help the client by distracting him from his main problem, but he should take care that she does not upset his domestic situation. A widow, perhaps his mother, will give him sound advice and he should attempt to visit her.

The client will eventually be happy and have peace of mind, but not before an ill-mannered young man of professional standing causes more trouble by trying to stir up past secrets. Financially, things will improve slowly after a long correspondence solves an old business problem.

A small gift will be much appreciated, but could bring about problems related to the giver, who is a fair-haired woman: there is a warning that her feelings toward the client may well cause jealousy. His social life will improve and through this he will lose some of his worries. He will make new resolutions that will inevitably cause changes in his plans, and a long-awaited letter will bring very good news that will increase his confidence. There is also mention of a ring, which suggests the possibility of marriage.

Although the present is full of trouble and difficult people for the client, he can be confident that things will improve in the future.

Great Star

This is the most detailed of the traditional star spreads. The 32-card deck is used, and the client card (**C**) is chosen and placed face up on the table. The client then shuffles the deck and divides it into three. Turn each of these piles face up and read the three cards exposed, first singly and then in combination. These cards (**a**, **b**, **c**) are called the indicators and give the general tone of the reading. Remove them from the deck and place them to the left of the table. Reshuffle the deck and deal the star in the order shown. Interpret each group of three cards in conjunction, beginning with the group immediately above the client card and continuing in a counterclockwise direction. Finally, study the spread as a whole and summarize your interpretation.

Interpretation

The client card is the queen of diamonds. The special combinations that should be noted are the two eights (**9**, **17**), the two queens (**13**, **21**), and the two aces (**8**, **16**). The three indicator cards (**a**, **b**, **c**) show that the client's future troubles will be of only a temporary nature. She will share them with a dark-haired young man.

Cards **1**, **9**, and **17** indicate joy, happiness, and love shared with a dark-haired young man, reinforcing the message of the indicator cards. A holiday will come as a welcome surprise. Cards **2**, **10**, and **18** suggest that bad news will bring disharmony and disputes, but these will

not be serious. Cards **3**, **11**, and **19** indicate a major change, a move, and a journey. During this upheaval a dark-haired woman will prove to be a good friend. Cards **4**, **12**, and **20** warn of treachery and deceit outside the home casting a shadow over domestic life, but a friend's wedding brings a brief diversion. Cards **5**, **13**, and **21** show the client worried by her friends' troubles. The unhappiness of an older lady, possibly a widow, causes concern. Cards **6**, **14**, and **22** show the client's life improving after a minor illness, and a letter bringing good news about money. Cards **7**, **15**, and **23** reveal a generous fair-haired man and a reliable dark-haired man helping the client with a problem associated with gossip or even scandal. Cards **8**, **16**, and **24** promise good news about money and security at home.

Summarizing this information, we see that the client is mainly interested in her home and her marriage. She is striving for happiness, but needs to accept that life has its ups and downs. Relationships with those close to her will not always be as easy as she once thought, and she must expect some dramatic changes. She has many friends who sometimes inflict their problems on her. She should take note of the possibility of a minor illness, but otherwise her future looks promising, and she can expect improvements in her finances and in her home life.

Sortilege

Sortilege is divination by the casting or drawing of lots, and comes from the Latin – *sors,* the word for a lot, and *sortilegus* meaning a diviner. Nearly everyone has unthinkingly determined their future by lot at some time in their lives – tossing a coin to make a decision, for example, or drawing straws to select a person to carry out a particular action. Many forms of gambling – sweepstakes, lotteries, bingo, roulette, etc – also depend on casting or drawing lots.

Cleromancy, an alternative name for sortilege, comes from *kleros,* the Greek word for lot. Greek lots were often specially marked wooden counters that were drawn from an urn or cast on the ground. Cleromancy was also used to supplement prophecy: the oracle at Delphi used beans as lots. The enquirer's question was written on a strip of lead, and placed in a jar containing

SOME SORTILEGE TECHNIQUES

1 Aleuromancy This is said to have been in common practice until the ninth century. All the possible answers to a specific question were written on slips of paper, and these were then rolled up and baked inside small balls of dough. The querant chose a ball at random, and broke it open to find the answer.
The tradition survives today in the "fortune cookies" available in some Chinese restaurants. Customers choose one of the small hollow pastries, and break it open to find the slip of paper that tells their fortune.
2 Astragalomancy is divination by casting small bones called astragals, which were usually the vertebrae or ankle bones of sheep.

3 Belomancy is divination by arrows. The specially marked arrows could be cast on the ground or drawn from a container. This form of divination probably dates back to the Babylonians, and was also practiced by the Scythians, Arabs, and some North American Indian tribes.
4 Pessomancy, psephomancy is divination by drawing or casting colored or specially marked pebbles. Many African witch doctors keep bags of "wise stones" that they cast to foretell the future. In the Arab tradition, the pebbles are turned out into a heap, and the omens read one at a time as the stones are drawn at random.

READING THE STONES

Listed in the table *right* are the colors, symbols, and interpretations of a set of "talking stones" suitable for fortune telling. Choose small stones with rounded edges; you should be able to hold all nine together in your hand. The symbol should be marked on only one side of the stone.
Concentrate on your question while you shake the stones in your hand and cast them in front of you. The answer to your question can then be read in the stones whose symbols are showing. The symbols close to you represent events in the near future; those farther away foretell the more distant future. Stones that touch each other or that are very close together should be read in conjunction.

	Color	Symbol	Interpretation
a	White	Eye	"I," the questioner
b	Red	Swords	Drive, energy, strife
c	Yellow	Sun	Health, the outer life, men
d	Blue	Flower	Success, prosperity
e	Green	Rings	Relationships, harmony
f	Blue-green	Waves	The intellect, travel
g	Gray	Moon	The inner life, women
h	Brown	Bird	Communications, visitors
i	Black	Fence	Delay, restrictions, old age

a mixture of black and white beans. The lead strip was then withdrawn together with a single bean: if the bean was white, the answer to the question was yes; if black, the answer was no.

Many different objects have been used as lots. In Japan, slips of paper inscribed with omens for the future were placed in containers and drawn at random. In Polynesia, a coconut was spun, and answered questions by how it fell. In Africa, the tradition varies from tribe to tribe: lots could be sacred stones, or carved wooden or bone divining sticks. Divining sticks are also known in parts of Asia, and sacred stones among the North American Indians.

CHAPTER AND VERSE

Opening a book at random and taking an omen from the first words read – bibliomancy – is another form of sortilege. Bibliomancy is also called stichomancy: a "stich" is a line of verse or a short section of prose. Divination from a book of poetry is sometimes known as rhapsodomancy.

Although in theory any book can be used in bibliomancy, in practice it is only the works of major writers that are consulted – the epics of the Greek writer Homer, for example, or the works of the Persian poet Hafiz (where the omen is traditionally selected with a knife), or the plays of Shakespeare. In the late Middle Ages the works of the Roman writer Virgil were the most popular choice, and bibliomancy was known as the *sortes Virgilianae* – the "Virgilian lots." The Bible has long been used for bibliomancy: both words are derived from the same Greek word *biblia*, meaning books. Some bibliomancers use the whole Bible; others take their omens only from the 31 verses of the last chapter of the book of Proverbs.

BIBLIOMANCY

Allow your intuition to direct your choice of book. Close your eyes, concentrate on your question, and open the book at random. Open your eyes: the first words you read should form an answer to your question. You may prefer to use some form of pointer – your finger will do – to indicate the words of your omen before you open your eyes to read them.

©DIAGRAM

Runes

In about the first or second century AD the Germanic peoples of Northern Europe began using an alphabet made up of characters called runes. Norse myth says that knowledge of these runes came from Odin, the one-eyed god of occult wisdom and the protector of heroes. Odin was said to ride through the sky on an eight-legged horse, and to be accompanied by a raven and a wolf. To humans, he would appear as a bearded man in a gray cloak, with a wide-brimmed hat pulled forward to shade his piercing blue eye. To gain knowledge of the runes, Odin is said to have hung from the world-tree Yggdrasil (the giant ash tree that in Norse myth supported the universe) for nine days and nights, without food and water and impaled on his own spear.

The Norse rune masters would use the runes to predict future events, and for many other purposes as well. Runes would be used to heal, to protect, to control the weather, or to help a prisoner escape from his enemies. They would also be engraved on swords to improve a warrior's fighting ability, and on amulets or talismans worn to attract love, happiness, and prosperity.

Making the runes
Sets of runes can sometimes be bought in specialist shops, but it is quite possible to make your own. Traditionally, the runes are carved or burned into small oblong pieces of wood (Norse rune masters would have used the wood of a fruit tree), or engraved on copper, bronze, or gold disks. The runic symbols should be inscribed on one side only; the other side remains blank. Alternatively, you can make rune cards by drawing the runes on small squares of white board.

Reading the runes
Clear your mind of thoughts, and scatter the runes face down in front of you. Ask the enquirer to shuffle the runes (as if they were dominoes) and then to arrange 13

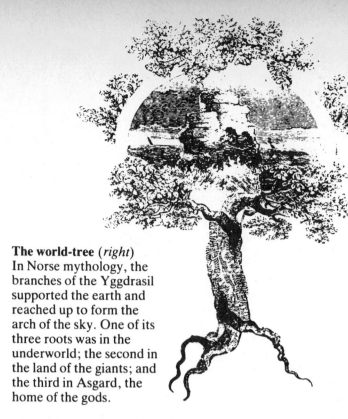

The world-tree (*right*)
In Norse mythology, the branches of the Yggdrasil supported the earth and reached up to form the arch of the sky. One of its three roots was in the underworld; the second in the land of the giants; and the third in Asgard, the home of the gods.

of them in a circle, still face down. The layout of this circle – called the runic wheel – and the order in which the runes should be set out are shown in the diagram *below*.

Turn the runes in the wheel face up and begin your interpretation. Each rune should be related to the rune on either side of it, to the rune immediately opposite it, and to the center rune. Runes are in their upright position if their tops face the center of the wheel; the tops of reversed runes face the outside of the wheel. Each position on the runic wheel is also connected with a different aspect of life: these are listed *below* and should be taken into account in your reading.

Positions on the runic wheel
1 The self, the personality.
2 Money, possessions.
3 Family.
4 The home.
5 Creativity, self-expression.
6 The outside world, physical health.
7 Love and marriage.
8 Inheritance, death.
9 Education, travel.
10 Careers, social status.
11 Friendships, pleasure.
12 The inner life, psychic qualities.
13 The enquirer.

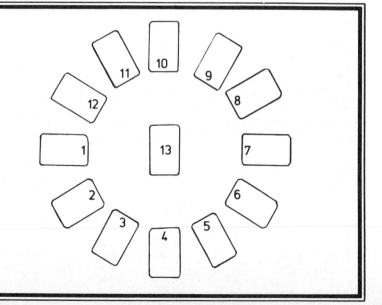

Rune interpretations

a *Upright* Be careful and plan ahead.
Reversed Impatience will lead to failure.
b *Upright* Romantic fulfillment.
Reversed Romantic difficulties.
c *Upright* Intuition, premonitions coming true.
Reversed Be cautious with money.
d *Upright* Old age, wisdom
Reversed Bad advice, senility.
e *Upright* A passionate love affair.
Reversed A parting, sadness caused by friends.
f *Upright* An old problem solved.
Reversed An old problem causing new difficulties.
g *Upright* Changes at work.
Reversed An offer that should be refused.
h *Upright* Wills, inheritances, legacies.
Reversed Accidents, damage.
i *Upright* News, a stranger.
Reversed Problems in communication.
j *Upright* New relationships, partnerships.
Reversed Loss of a friend.
k *Upright* Moving house, crossing water.
Reversed An unpleasant journey.

l *Upright* Happiness and success.
Reversed Self-sacrifice, delay.
m *Upright* Holidays, travel, visits.
Reversed Sudden journeys and changes.
n *Upright* Family, marriage, fertility, children.
Reversed Ill health, sterility, divorce.
o *Upright* Financial good fortune, promotion.
Reversed A lost opportunity.
p *Upright* A flash of inspiration.
Reversed An inability to see the obvious.
q *Upright* Minor delays and family disagreements.
Reversed Major delays and family quarrels.
r *Upright* A gift, windfall, or pleasant surprise.
Reversed Unreliable confidants.
s *Upright* Legal documents, contracts.
Reversed Enemies.
t *Upright* Major changes leading to prosperity.
Reversed Isolation, detachment.
u *Upright* Certain success.
Reversed A failure that leads to a new opportunity.
v Fate, "karma," the inevitable.

©DIAGRAM

Dice

Dice – of which each individual is called a die – have existed since at least 2000BC. They seem to have been universally popular, and have been found in one or other of their many forms all over the world. Early dice accompanied a wide range of games, usually of the board-and-counters type, or were used alone for gambling – "loaded" dice, specially made for cheating, have been found in ancient tombs in Egypt and the Far East.

The use of dice for divination probably evolved from sortilege, which is divination by the casting of lots. One form of sortilege, astragalomancy, made use of the direct ancestors of the dice we know today. These were astragals, the vertebrae or the ankle-bones of sheep. As

Early dice
a Astragal.
b Ancient Egyptian die.
c Etruscan dice.
d Roman long die, marked *malest* (ill luck) on one side.
e Roman die with 14 faces.
f Die in the form of a six-sided figurine.
g Asian long dice.

Astragalomancy

Today this is a form of divination using two dice, but originally a pair of astragals (probably the left and right ankle-bones of a sheep) would have been used. This method allows you to use the dice to answer a specific question.

Concentrate on your question, and then throw the dice into the circle. Add the numbers on the two dice, and then consult the list of answers. If a die falls outside the circle it is not counted.

One Yes.
Two No.
Three Take care.
Four Be wise.
Five Good luck.
Six Of course.
Seven Have faith.
Eight Be patient.
Nine Certainly.
Ten Doubtful.
Eleven Nonsense.
Twelve A chance.

Reading the dice

Some people believe that the dice should be thrown only on behalf of someone else, and not to predict your own future. Another belief says that the dice should be thrown in complete silence, and yet another holds that cool weather and a calm atmosphere are the best conditions for a good reading.

The most usual modern method is to draw a circle 12in (30cm) in diameter on a table or other flat surface. You then throw three dice out of your hand or from a cup to land inside this circle. If all the dice land outside the circle, pick them up and throw them again. If the same should happen a second time, the dice should be abandoned and you should wait for a more propitious time – do not throw them a third time.

Add together the numbers on the three dice and look up the meaning of the total. Any dice that fall outside the circle are not counted. If one falls outside, add together the numbers on the other two, but remember that the die outside the circle means that your plans may go wrong. If two dice land outside the circle, trouble or a quarrel may be coming. If a die falls on the floor there are troubled times ahead; two dice on the floor suggest serious trouble. If one or more dice land outside the circle and the remaining dice in the circle total less than three, there is no reading – only the numbers from three to 18 are read.

If a number recurs during a reading, it indicates that significant news is on the way. In the rare event that one die lands on top of another and stays there, you may receive a gift – but you must also take care, both in business and in love.

INTERPRETING THE TOTALS

Three A surprise or some unexpected news may be on the way, but it will be favorable.
Four Disappointment or unpleasantness could be in store, and possibly bad luck, too.
Five Your wish will come true, but perhaps in an unexpected way. A stranger may bring happiness.
Six There will be loss and misfortune, probably in money and business matters.
Seven You will suffer setbacks and maybe unhappiness through scandal or gossip – be careful.
Eight Outside influences are strong, and you might be the victim of unfair blame or injustice.
Nine Lucky for love and marriage; you can expect reconciliation and forgiveness after a quarrel.
Ten A strong prediction of birth, also domestic happiness and a promotion or business success.

they had four easily-distinguishable faces, they were convenient for throwing – each face could be given a set value. Astragals were used in ancient Greece and Rome and, in fact, persisted in use alongside more recognizable forms of dice until the tenth century. Dice have been made in a variety of shapes and sizes, sometimes with up to 20 faces. In the past most were made of wood, bone, or ivory, but more precious materials were sometimes used and were considered to enhance the latent power of the dice. Modern dice are usually cubes and made of plastic. The standard western marking has the 1-spot on the face opposite the 6-spot, 2 opposite 5, and 3 opposite 4, but other numberings are still in use in other parts of the world.

Eleven A parting, perhaps from someone close to you; there may be an illness.
Twelve Good news will arrive, probably by letter, and you should take advice before replying.
Thirteen This dark number predicts grief and sorrow, which may last a very long time.
Fourteen A friend will help you, or you may meet a new admirer or stranger who will become a close friend.
Fifteen You need to take great care, perhaps against some temptation into dishonesty.
Sixteen This number tells of travel, and the omens for the journey are very good.
Seventeen A change of plan may come about through a person from overseas or who is associated with water.
Eighteen This number is the best omen of all, bringing success, prosperity, and happiness.

Specific predictions
It is possible to make predictions about particular areas of your life by dividing the circle into 12 equal sections *below*. The overall message gained from the total of the numbers on the dice can now be applied with special relevance to the sections in which the dice fell. In addition, a special prediction can be made for each section by reading the number on the individual die within it. If two or three dice fall into the same section,
this makes the message much more forceful. Interpret the numbers on the individual dice as shown here, and integrate these meanings with your earlier readings to give a coherent prediction.
One Generally favorable, but bear the overall prediction in mind.
Two Your success depends on your friends.
Three An excellent omen for success.
Four Disappointment and trouble.
Five Good indications.
Six Uncertainty.

Sections of the circle
A Next year.
B Money matters.
C Travel.
D Domestic matters.
E The present.
F Health.
G Love and marriage.
H Legal matters.
I Your present state of mind.
J Work and career.
K Friends.
L Enemies.

© DIAGR·

Dominoes

Dominoes are small, oblong-shaped tiles of wood, ivory, or plastic. Each tile is divided in half, and each half has spots indicating numbers from zero to six. Modern sets consist of 28 tiles – one tile for every combination from double-blank to double-six. They are used to play a number of different games but, like dice, the numbers on the pieces can be used to predict the future.

Dominoes were first recorded in China in the twelfth century BC, and these early examples would probably have been used for divination rather than for gaming.

Dominoes are closely related to dice and may indeed have evolved as a form of dice for safe use in occult matters: using dice for both gambling and fortune telling could have been considered dangerous. Dominoes are still used extensively for prediction in India and Korea, and some Indian and Chinese games combine gambling and fortune telling – certain tiles are thought to bring good luck even if the player loses a bet!

In China the dominoes, like the dice, have red spots as well as black. A set of Chinese dominoes has 32 pieces:

How to read the dominoes

Lay all the tiles face downward and shuffle them well. Draw three tiles, and read the meaning of each one. These interpretations must be organized into a coherent picture, and this will require imagination and subtlety on your part.

According to one method you should pick all three dominoes before looking at any of them, although you should re-shuffle the remaining tiles before each draw. Another way is to pick one domino and to consult its meaning. Then return the tile to the set and re-shuffle before picking for the second time. Repeat for the third draw. With this method you may draw the same tile more than once – if this happens, it presages a very quick fulfillment of the prophecy.

Whichever method you choose, it is important not to draw more than three dominoes at a consultation, or to consult the dominoes more than once a week, or it is said that the messages will become meaningless.

DOMINO MEANINGS

Six-six This is the best domino in the set, with strong omens for success and happiness in every area of life.

Six-five A close friend or maybe a benefactor, but patience and perseverance are also indicated. A kind action will bring you great regard.

Six-four All the signs point to a quarrel, or maybe even a lawsuit, with an unsuccessful outcome.

Six-three You are going to travel, or a journey will affect your life. A holiday will be happy, and a journey may bring a gift.

Six-two Very good luck is coming your way, and your circumstances may be improved. But this tile is only lucky for the honest!

Six-one There will be an end to your problems. A good friend could be involved in this; a wedding is foretold.

Six-blank Be careful of false friends or a deceitful person. You could suffer some unhappiness because of gossip.

Five-five A strong omen for change, and the change will bring success. You might move to a new place where you will be happy, or make money from a new idea.

Five-four Profits and good fortune in material terms, possibly unexpected, but don't take any chances – it is not a good time for investments.

Five-three A calm and well-adjusted atmosphere here – you will get some good news or helpful advice from a visitor or from your boss.

Five-two A true friend will have an influence on your life, maybe because of their patience and tolerance. This is also an omen for birth.

11 identical pairs, 10 single dominoes, and no blanks. European dominoes probably came from China, and appeared in Italy and France in the eighteenth century. Their name was probably derived from a long black cloak and face mask called a domino. French prisoners introduced dominoes into England at the end of the eighteenth century. The colored spots and duplicate tiles were dropped in western sets, blanks were added, and a 28-tile set in black with white spots became standard. Sets running up to nine-nine and even 12-12 do exist, but they are uncommon. In the move to the west some of the occult subtleties of dominoes were also lost: in the east the names given to the tiles – "Leaping Gazelle," "The Little Snakes," and so on – carry a strong mystic element.

Five-one A love affair, or an interesting meeting with a new friend, is in store. Things may not end happily for those in love.

Five-blank There will be some sadness – you may have to give comfort to a friend in trouble. But you need caution, so think carefully about what you say.

Four-four Happiness, fun, relaxation, and celebration are the signs in this domino. There may be a party in a big building.

Four-three You might have expected some problems or disappointments, but instead you will find happiness and success.

Four-two A change of some sort, but not a happy one – setbacks, losses, or maybe even a robbery. Someone you know is deceitful – be careful!

Four-one This domino is a sign that there will be some financial problems ahead – be sure that you pay any outstanding debts.

Four-blank Some news will not be favorable – you may be disappointed in a love affair, or something you want could be postponed. Try to reconcile a quarrel.

Three-three This domino predicts obstacles in your emotional life – jealousy or distress. But money is well favored.

Three-two Some pleasant changes may be coming, but you need to be cautious just now, especially in financial matters.

Three-one The answer to the question in your mind is "no." Some surprising news might be useful, but beware of unhappiness caused by outsiders.

Three-blank This domino is not a good omen, and you could experience unexpected problems both at home and at work.

Two-two You will get what you want, as this is a good domino. Business success and personal happiness are predicted, but enemies might try to spoil it for you.

Two-one Financial problems and maybe a loss of money or property are indicated, but this domino is good for social life and old friends.

Two-blank This is a good omen for travel and meeting new friends, but something is worrying you and someone could cause difficulties for you.

One-one Harmony and affection are predicted, and a stranger could be involved. You have an important decision to make – don't put it off.

One-blank A stranger or outsider will bring some interesting news that could mean financial gain, but don't be too trusting.

Blank-blank This is the blackest domino in the set, and it carries the worst omens. The double blank will have a negative effect on all your activities.

Tablets of fate 1

Magic tablets combine the random element of casting lots with the occult significance of numbers. No-one is sure how old they are, but they are believed to have developed as a simple method of predicting the future for those who could not afford the services of oracles and other fortune tellers. They were certainly popular in the seventeenth century when they were on sale in the form of chap books (cheap pamphlets sold in the street). The tablets enjoyed renewed popularity in the nineteenth century, although more in the form of parlor games than a serious means of divination. Although the tablets are possibly one of the least sophisticated ways of predicting the future, this does not necessarily imply that they are ineffective. One advantage of this method is that a tablet can be devised so that its answers have particular relevance to your lifestyle. It is quite possible and permissible to construct your own tablet, by devising your own number sequence and list of answers.

6	13	16	8
15	5	1	12
3	10	9	4
14	2	7	11

HOW TO USE THE TABLETS

All the tablets shown here are used in essentially the same way, although experts may differ over the details of the ritual to be used and the frequency with which you may ask questions.

The Tablet of the Sphinx must be consulted first of all, as it will tell you if the present moment is an auspicious one for using this method of divination. If the Sphinx gives a positive answer, you may put your question to the tablet appropriate to the subject. We reproduce six tablets as well as the Sphinx, covering the fields of love, home and family, time, justice, work and finance, and travel. All the equipment you will need is a pencil or similar pointer.

Shut your eyes and concentrate on the question you wish to ask. If someone else is present, ask them to turn the book around three times, keeping it open at the appropriate page throughout (you may turn it yourself, but it is less satisfactory). Meanwhile, take the pencil by the blunt end with the thumb and forefinger of your left hand, and dangle it over the table. Your helper, having turned the book, should place it so that the tablet is approximately under the pencil point. Some authorities say you should now move the pencil point as if to trace out a square or circle in mid-air three times. In any case, remember to concentrate hard on your question. Then bring the point down on to the page, after which you may open your eyes.

Now check which numbered area the pencil point has come down on, and look up that number in the key below the tablet to find what the answer is. If the page was upside down when you opened your eyes, take the answer given after the word "reversed." If the pencil misses the tablet completely three times, do not try again for at least 24 hours.

THE TABLET OF THE SPHINX

This tablet should be consulted first of all, as it tells you whether the other tablets will give true answers at the present time.

1 *Upright* Now is the time to test your fate.
Reversed Today is not the time.
2 *Upright* Tomorrow will be preferable.
Reversed Yes, straight away.
3 *Upright* Thursday is the best day.
Reversed Try any day but Thursday.
4 *Upright* You are too impatient.
Reversed Leave it as it is.
5 *Upright* Try on Sunday.
Reversed Not on Sunday.
6 *Upright* Lose no time.
Reversed Wait one week exactly.
7 *Upright* The answers are waiting.
Reversed Do not even try.
8 *Upright* Try on Tuesday.
Reversed Not until next week.
9 *Upright* Try on the day on which you were born.
Reversed Soon, if you do not lose your temper.
10 *Upright* Saturday is preferable.
Reversed No Saturday is suitable.
11 *Upright* There is nothing to say.
Reversed Secrets wait.
12 *Upright* Monday will be auspicious.
Reversed Monday is inauspicious.
13 *Upright* Lose no time.
Reversed First be sure of your own mind.
14 *Upright* Try on Friday.
Reversed Good fortune awaits you.
15 *Upright* Try on Wednesday.
Reversed Certainly not.
16 *Upright* Straight away.
Reversed Do not try at all.

5	11	1	9
14	7	4	12
8	3	16	2
6	15	10	13

THE TABLET OF VENUS

This tablet will answer questions connected with love.

1 *Upright* This love is true.
Reversed Think hard – this person disagrees with you.
2 *Upright* Expect some delay.
Reversed Not the kind who is easily deceived.
3 *Upright* Follow your own heart.
Reversed Flatterers are dangerous.
4 *Upright* Yes, if you're sure of your own mind.
Reversed If you knew the truth you'd forgive.
5 *Upright* All's well.
Reversed Yours was a hasty judgment.
6 *Upright* You will be to blame if you lose this love.
Reversed True love can weather misfortune.
7 *Upright* You are causing unhappiness.
Reversed Look beyond appearances.
8 *Upright* Do not let jealousy come between you.
Reversed A friend who loves you truly.
9 *Upright* You are the only one who is loved.
Reversed You are too fond of amusements.
10 *Upright* You are in someone's thoughts now.
Reversed Beware of a flirt.
11 *Upright* A passing cloud.
Reversed A misunderstanding on both sides.
12 *Upright* Someone has had a change of mind.
Reversed Evil tongues, evil minds.
13 *Upright* Yes, but not the one you are thinking of.
Reversed You should not act hastily.
14 *Upright* What reason is there for doubt?
Reversed It was an infatuation – forget it.
15 *Upright* Remember what was said as you parted.
Reversed There is no reason to be jealous.
16 *Upright* It is true love.
Reversed Be sensible before it is too late.

THE TABLET OF THE MOON

This tablet will answer questions concerning your home, relatives, and friends.

1 *Upright* All is well, so be patient.
Reversed You are your own worst enemy.
2 *Upright* The fault is yours.
Reversed Less than ever.
3 *Upright* Do not let them worry you.
Reversed If you can do so with a clear conscience.
4 *Upright* Love will find a way.
Reversed There'll be none.
5 *Upright* It's a question of jealousy.
Reversed It may possibly come about.
6 *Upright* You are indulging in fantasy.
Reversed None if you are discreet.
7 *Upright* A fair woman.
Reversed Sometimes, but very rarely.
8 *Upright* It's most unlikely.
Reversed Something will occur that improves matters.
9 *Upright* You will be disappointed in this matter.
Reversed You will do more harm than good.
10 *Upright* Hasty words will be regretted.
Reversed Do not take any of them into your confidence.
11 *Upright* Groundless suspicions.
Reversed Current gossip maligns you.
12 *Upright* There is a marvellous friend to help.
Reversed The secret is at risk.
13 *Upright* Be content.
Reversed Trust the woman who speaks her mind.
14 *Upright* Your neighbor is a true friend.
Reversed It will soon be over.
15 *Upright* You will have your wish.
Reversed There is no reason for doubt.
16 *Upright* A removal.
Reversed Everything is for the best.

Tablets of fate 2

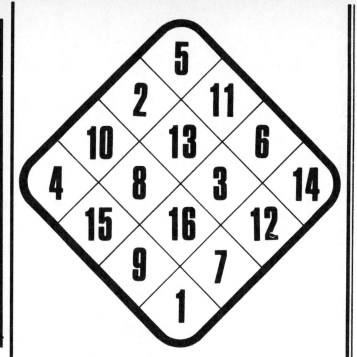

10	3	6	13
8	15	1	5
9	11	7	16
2	14	12	4

THE TABLET OF THE SUN

This tablet answers questions concerning time.

1 *Upright* In six months' time.
Reversed Wait exactly one week.
2 *Upright* Never.
Reversed In two weeks.
3 *Upright* It will soon come about.
Reversed Time will tell.
4 *Upright* Soon.
Reversed Not for a long time.
5 *Upright* Continue and you will flourish.
Reversed Not yet.
6 *Upright* In less time than you think.
Reversed Very gradual change.
7 *Upright* This year.
Reversed The hundredth day of the year.
8 *Upright* Yes.
Reversed The fifteenth day of the month.
9 *Upright* There is some cause of delay.
Reversed In two years' time.
10 *Upright* You are wrong to be impatient.
Reversed Never.
11 *Upright* Straight away.
Reversed In months rather than days.
12 *Upright* Very soon.
Reversed Three times.
13 *Upright* Find your lucky day.
Reversed Sooner than you imagine.
14 *Upright* There is not much longer to wait.
Reversed Leave well alone for as long as you can.
15 *Upright* It seems to have no chance of happening.
Reversed Highly improbable.
16 *Upright* In one year's time.
Reversed In a while.

THE TABLET OF JUPITER

This tablet answers questions concerned with doubts, worries, legal problems, and justice.

1 *Upright* You have been misjudged.
Reversed Your judgment was hasty.
2 *Upright* The truth will out.
Reversed You will not play a major part.
3 *Upright* Your judgment was much too hasty.
Reversed You could not escape this trouble.
4 *Upright* This cloud will pass.
Reversed Things will soon improve.
5 *Upright* You are in the wrong.
Reversed Be brave, you have done no wrong.
6 *Upright* You are most certainly right.
Reversed This is an injustice.
7 *Upright* Learn from your own experience.
Reversed Take care.
8 *Upright* You already know the truth.
Reversed There is no danger.
9 *Upright* No-one can answer the question for you.
Reversed Justice will triumph in the end.
10 *Upright* There will be little delay.
Reversed Do not be afraid without reason.
11 *Upright* Try once more.
Reversed Speak out boldly.
12 *Upright* Do not be afraid.
Reversed No, which is a good thing.
13 *Upright* Yes, and right will prevail.
Reversed You are not in error.
14 *Upright* Things are not as black as you think.
Reversed Make your plans slowly and carefully.
15 *Upright* It is a foolish scandal.
Reversed Do not be anxious.
16 *Upright* You were in the wrong.
Reversed Everything will come right in the end.

8	13	6	2
3	5	12	16
10	7	9	4
14	1	15	11

THE TABLET OF MARS

This tablet will answer questions to do with work, business, or money.

1 *Upright* Many changes.
Reversed Friends are more valuable than money.
2 *Upright* New work.
Reversed It will be very expensive.
3 *Upright* It's up to you.
Reversed There is a high risk.
4 *Upright* Happiness is preferable to wealth.
Reversed Do not rely on it.
5 *Upright* The bad times will soon be over.
Reversed There is the prospect of wealth.
6 *Upright* A big surprise.
Reversed Be ready to take some blame.
7 *Upright* Think hard before giving your consent.
Reversed Look at it from a different angle.
8 *Upright* Hard work is what is needed.
Reversed Be less selfish and more considerate of others.
9 *Upright* Prove that you can be trusted.
Reversed If you persevere no-one can rob you of success.
10 *Upright* Be very careful.
Reversed Turn back.
11 *Upright* Expect problems ahead.
Reversed Take counsel of your second thoughts.
12 *Upright* Your worries will soon be over.
Reversed Exactly what you deserve.
13 *Upright* Expect good luck.
Reversed Money.
14 *Upright* Be bold.
Reversed It will be an improvement.
15 *Upright* All's well.
Reversed You will gain by an accident.
16 *Upright* Have patience.
Reversed Be brave.

THE TABLET OF MERCURY

This tablet answers questions about journeys.

1 *Upright* In a while.
Reversed Wants to be with you.
2 *Upright* Yes, it's all for the best.
Reversed It's inadvisable.
3 *Upright* Better to stay where you are.
Reversed You will decline.
4 *Upright* The prospect of a long journey.
Reversed When you least expect it.
5 *Upright* Distant thoughts are turned to you.
Reversed Some loss and some gain.
6 *Upright* A disappointment.
Reversed It should not be long now.
7 *Upright* Not far.
Reversed An enjoyable time.
8 *Upright* Yes, though it's not so very important.
Reversed After careful thought.
9 *Upright* Modern transport has made the world shrink.
Reversed Very doubtful indeed.
10 *Upright* It will happen very suddenly.
Reversed An unexpected route to happiness.
11 *Upright* Definitely for the better.
Reversed Westward.
12 *Upright* Expect many changes.
Reversed All will not be happiness.
13 *Upright* Your hopes will be fulfilled.
Reversed The distance is great.
14 *Upright* Wait awhile.
Reversed Soon.
15 *Upright* All's for the best.
Reversed The east beckons.
16 *Upright* Don't go.
Reversed Not yet.

Numerology 1

Numerology is believed to be one of the oldest forms of occult lore. Its origins cannot be traced, but the Babylonians, the ancient Egyptians, and many other peoples are all thought to have held theories of the occult significance of numbers. This concept is closely related to astrology, and to the observation of numbers found in natural phenomena – the five senses, the seven colors of the spectrum, the 12 signs of the zodiac, and so on. Numbers were especially important to the Cabalists, both in ancient times and in the Middle Ages. The Cabala, the secret mystical lore of the Jews, contains a magico-philosophical science of numbers known as *gematria,* based on the 22 letters of the Hebrew alphabet.

Although there are some variations between the numerological systems that have come down to the

Finding the primary number

The primary numbers from 1 to 9 are the basis of all numerological systems. Every number can be reduced to its primary by a simple process of left-to-right addition. Thus 25 becomes 2+5=7, and 7 is its primary number. Similarly, 198 becomes 1+9+8=18, which is further reduced to 1+8=9. The same simple process can be applied to dates, names (by a system of number-letter equivalents), events, and so on.

All numerologists agree about the fundamental importance of the primary numbers, but some also offer meanings for secondary numbers (ie 10 and above). The secondary numbers, if used, are also arrived at by a process of addition.

Birth numbers

Your most important number is your birth number. This is calculated by adding up the numbers of your date of birth. For example, if you were born on June 11, 1952, add 6 (because June is the sixth month) +1+1+1+9+5+2, which gives 25. Then add 2+5, giving 7. Number 7 is therefore your birth number. This number is of course unchangeable, and it shows the numerical influence at birth. By looking up the meanings ascribed to 7, you can find your natural characteristics and basic personality traits.

1 2 3 4 5

Other important numbers

Many other significant numbers can be calculated in the same way as the birth and name numbers. By comparing numbers and interpreting their meanings, it is possible to gain knowledge about your life and future events. For example, if you want to know whether a certain job is the right one for you, compare the primary number obtained from the job title with your name number. Do the two numbers fit together well? What do the two numbers tell you? As another example, you might want to know whether a certain date will be a good one for you: add the primary number of the date to your birth and name numbers, and interpret your answer.

You may also influence future events by the use of numbers. Suppose that Jenny Brown wants to be successful in her career as a journalist. She might decide to adopt her middle initial, C, in her working name – Jenny C. Brown gives her a name number of 6, which matches the number 6 given by the letters of the word journalist. Furthermore, 6 is a balanced and harmonious number.

Numerological analysis

If possible, begin your analysis with the birth number. It represents your subject's inborn characteristics, and is known as the "number of personality."

Next analyze the name number for the name by which your subject is best known. It shows the traits developed during life, and is known as the "number of development." If your subject uses another name at work – initials instead of a first name, perhaps, or a stage name – calculate its number as well: it shows your subject's achievements, and is called the "number of attainment."

Your subject's inner nature is shown by the vowel number, known as the "number of underlying influence." It is found by adding up the number equivalents of the vowels in a name and reducing them to the primary.

Finally, take into account any number that occurs frequently and strongly when you are calculating the birth, name, and vowel numbers. This is the frequency number, which has a modifying effect on the analysis, and is known as the "number of added influence."

present day, most seem to be based on the theories of the Greek mathematician and philosopher Pythagoras. He believed that the whole universe was ordered mathematically, and that as everything in it could be expressed in terms of numbers, numbers were therefore the key to the universe.

Numerology, which was also known as numeromancy or arithomancy, used to be practiced as a form of general divination; today its practitioners are mainly concerned with character analysis and potential. The basis of numerology is the belief that numbers – especially the primary numbers from 1 to 9 – exert an influence on every facet of our lives and personalities. Each person has numbers that relate to the significant events in their lives, the most important being the birth number and the name number.

Name numbers

To find your name number, convert the letters of your name to figures, using number-letter equivalents (see box *below*). You should work from the name you usually use, not necessarily your full, formal name. For example, using the older system of equivalents, Jenny Brown becomes

J E N N Y
1+5+5+5+1 = 17, 1 +7 = 8

B R O W N
2+2+7+6+5= 22, 2+2=4

8+4 =12, 1+2=3

Jenny Brown's name number is therefore 3.

A person's name number tends to show acquired or developed traits, and unlike the birth number, it can of course be changed. It is considered ideal if a person's birth and name numbers coincide; this will reinforce the characteristics of the birth number, but in a harmonious way. If there is a serious mismatch between the two numbers, it may indicate inner conflicts that remain unresolved. Let us suppose that Jenny Brown has a birth number of 9. Although 3 is not unharmonious with 9, Jenny might find that she enjoyed more success in her life if she used her full name, Jennifer, because Jennifer Brown gives a name number of 9 to match her birth number.

67890

Number-letter equivalents

The older system of number-letter equivalents *left* omits the number 9. It was omitted because it was held to be of special significance; in the Cabalistic tradition it was considered to be the numerical equivalent of the name of God.

The more modern system of equivalents *below* uses all the primary numbers, including the number 9.

1	2	3	4	5	6	7	8
A	B	C	D	E	U	O	F
I	K	G	M	H	V	Z	P
Q	R	L	T	N	W		
J	S			X			
Y							

1	2	3	4	5	6	7	8	9
A	B	C	D	E	F	G	H	I
J	K	L	M	N	O	P	Q	R
S	T	U	V	W	X	Y	Z	

Numerology 2

Many of the characteristics associated with the primary numbers are related to personality, so allowing you to assess the character of any individual whose name or birth number you have calculated. When you use the numbers for other purposes (for example, to find out if a certain plan will be a good one) their meanings should be interpreted according to their more general characteristics.

Each number is associated with a planet, and with a day of the week – this day is said to be auspicious for those whose birth number is linked with it. The numbers also have positive connections with dates containing the

1 2 3 4 5

Interpreting the numbers

1 Number 1 stands for the Sun, and all that is strong, individual, and creative. Number 1 people are born leaders; they are ambitious and active, and often dominant and aggressive. This is a powerful number, and it augurs success. It is the number of innovators, leaders, winners – but also of tyrants! Number 1 people can be very self-centered, ruthless, and stubborn if crossed, and their chosen career or activity will probably receive more energy and attention than their personal relationships. Sunday is the day associated with the Sun and with the number 1.

2 The Moon, and Monday, are associated with the number 2. Number 2 people are more gentle, passive, and artistic than the stronger number 1 characters. Number 2s are more geared to thought than to action, and although they are inventive, they will be less forceful in carrying out their plans. They are likely to have charm and powers of intuition, but they may suffer from a lack of self-confidence. Number 2 people can be changeable – perhaps even deceitful – and may be over-sensitive and depressive. Number 2 people get on well with their opposites, the number 1 people.

3 Energetic, disciplined, talented, number 3 people often achieve success in their chosen fields. In fact, they are seldom satisfied with less, as they are conscientious,

very proud and independent, and they love to be in control. They may be too fond of telling other people what to do, but they have many good qualities. A superficial show may hide considerable spirituality, since 3 is the number of the Trinity. Number 3 people have good relationships with other 3s, and those born under 6 and 9. Jupiter is the planet of this number, and Thursday is the luckiest day for number 3 people.

4 Number 4 – number of the seasons, the elements, the points of the compass – is oriented to the earth, and its people may be steady and practical, with great endurance. Yet number 4 – the square – contains its own opposite, and number 4 people often see everything from the opposite point of view, making them rebellious and unconventional. They are seldom interested in material things. Making friends is hard for 4s, and they may feel isolated. People whose numbers are 1, 2, 7, and 8 are the best friends or partners for 4s. Number 4 is associated with the planet Uranus, and with Sunday.

5 Number 5 – the number of the senses – symbolizes the planet Mercury, and people born under this number are mercurial in all their characteristics. Lively, sensual, pleasure-seeking, impulsive, quick-thinking and quick-tempered, these highly-strung number 5 people may have trouble with their nerves. They are

The secondary numbers

Some numerologists take into account the meanings of the secondary numbers as well as the nine primaries. There are many ways to do this, as well as many different interpretations of the secondary numbers themselves.

Normally a secondary number will be taken into account only as additional information, or to add a further dimension to the interpretation of the primary

number. Suppose, for example, that the letters of a name add up to 11 (which when further reduced gives a name number of 2), and the person's birthday falls on November 11. Such a strong coincidence of the number 11 (November is the eleventh month) cannot be ignored, although 11 is not the occult primary birth or name number. The implications of 11 can be added to the meanings of the primary to fill out the total picture. The more mystically-minded numerologists have same number: for example, the 5th, 14th, and 23rd of each month are seen as good days for anyone whose birth number is 5.

6 ♀ 7 ♆ 8 ♄ 9 ♂

good at making money, especially by risk or speculation, and they bounce back easily from any failure. They make friends easily with people born under any other number, but close friends will probably be fellow number 5s. Wednesday is the luckiest day for the quicksilver number 5.

6 A "perfect" number because it is the sum of its factors (1,2,3), 6 is balanced and harmonious, and is associated with family love and domesticity. Number 6 people are very reliable and trustworthy, but they may also be obstinate. Their planet, Venus, governs devotion in love, but number 6 people are romantic rather than sensual. They have a great love of beauty; they are usually attractive and have a greater ability to make friends than any other number. Despite a hatred of any sort of discord, they can be obstinate fighters. Their luckiest day is Friday.

7 Number 7 is thought to have occult significance, and people born under its influence often have a strongly philosophical or spiritual outlook – they are not usually interested in material things. They may be highly intuitive, even psychic. Number 7 people often exert a mysterious influence over others, but may also have a tendency to become too introverted. They are original thinkers, and have the luck associated with their number. Their planet is Neptune, which is

associated with water, and number 7 people often have a restless love of travel and of the sea. Monday is their luckiest day.

8 Number 8 is a strange, difficult number. It is twice 4, and so incorporates the rebellious contradictions of that number. Number 8 may mean sorrow, yet it is also associated with worldly success. Number 8 people have great willpower and individuality, but they may appear cold. In fact they have deep and intense feelings, and are often misunderstood by others. Their planet is Saturn, and Saturday is their most important day.

9 Number 9 is sometimes considered the ultimate number, with special or even sacred significance. When multiplied by any number, it reproduces itself (eg 3×9=27, 2+7=9). Number 9 symbolizes the planet Mars, and its people are fighters – active and determined, they usually succeed after a struggle, but they are also prone to accident and injury, and may be quarrelsome. But at its best, number 9 will influence the highest qualities of courage and brotherly love. Number 9 people should try to carry out their plans on Tuesday, the day governed by their planet, Mars.

11, 12, 13, 22, 40

offered a vast list of meanings for secondary numbers. Another school of thought recognizes only the secondary numbers up to 22 (there are 22 letters in the Hebrew alphabet). More often, however, just a few significant secondaries are taken into account, as listed below.

11 This is the number of special mystical awareness, possibly balanced between good and evil.

12 A powerful sign of completeness, being the number

of signs of the zodiac, the months, the apostles, etc.

13 One more than the "perfect 12," this number is usually associated with ill fortune and the black arts, but it can also be a positive force.

22 This number, like 12, has a strong sense of fullness and completeness. It is the number of letters in the Hebrew alphabet, and of the cards in the major arcana of the tarot.

40 Another potent number suggesting completeness.

I Ching 1

The I Ching or Book of Changes has existed in some form for 4000 years. It has meant many different things to different ages and cultures, which in view of its name ought not to surprise us. Before examining the changes that have taken place within the book and in the significance that people have found in it, there are two fundamental ideas that have to be grasped. Firstly it is considered to be much more than a means of prediction; it is regarded as a book of wisdom that offers advice on how to cope with your fortune. Secondly, it is the product of a culture very different from ours: in order to understand the I Ching we need to accept the ancient Chinese way of thinking about the world, especially on the subjects of change and chance.

The central feature of the I Ching is the hexagram, a pattern of six horizontal lines, to be read from the bottom upward. The hexagram is formed by the questioner in what to western minds seems a purely random manner, using yarrow stalks, coins, or wands. To the Chinese mind, though, there is nothing random about it: the pattern formed is the unique and inevitable product of the moment, a fingerprint of the questioner's

The history of the I Ching

Like many ancient books, the I Ching is the product of more than one hand. The two symbols used in the hexagram, the broken and unbroken lines, pre-date recorded history. They have thus long been ascribed to the mythical figure Fu Hsi, said to have been the first Emperor of China. The eight trigrams formed from them and found as the two halves of the hexagrams are said to have been discovered on the shell of a sacred tortoise. Two early books of changes were used for divination under the Hsia Dynasty (2205–1766BC) and the Shang Dynasty (1766-1150BC), but the present set of 64 hexagrams is said to have been compiled by King Wen (died c.1150BC). He also began the process of adding explanatory text, which was continued by his son the Duke of Chou, to form an oracle that was used throughout the Chou Dynasty (1150-249BC). This is thought to have been the form in which Confucius knew and studied it. Confucius is believed to have written one of the additional commentaries, and in time the rest came to be attributed to him as well.

In the next few centuries there were many more textual accretions, only parts of which survive. Under the Ch'in (221–206BC) and Han (206–220AD) Dynasties the I Ching was practically submerged under an overlay of magic and the Yin-Yang doctrine. It was a scholar called Wang Pi (226–249AD) who rescued it from these later interpretations and argued that it should be used as a fund of wisdom, not merely a means of divining the future. It then developed into a guide to statecraft. Present texts are based on the early eighteenth century AD edition called Chou I Che Chung. In the west the most widely used translations have been those of James Legge (into English, 1899) and Richard Wilhelm (into German, 1924, and thence into English).

Fu Hsi *below*
The legendary first Emperor of China, depicted inventing the eight trigrams.

predicament, bound up with and reflecting that person's past and future. Once complete, the hexagram is looked up in the Book of Changes, where interpretation and advice will be found.

The ancient users of the I Ching believed that spirits were communicating with them through the medium of chance, as expressed in the fall of the stalks, coins, or wands. Modern users may prefer C.G. Jung's explanation that it is the unconscious mind that is being consulted. Whichever view you prefer, the I Ching seems to have its own personality, one that accepts changing explanations with perfect equanimity, because the acceptance of change as the greatest natural law is the very basis of its philosophy. It is a guide to the world of flux in which we have our existence.

Please note that here we can merely help you to understand the I Ching. There is no substitute for the book itself, and you will need to buy or borrow a copy of one of the English translations.

Confucius

Confucius lived from 552 to 479BC. His name was more properly K'ung-fu-tzu, and he came from the state of Lu in the south of what is now the Shantung province of China. Although he is commonly thought of as a scholar and writer, he in fact devoted more time to formulating and teaching an ethical theory of statecraft. His aim was to see his humane reforms applied in his lifetime, but he was denied any influential post and had to transfer his hopes to the careers of his pupils. Yet in time his teachings, although encrusted with wrongly attributed texts and dubious reinterpretations, came to dominate the thought of China for two thousand years. He undoubtedly studied the I Ching, and is said to have remarked that if he could have his life extended he would devote fifty years to it, and thereby avoid many errors. It came to be regarded as one of the classics of Confucianism, but his authorship of most of the commentaries is now disputed.

The portrait of Confucius *right* is composed of lines of Chinese calligraphy.

I Ching 2

Here we explain the makeup of the trigrams that will later go to form the all-important hexagrams.

Trigrams are formed from three broken or unbroken lines, and each sort of line has significance at various levels. The lines are grouped in threes in every possible permutation, making eight trigrams in all.

Each trigram has a name and is further elucidated by an attribute, an image, and a family relationship.

It is vital to remember that the trigrams are regarded as symbols of change, not of a set of static conditions, and one trigram is constantly changing into another.

Studying the trigrams on their own will help considerably in later grasping the full subtlety of the complete hexagram.

The unbroken line *above*
This began as a simple sign for "yes" in divination. It is now called Yang, heaven, or "the firm," and is associated with the positive, active, and masculine side of nature.

The broken line *above*
This sign stood at first for "no," and is now called Yin, earth, "the yielding," and is linked with the negative, feminine, passive side of nature.

The eight trigrams *right*
Each of the eight trigrams combines the two types of line in a different way, ranging from the complete dominance of Yang to the supremacy of Yin. The trigram must be read from the bottom up, line by line, to grasp the idea of flux or continual change from one principle to the other.

The name of each trigram in Chinese characters is also shown.

Circular symbol *right*
This design is common in Chinese art as a symbol of the trigrams in never-ending interaction about the emblem of Yang and Yin.

122

Ch'ien (The creative)	Strong	Heaven	Father
K'un (The receptive)	Devoted, yielding	Earth	Mother
Chen (The arousing)	Inciting movement	Thunder	First son
K'an (The abysmal)	Dangerous	Water	Second son
Ken (Keeping still)	Resting	Mountain	Third son
Sun (The gentle)	Penetrating	Wind, wood	First daughter
Li (The clinging)	Light-giving	Fire	Second daughter
Tui (The joyous)	Joyful	Lake	Third daughter

Names *above*
The names of the trigrams do not appear elsewhere in Chinese, which suggests either extreme antiquity or that they are of foreign origin.
The English translations are not universally agreed upon, but those given here are in common use.
The Wade system of spelling that is used here to render the sound of the name in our alphabet is now officially obsolete, but is still the system found in most editions of the I Ching.

Attributes *above*
Each trigram has an attribute, a word or two indicating the kind of action that is latent in the particular combination of lines. The attributes are particularly helpful in conveying to the Western mind the idea of potential change implicit in every trigram.

Images *above*
The images associated with the eight trigrams include heaven and earth and all the major features and phenomena that occur between the two. Each image brings with it associated ideas that can add depth and resonance to the interpretation of that trigram when it is found as part of the hexagram.

Family relationships *above*
Certain relationships from within the family are linked with the trigrams (the ones shown are those given by King Wen). Their significance is usually figurative, the sons being associated with movement, the daughters with devotion.
(Some authors link many more themes with the trigrams: animals; parts of the body; time of day; points of the compass.)

©DIAGRAM

I Ching 3

The makeup of the hexagrams

The 64 hexagrams devised by King Wen can be subdivided in various ways to extract information on various themes.

The table below shows which trigrams combine to form which hexagrams. It will be useful also for finding the name and number of a hexagram when you begin casting them yourself later. To use it for this purpose, first divide your hexagram into its two trigrams. Find the lower trigram in the left hand column and read across, then find the upper trigram in the top row and read down. Where the two cross you will find the name and number of your hexagram, which can then be looked up in your copy of the I Ching.

For example, the hexagram shown right (**A**) is composed of the lower trigram Sun (**B**) and the upper trigram Chen (**C**). Checking on the table across from Sun and down from Chen reveals that the hexagram is Heng, number 32.

Upper trigram / Lower trigram	Ch'ien	Chen	K'an	Ken	K'un	Sun	Li	Tui
Ch'ien	Ch'ien 1	Ta Chuang 34	Hsu 5	Ta Ch'u 26	T'ai 11	Hsiao Ch'u 9	Ta Yu 14	Kuai 43
Chen	Wu Wang 25	Chen 51	Chun 3	I 27	Fu 24	I 42	Shih Ho 21	Sui 17
K'an	Sung 6	Chieh 40	K'an 29	Meng 4	Shih 7	Huan 59	Wei Chi 64	K'un 47
Ken	Tun 33	Hsiao Kuo 62	Chien 39	Ken 52	Ch'ien 15	Chien 53	Lu 56	Hsien 31
K'un	P'i 12	Yu 16	Pi 8	Po 23	K'un 2	Kuan 20	Chin 35	Ts'ui 45
Sun	Kou 44	Heng 32	Ching 48	Ku 18	Sheng 46	Sun 57	Ting 50	Ta Kuo 28
Li	T'ung Jen 13	Feng 55	Chi Chi 63	Pi 22	Ming I 36	Chia Jen 37	Li 30	Ko 49
Tui	Lu 10	Kuei Mei 54	Chien 60	Sun 41	Lin 19	Chung Fu 61	K'uei 38	Tui 58

Reading the hexagram
right The hexagram is read from the bottom line upward, and the lines are accordingly numbered for reference as shown.

Primary trigrams *right*
The two trigrams of which a hexagram is composed are referred to as the lower (**d**) and upper (**e**) primary trigrams.

Pairs of lines *right*
The hexagram may be divided into pairs of lines. The lower pair (**a**) refers to earth, the middle (**b**) to man, and the upper (**c**) to heaven.

Nuclear trigrams *right*
There are two trigrams interlocked within the hexagram, known as the lower (**f**) and upper (**g**) nuclear trigrams.

The sovereign hexagrams *below*
The twelve hexagrams shown below are regarded as particularly significant. They represent the twelve lunar months in the Chinese year and at the same time reflect the rise and fall of Yang and Yin through the seasons. In numbers one to six in the sequence shown, Yang is predominant, as represented by the unbroken lines. In numbers seven to twelve the rise of Yin is apparent in the increasing proportion of broken lines.

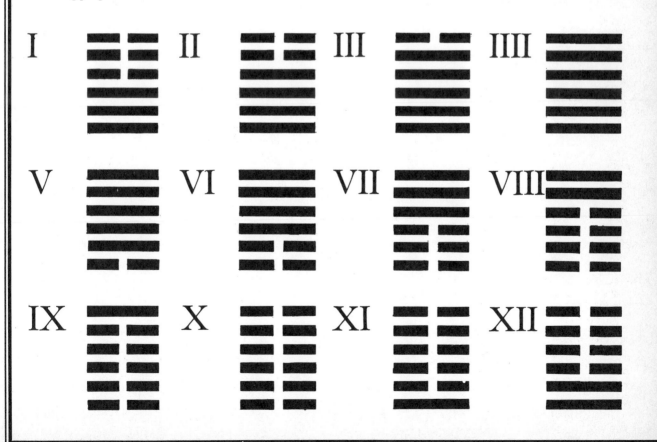

©DIAGRAM

I Ching 4

Here we list the names of all the 64 hexagrams and illustrate the hexagrams themselves in two traditional arrangements.

The order in which the names are listed is that in which they appear in the I Ching itself. The numbers against the names allow you to find the hexagrams themselves on the circular diagram. The order in which they appear in the circle is regarded as the natural development of the lines. The arrangement of the square is also logical, each horizontal row having the same lower primary trigram and each vertical row the same upper primary trigram. Over the centuries Chinese scholars have read much significance into the symmetry that is inherent in the hexagrams.

Studying the list and diagrams will help you both to appreciate the subtle variety of the hexagrams and gradually to learn to recognize them; however, you will still need to consult a copy of the I Ching itself in order to bring out their meaning.

NAMES OF THE HEXAGRAMS

1 **Ch'ien** The creative.
2 **K'un** The receptive.
3 **Chun** Difficulty at the beginning.
4 **Meng** Youthful folly.
5 **Hsu** Waiting.
6 **Sung** Conflict.
7 **Shih** The army.
8 **Pi** Holding together.
9 **Hsiao Ch'u** The taming power of the small.
10 **Lu** Treading.
11 **T'ai** Peace.
12 **P'i** Standstill.
13 **T'ung Jen** Fellowship with men.
14 **Ta Yu** Possession in great measure.
15 **Ch'ien** Modesty.
16 **Yu** Enthusiasm.
17 **Sui** Following.
18 **Ku** Work on what has been spoiled.
19 **Lin** Approach.
20 **Kuan** Contemplation.
21 **Shih Ho** Biting through.
22 **Pi** Grace.
23 **Po** Splitting apart.
24 **Fu** Return.
25 **Wu Wang** Innocence.
26 **Ta Ch'u** The taming power of the great.
27 **I** The corners of the mouth.
28 **Ta Kuo** Preponderance of the great.
29 **K'an** The abysmal.
30 **Li** The clinging.
31 **Hsien** Influence.
32 **Heng** Duration.
33 **Tun** Retreat.
34 **Ta Chuang** The power of the great.
35 **Chin** Progress.
36 **Ming I** Darkening of the light.
37 **Chia Den** The family.
38 **K'uei** Opposition.
39 **Chien** Obstruction.
40 **Hsieh** Deliverance.
41 **Sun** Decrease.
42 **I** Increase.
43 **Kuai** Breakthrough.
44 **Kou** Coming to meet.
45 **Ts'ui** Gathering together.
46 **Sheng** Pushing upward.
47 **K'un** Oppression.
48 **Ching** The well.
49 **Ko** Revolution.
50 **Ting** The caldron.
51 **Chen** The arousing.
52 **Ken** Keeping still.
53 **Chien** Development.
54 **Kuei Mei** The marrying maiden.
55 **Feng** Abundance.
56 **Lu** The wanderer.
57 **Sun** The gentle.
58 **Tui** The joyous.
59 **Huan** Dispersion.
60 **Chieh** Limitation.
61 **Chung Fu** Inner truth.
62 **Hsiao Kuo** Preponderance of the small.
63 **Chi Chi** After completion.
64 **Wei Chi** Before completion.

I Ching 5

The process of "casting" by which the hexagram is formed is crucial. We show two methods, one using coins, the other using yarrow stalks. Although the coin method is quick, simple, and quite adequate, many feel that the best results are obtained through the yarrow stalks. This is because the lengthier ritual helps to concentrate the mind during this most vital stage in the process.

Strong lines *right*
Whether you use the coins or the yarrow stalks, you need to understand the function of "strong" or "moving" lines. A strong Yang line is shown with a circle over the center (**a**); a strong Yin line has a cross in the gap (**b**). If one or more of these lines occurs when you cast your hexagram, first look up the hexagram in the I Ching as if all lines were normal and interpret it. Then the strong lines turn into their opposites, strong Yang becoming Yin and strong Yin becoming Yang, so forming a second hexagram which must also be interpreted.

For example, the hexagram (**c**) is interpreted as it stands, as number 42, called I. Once the strong lines have been changed it becomes number 41, Sun (**d**), whose meaning will add to and modify that of number 42.

The yarrow stalks
The yarrow is a plant traditionally associated by the Chinese with divination. Sometimes prepared strips of bamboo can be bought as a substitute. In either case 49 are needed, though it is customary to have one spare to round out the set.

The basic procedure *below*
1 Place the 49 stalks on a flat surface and divide them arbitrarily into two piles.
2 With your right hand take one from the right hand pile and place it between the little finger and ring finger of your left hand.

3 Again with your right hand, discard stalks from the left hand pile four at a time, until four, three, two, or one remain. Place these remaining stalks between the ring and middle fingers of your left hand.
4 Now reduce the right hand pile four by four until four or fewer stalks remain, and put these between the middle and index fingers.
5 All the stalks in your left hand should now be put carefully to one side.
6 Heap together all the stalks that were discarded four by four.

The coins

Three coins are needed, ideally old Chinese cash (**A**), which are round with a square central hole and have characters on one side only. That side is given the value two, and the plain side the value three. If ordinary coins are used, the side showing the monetary value is regarded as the side with characters and thus counts two. Special I Ching coins are also available.

The three coins are shaken in the hands (in China the shell of a tortoise is often used) and dropped onto a flat surface. The total value of the uppermost sides (which will be six, seven, eight, or nine) should be written down. The coins are thrown a total of six times, and each number obtained is written above the previous one. The six numbers must now be converted into Yang and Yin lines (which may be strong or normal) as shown in the key (**B**).

In the example shown, the numbers (**C**) give the hexagram number 46, called Sheng (**D**), with strong lines in second and fifth places.

Repeating the basic procedure *left and below*

The diagram (**a**) shows how the basic procedure (stages 1 to 6) must be repeated twice more, making a total of three times. You will then have three groups of stalks, set aside as you reached stage 5 each time. Add these together (**b**) and you will find they total 13, 17, 21, or 25. This number converts to a Yin, Yang, strong Yin, or strong Yang line, as shown in the key (**c**). The type of line indicated by your number is now entered as the bottom line of the hexagram (**d**).

The whole of this triple process must be repeated for each line of the hexagram.

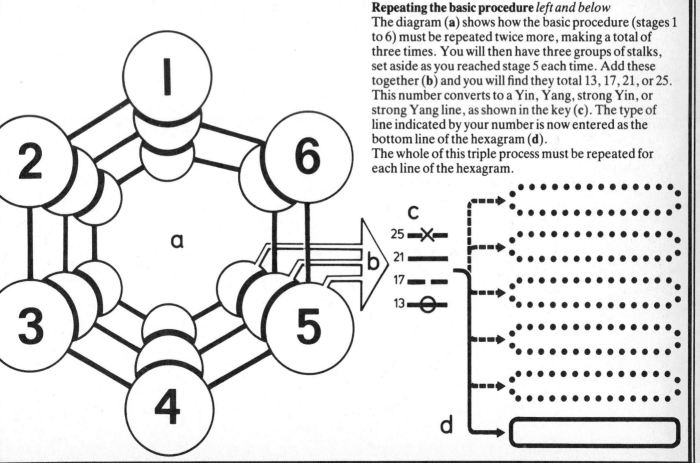

I Ching 6

With the hexagram formed, the most difficult part in the process of consulting the I Ching still lies ahead. The text of the I Ching is complex and couched in cryptic terms; there is no substitute for long experience in interpreting it, and it is for this reason that many enquirers pay for the services of a professional reader. Here it is possible to give only brief initial guidance by describing the parts into which the text is divided and explaining some of the more obscure expressions that will be encountered.

READING THE TEXT
Depending on which edition of the I Ching you use, you may find up to five parts to the text under the entry for each hexagram.

The judgment (or decision)
This gives the essence of the situation, expressed in a few cryptic lines said to have been composed by King Wen.

The commentary on the judgment
This is of Confucian or post-Confucian origin and is self-explanatory.

The image (or the symbol)
This is also ascribed to King Wen, and takes the judgment a stage further by supplying images that link it with the human sphere.

The lines
These are interpretations of the strong or moving lines, made by King Wen's son, the Duke of Chou. They are more explicit in offering advice than most of the other parts, but remember they do not apply to the weak or normal lines.

Other commentaries
The modern editor will have added clarifying remarks to some or all of the older sections of the text. The remarks may well reflect a bias toward some particular view of the I Ching, such as the application of C.G. Jung's theory of the unconscious mind.

COMMON EXPRESSIONS EXPLAINED
Advantage will come from being firm and correct You must persevere in the course the I Ching indicates.
Correct A Yang line in first, third, or fifth place, or a Yin line in second, fourth, or sixth place in the hexagram.
Crossing the great water Overcoming a major obstacle.
Evil The strongest indication of a dangerous course.
Inner The lower primary trigram.
Misfortune A mild indication that your course is wrong.
Movement Associated with Yang.
No blame/no error You can still correct your course without incurring permanent harm.
Outer The upper primary trigram.
Peril An intermediate warning of a dangerous course, between evil and misfortune.
Regret Acknowledging that you are at fault.
The superior man/great man/sage The paragon of correct behavior, fully in accord with the doctrine of Tao.
Supreme success The most favorable indication that you are on the correct course of action.

CONSULTING THE ORACLE

To demonstrate the whole process of consulting the I Ching, a woman was asked to pose a question using the coins method, and to interpret the resulting hexagrams with the aid of Richard Wilhelm's translation of the text.

Question

Things aren't as we would both like them to be. What is happening in our relationship?

Hexagram thrown (A)

6th line	3+3+2=8	Yin line
5th line	2+3+2=7	Yang line
4th line	3+3+3=9	strong Yang line
3rd line	3+3+3=9	strong Yang line
2nd line	3+3+2=8	Yin line
1st line	3+2+2=7	Yang line

This is hexagram number 49 called Ko (Revolution or Molting).
Primary trigrams:
Above Tui. The joyous, lake, third daughter.
Below Li. The clinging, fire, second daughter.

The judgment

Revolution. On your own day
You are believed.
Supreme success,
Furthering through perseverance.
Remorse disappears.

The Image

Fire in the lake: the image of revolution.
Thus the superior man
Sets the calendar in order
And makes the seasons clear.

The strong or moving lines

Nine in the third place means:
Starting brings misfortune.
Perseverance brings danger.
When talk of revolution has gone round three times,
One may commit himself,
and men will believe him.

Nine in the fourth place means:
Remorse disappears. Men believe him.
Changing the form of government brings good fortune.

Second hexagram (B)

When the strong or moving lines have been changed, number 49, Ko, becomes number 3, Chun (Difficulty at the beginning).
Primary trigrams:
Above K'an. The abysmal, water, second son.
Below Chen. The arousing, thunder, first son.

The judgment

Difficulty at the beginning works supreme success, furthering through perseverance.
Nothing should be undertaken.
It furthers one to appoint helpers.

The Image

Clouds and thunder:
The image of difficulty at the beginning.
Thus the superior man
Brings order out of confusion.

The answer as interpreted by the questioner

I thought that we were basically devoted to each other, but at the moment there is so much misunderstanding that we are in conflict. We are fighting a lot more than we did before. I have a need to make him see and understand how I am changing, my internal conflict, my need for a peaceful relationship. He seems to have a similar conflict, but for very different reasons that I am only just beginning to appreciate. Perhaps we need this revolution in our relationship, to bring it onto a new footing.

The image is very helpful. I must not push things, but let them take their own course. I must make it clear to him what I am feeling and doing, and talk to him about the ideas that are beginning to form in my mind. If I am careful, and move slowly but persistently, it will all work out in the end. Things are chaotic for both of us, so it really is important to discuss changes thoroughly and not just to rush ahead as I usually do.

The third moving line is important. I always do want to make things happen immediately, and then wish I hadn't.

The fourth moving line seems to mean that if we wait and sort things out first, the changes that are happening to us and that we need will work out well.

I feel a sense of loss, but I begin to see that the breakdown in our current relationship can be the beginning of a new – and I hope better – one, and of a new life for me.

Second hexagram

I do need help to sort out my ideas, and to get good advice and sound information about starting on a new career now that the children have grown up and left home. I realize that much of my confusion and chaos is because I have not taken the time to organize my thoughts and my needs properly – in fact I must make the time for it now.

Does this hexagram imply that we also need to get help in our relationship? I feel it means that I should ask him for his help, so that we can sort out our problems together, and make it clear what our wants and expectations are. It will be difficult at first, but we can work toward a new perspective. One thing at a time.

Part 3
FORTUNES FROM NATURE

1 Reading the tealeaves was a popular form of fortune telling in the last century, as shown in this 1895 engraving.

2 Specially-marked cups intended to make reading the tealeaves easier are commercially available, although disapproved of by purists!

3 The cycle of the 12 animals of the oriental zodiac is shown in this Chinese woodblock print.

4 Astrologers have long believed that each planet and sign of the zodiac has a special relationship with a specific part of the body. This example of "zodiacal man" is from a fifteenth-century Spanish woodcut.

5 Dürer's engraving *The Northern Hemisphere of the Celestial Globe* (c. 1515) shows the 12 zodiac constellations around the circumference.

Common omens and superstitions 1

Some omens – today we call them superstitions – have been passed down from ancient times. The correct interpretation of signs from the gods used to be the province of the augurs and other soothsayers, but some of their knowledge became common property and has since passed into folklore. Other superstitions have grown up because, say, an unusual occurrence led to a particular piece of good or bad luck, or because a fairly common occurrence seemed always to be followed by a particular type of weather (usually rain).

Walking under a ladder has long been believed to bring bad luck. The Egyptian god Osiris was said to have ascended to the sky by means of a ladder, as was the ancient Persian god Mithras, who was later much worshiped by the soldiers of the Roman army. Since ladders were so much in use by the gods, walking under them became taboo for humans in order to prevent the gods becoming angry.

Salt, too, was precious to the gods – and to humans, as it was an important trade commodity. It was sprinkled on the heads of animals to be sacrificed, and was used in the making of solemn and binding agreements. Spilling salt was unlucky in many ways: it offended the gods, was a sign of broken faith, and, on a more mundane level, was a waste of money.

Omens and their interpretations can vary considerably from country to country, and can even be completely reversed in their meaning. The commonest example of this is probably the black cat: if one crosses your path it is regarded as lucky in England, but is considered unlucky in other parts of Europe and in the USA.

a

b

c

d

Omens of good luck
Bats flying at twilight.
A gift of a hive of bees (**a**).
A robin flying into the house.
A white butterfly (**b**).
A four-leaved clover.
Hearing crickets singing.
Burning your fingernail parings.
Cutting your hair during a storm.
Finding a hairpin and hanging it on a hook.
Seeing a load of hay.
Looking at the new moon over your right shoulder.
Picking up a nail that was pointing toward you.
Picking up a pencil found in the street.
Keeping a piece of oyster shell in your pocket.
Carrying a rabbit's foot.
Walking in the rain (**c**).
Sleeping on unironed sheets.
Spilling your drink while proposing a toast.
Breaking uncolored glass other than a mirror.
Sleeping facing south.
A sprig of white heather.
Meeting sheep.
A ladybird.
A bluebird.

A strange dog following you home (**d**).
Putting your dress on inside out.
Rubbing two horseshoes together.
A peapod containing nine peas (**e**).
A horseshoe.
Picking up a pin.
A wishbone.
Catching two rats in the same trap.
Sneezing three times before breakfast (**f**).
Meeting a chimney-sweep.

e

f

Omens of rain

Bats hitting a building.
Bees staying in the hive.
A frog croaking in the daytime.
Killing a spider.
A crescent moon upside down.
A halo around the moon (**A**).
A rainbow on a Saturday.
Smoke accumulating close to the ground.
Snakes crawling to higher ground.
A spade stuck in the ground (**B**).
An itching corn.
Dropping a piece of buttered bread.
Burning ferns.
Cattle lying down.
Leaves turning up.
A red sky in the morning.
Donkeys braying (**C**).
Cocks crowing in the evening (**D**).
Soot falling down the chimney.

Omens of bad luck

Emptying ashes after dark.
A bat entering the house.
Putting a hat on a bed.
An owl hooting three times (**1**).
Wearing an opal unless you were born in October.
Singing before breakfast.
Giving away a wedding present.
Borrowing, lending, or burning a broom.
A five-leaved clover.
Bringing eggs into the house after dark.
Cutting your nails on Friday.
Dropping a glove.
Bringing white lilac or hawthorn blossom into a house.
Looking at the new moon over your left shoulder.
Taking anything out of the house on New Year's Day.
Peacock feathers.
Removing your wedding ring.
A rooster crowing at night.
Killing a seagull.
Mending a garment while you are wearing it.
Putting shoes on a chair or table.
Dropping an umbrella.
Seeing an owl in daytime.
Keeping your slippers on a shelf above head height.

Putting an umbrella on a table (**2**).
Blossom and fruit growing together on the same branch (except on orange trees).
Meeting a hare on the road (**3**).
Violets flowering out of season.
Meeting a pig immediately after a wedding.
Meeting a grave-digger.
Buttoning a button into the wrong buttonhole.
Opening an umbrella indoors.
Putting on your left shoe before your right.
Sitting on a table without keeping one foot on the ground.
Killing a cricket.
A picture falling.
Breaking your glass when proposing a toast (**4**).
Putting your shirt on inside out.
Getting out of bed left foot first.
Putting a pair of bellows on a table.
A ring breaking on your finger.
Three butterflies together.
Red and white flowers in the same arrangement.
Bringing Christmas greenery into the house before December 24.
Leaving Christmas decorations up after Twelfth Night.

Common omens and superstitions 2

1

1 HORSES (HIPPOMANCY)
One white horse Ill luck.
Two white horses together Good luck.
One white horse seen by a pair of lovers Good luck.
A piebald horse Good fortune.
The tail of a piebald horse Misfortune.

2

2 CATS (AILUROMANCY)
A cat washing its face or ears Rain.
A cat washing one ear three times Expect visitors from the direction in which the cat is looking.
A cat following you Money.
A cat climbing the furniture Rain.
A cat that unaccountably leaves home Disaster.
A gray cat Good luck.
A black cat entering your house Good luck.
A black cat crossing your path Lucky in Britain; unlucky in the USA and some European countries.
A white cat crossing your path Illness.
A black cat walking under a ladder Bad luck for the next person to climb the ladder.
A cat sneezing on the day before a wedding Unlucky for the bride in the USA; lucky for her elsewhere.
Cat appearing around a door Think of a question and call for your cat. If his right paw appears first around the door, the answer to your question is yes. If the left paw is first, the answer is no.
Meeting three black cats in succession Good luck.
Cat sleeping with its back to the fire Rain.

3

3 SPIDERS (ARACHNOMANCY)
Seeing a spider in the morning Grief.
Seeing a spider at noon Anxiety.
Seeing a spider in the evening Financial loss.
Seeing a spider spinning a web Some sources say this indicates that there is a plot against you, others that you will receive a gift, probably new clothes.
Seeing a spider spinning in the morning Good luck.
Seeing a spider spinning in the afternoon A journey.
Finding a spider's web in a doorway A visitor.
Seeing a spider climbing its thread Good news.
Seeing a spider dropping on its thread Good luck, unless it reaches the floor, when it is bad luck.
Finding a spider on your clothes Money, a letter, or both.
Finding a spider on your body Good fortune.
Finding a small red "spider" Money.
Killing a spider Bad luck.
Seeing a spider cross a wall Good luck.

4 ITCHES

1 **Top of head** Promotion, good luck.
2 **Left cheek or left ear** Compliments.
3 **Right cheek or right ear** Derogatory remarks.
4 **Left eye** Disappointment.
5 **Right eye** A meeting.
6 **Inside nose** Grief, bad luck.
7 **Outside nose** "Crossed, vexed, or kissed by a fool."
8 **Mouth** Insults.
9 **Neck** Illness.
10 **Back** Disappointment.
11 **Left shoulder** Unhappiness.
12 **Right shoulder** An inheritance.
13 **Left elbow** Bad news.
14 **Right elbow** Good news.
15 **Left palm or left ankle** Bills to pay.
16 **Right palm or right ankle** Expect money.
17 **Abdomen** An invitation.
18 **Loins** A reconciliation.
19 **Thighs** A move.
20 **Left knee** Gossip.
21 **Right knee** Good news.
22 **Shins** An unpleasant surprise.
23 **Left foot** An unprofitable journey.
24 **Right foot** A profitable journey.

5 KNIVES AND SCISSORS

Dropping a knife on the floor A male visitor.
Dropping a pair of scissors A disappointment, which can be averted by stepping on the scissors before picking them up.
Scissors landing point down when dropped Illness.
Crossed knives Bad luck.
Breaking a pair of scissors Bad luck.
A knife left blade upward Danger.
Giving a gift of a knife or scissors This can cut the friendship unless a pin or a penny is given in exchange.
A new knife used first on anything other than paper or wood Bad luck.
Scissors hanging on a hook Good luck.
Placing or finding a knife in the cradle of a newborn child Good luck.

Common omens and superstitions 3

1 LAMPADOMANCY

This involves taking the omens from a single oil lamp, or from a torch flame.

Flame with a single point Good luck.
Flame with two points Bad luck.
Flame with three points Good luck.
Flame bending Illness.
Flame unexpectedly extinguished Disaster.

2 LYCHNOMANCY

This is divination from the flames of three wax candles. Arrange the three candles in an equilateral triangle, and light a fourth candle some distance away to provide enough light for the reading. Switch off all the other lights in the room, and light the three candles from one match. Read the omens from the appearance of their flames.

A flame wavering from side to side Travel.
One flame burning brighter than the others Great success.
A glow or radiance at the tip of the wick Prosperity.
A curling or spiraling flame Enemies plotting.
Sparks Be cautious.
Rising and falling flames, or candles burning unevenly Danger.
Flame spluttering Disappointment.
Flame unexpectedly extinguished Great misfortune.

3 LITHOMANCY

This is divination using precious stones, one form of which involves candlelight.

Scatter gemstones of different colors around a candle. Darken the room, light the candle, close your eyes, and clear your mind of thoughts. When you open your eyes, notice which color of stone first reflects the light back to you. (In the absence of a good selection of gems, colored glass beads can be used as an alternative.)

Colorless Success and happiness.
Red Romance
Dark red A wedding.
Yellow Infidelity.
Green A wish will come true.
Turquoise An unexpected opportunity.
Blue Good luck.
Violet Grief.
Purple A quarrel.
Black Ill luck.

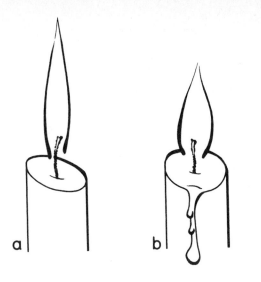

OTHER CANDLE OMENS

a) A candle burning with a tall straight flame Expect the arrival of a stranger.

b) A dripping candle A drip of wax on the side of a candle indicates ill luck for the person sitting on that side.

c) Birthday cake candles Your cake should carry a lighted candle for each year of your age. Make a wish, and try to blow out all the candles in one breath. If you succeed, the wish will come true.

d) To know if your lover is true Take two halves of a walnut shell, two small candles or wax matches, and a bowl of water. Stand a candle upright in each half of the walnut shell, fixing it into place with a little melted wax. Set the walnut shell boats in the middle of the bowl of water, naming one candle for yourself, and the other for your lover. Light the candles. If the two boats float side by side with the candles burning evenly, you will be true to each other. If the boats drift apart, overturn, or the flame goes out, the relationship is doomed. If your candle burns for longer than that named for your lover, then you love more than you are loved, and vice versa.

e) To know your luck for the next year
Arrange 12 lighted candles in a large circle on a wood or concrete floor, having first carefully removed any furnishings that might catch fire. Name a candle in turn for each month of the year. Beginning at the January candle, jump over each in turn until you have completed the circle. Any candle knocked over or extinguished signifies bad luck for that particular month; a candle still burning indicates good luck.

Fortunes from food

Many of the special days that punctuate our calendar – Twelfth Night, Candlemas, May Day, and so on – date from pagan times, although they have since been absorbed into the Christian tradition. They would have been, and in some cases still are, holidays when food and feasting played an important part. So it is not surprising that many of the forms of prediction involving food are supposed to work best on one or other of these feast days.

Halloween, on October 31, was the pagan New Year's Eve. As such, it was an important time for attempting to discover the future. It was also the day dedicated to Pomona, the Roman goddess of the orchards, and so apples came to play an important part in the Halloween divination rites – most of which are concerned with whom and when you will wed.

The details of some of the forms of divination that involve food have been lost in history. Crithomancy, for example, involved reading the markings on freshly baked bread or cakes. And tyromancy was divination from cheese. Alphitomancy enabled the seers to detect lies or dishonesty with special cakes made of wheat or barley flour – these were supposed to be swallowed easily by those of a clear conscience, but to choke liars or wrong-doers. A similar ordeal was known in medieval English law, but the special cakes were replaced by a consecrated "trial slice" of bread and cheese.

ONIONS (CROMNIOMANCY)
To make a wish come true Wish while burning onion skins on the fire.

To find the name of the person you will marry Label several onions with different names and leave them to sprout. The first to sprout reveals the name of your future partner.

To answer a question Attach the possible alternative answers to your question to several onions; the first onion to sprout will give the answer to your question. Traditionally the onions were placed on a church altar on Christmas Eve.

APPLES
To know the initial of the name of your future partner
Peel an apple carefully, keeping the peel in one long piece. Then:
a) count off the twists by calling out the letters of the alphabet, and the last letter you call will be the initial of the name; or
b) throw the piece of peel over your left shoulder, and see which initial it most resembles.

To know the initial of the name of the next person to visit you Cut an apple into nine pieces, and throw the last piece over your left shoulder while reciting the alphabet aloud. The letter you have reached when the piece of apple touches the floor will be the initial.

Wishing on an apple Cut an apple in half through the center while you make a wish. If you have cut the apple without cutting any of the pips your wish will come true.

Apple breaking as you eat it Bad luck.

Bobbing for apples Fill a bowl with water, and cast in several apples. Several people at a time should attempt to secure an apple with their lips and teeth – hands may not be used. The first person to secure an apple will be the first to marry. If the apples are of different sizes, the prosperity you can expect in your life will be indicated by the relative size of your apple – the larger the apple, the more prosperous your life.

An alternative form of bobbing is for each woman present to make a secret mark on her apple before casting it into the bowl. The men then bob for the apples to find out which of the women present they will marry.

To know when you will marry Several people each tie an apple to a piece of string, and then whirl them around. Whoever has the apple that falls off the string first will marry first; whoever owns the last apple to fall will not marry at all.

To see your future partner On Halloween sit alone in front of a mirror, combing your hair and eating an apple. You will see in the mirror a reflection of your future partner looking over your left shoulder. Alternatively, cut the apple into nine pieces and eat eight of them with your back to a mirror. Then throw the ninth piece over your left shoulder and turn quickly to look in the glass. You should be able to see the reflection of your future partner.

140

PUDDINGS AND CAKES

Christmas pudding A small silver coin is stirred into the mixture before the pudding is cooked. Finding the coin in your slice of pudding means prosperity for the next year. Alternatively, a variety of charms are included in the pudding, and your future depends on the charm you find – a horseshoe for luck, perhaps, or a ring for a wedding.

Twelfth Night cake Keep a piece in a dry place for three months. If it has not become moldy, good fortune will be yours for the rest of the year.

Dreaming bannock On Shrove Tuesday evening, bake a bannock (a traditional unleavened oatcake) and include in the mixture some small silver charms and a silver ring. There must be complete silence during the mixing and cooking. As soon as the bannock is ready, cut it into as many pieces as there are unmarried people present. Your future for the next 12 months will be shown by the type of charm you find. The piece of bannock should not be eaten, but wrapped in your left sock or stocking, and placed under your pillow. You should then dream of your future partner.

Dumb cake On Midsummer's Eve, three people together mix, knead, and bake a cake from flour and water, with a little added sugar. The cake is then broken into three, and each person breaks their third into nine pieces. All the pieces are then passed through a wedding ring, borrowed from someone who has worn it for at least three years. Each person eats their nine pieces of cake, and the wedding ring is hung over the bed in which they should all sleep. Dreams of their future partners should then follow – providing that they have carried out the entire ritual in total silence.

Wedding cake Fast throughout Friday, and then fall asleep with a piece of wedding cake under your pillow. You should then dream of your future partner. Alternatively, if you wish to know if you will marry a particular person, pass the wedding cake three times through a borrowed wedding ring. Wrap the cake in a piece of paper on which you have written the name of the person concerned, and sleep with it under your pillow. You should then dream of your future partner.

NUTS

To dream of the occupation of your future partner Chop finely together a single walnut and a single hazelnut, and grate a piece of nutmeg. Mix them all together with a little dough or damp bread, form the mixture into nine small pills, and swallow all of them before going to bed. Your dreams are then said to show you a clear symbol of your future partner's occupation.

To know if your lover is true Place two nuts in the embers of a fire, or on the bars of the grate, naming one nut for yourself and one for your lover. If the nuts burn quietly together, the relationship will be a long and happy one. If, however, the nuts flare up fiercely, explode, or jump away from one another, the relationship will be ended by the person whose nut flares up or jumps away first.

EGGS

Egg whites Pour an egg white into a wine glass that is about three-quarters full of water. Place your hand on top of the glass, and swirl the mixture around gently. Leave it to stand for some time. The white will have formed into shaped clots from which it is possible for you to read your future.

Egg rolling On Easter Day, several people should take colored hard-boiled eggs to the top of a sloping grassy field. Each person should mark an egg with an identifying mark, and then roll it down the hill. Those whose eggs reach the bottom unscathed will have good luck for the next year; those whose eggs break can expect misfortune.

If all the eggs are released at the same time, the first egg to reach the bottom of the hill intact indicates the person who will marry first.

LETTUCE

When you are dressing a green salad, the number of lettuce leaves that fall from the bowl as you are tossing them in the dressing will tell you the number of years before you marry.

PEAS AND BEANS

On Care Sunday (the fifth Sunday in Lent, now called Passion Sunday) hide a small bean in a large dish of peas to be served with the main meal. The person who finds the bean on their plate will be the first to marry.

Augury

In Roman times, divination was the responsibility of the college of augurs, who consulted the omens to ascertain the wishes of the gods on any and every proposed plan of action. Omens could be read in almost anything from a sneeze to a shooting star, but the most common method was ornithomancy – predicting from the sound, appearance, and flight of birds.

The augur stood on a high hilltop, wearing his ritual toga with its scarlet stripes and purple border. He faced south, and used his special wooden staff to indicate the area of sky in which he would make his observations. Only certain birds were consulted, and not all in the same way. The flight of eagles and vultures was considered significant, for example, but it was the voices of crows, ravens, owls, and hens that were supposed to reveal the wishes of the gods. Signs occurring on the augur's left were usually considered favorable, those on his right the reverse. Interpreting the signs was not a simple matter – the number of birds seen, their speed of flight, whether they shed any feathers, the nature of their droppings, and many other details could all qualify the omen.

Predicting from the appearance of the entrails of animals is often thought of as part of augury, although it should more properly be referred to as haruspicy. It

DEPICTING THE ENTRAILS

The giant Humbaba was an important figure in Assyrian divination: his head (**1**) was entirely formed of intestines. The Babylonians used clay tablets (**2**) to show the meanings of the intestines of sheep, and clay models of the liver (**3**) to teach hepatoscopy. A later Etruscan bronze model of the liver (**4**) linked the reading of entrails with the study of astrology.

OTHER MEANS OF PREDICTION USED BY AUGURS

a Alectryomancy Predicting from the eating patterns of sacred chickens.

b Arachnomancy Predicting from the appearance and behavior of spiders.

c Cephalomancy Predicting from the skull or head of a donkey or goat.

d Entomomancy Predicting from the appearance and behavior of insects.

e Ichthyomancy Predicting from the shape and entrails of fish.

f Myomancy Predicting from the color and movement of mice.

was practiced extensively by the Assyrians, the Babylonians, and the Etruscans, by tribes in Africa and in Borneo, and by the Aztecs (who were known to read human entrails on occasion). Most predictions were made from the entrails of animals that had been dedicated and sacrificed to the gods. But some haruspices claimed to be able to tell the state of the intestines from the outward appearance of the animal – suggesting, for example, that sheep with red eyes had intestines with 14 turns, while sheep with black ears and a black nose had intestines with only 10 turns. And every turn of the intestine was held to have a special significance. Haruspices consulted not only the intestines but also the spleen, kidneys, lungs, gall bladder, and – most important of all – the liver. The liver was then regarded as the seat of life, and hepatoscopy (divination by the liver) was a highly respected art, carefully passed on from master to pupil. We have some idea of the complexities of hepatoscopy from models of the liver that date from as far back as 2000BC, and which were probably used as teaching aids. From them we can see that the liver was assumed to be divided into 40 or so zones, each governed by a separate god. And any marks, veins, or textures would have had their own specific meanings, depending on their location.

g **Oenomancy** Predicting from the patterns made by wine poured out as an offering to the gods.
h **Ophiomancy** Predicting from the color and movement of snakes.
i **Phyllorhodomancy** Predicting from rose petals.
j **Scapulomancy** Predicting from the patterns of cracks and fissures on the burned shoulder blade of an animal.
k **Tephromancy** Predicting from the patterns in the ashes of burnt offerings made to the gods.
l **Zoomancy** Predicting from the appearance and behavior of animals.

Pyromancy

Pyromancy – divination by fire – obviously played an important part in societies where burnt offerings were made to the gods, or where fire itself was regarded as a god. Seers studied the flames as the sacrifices were made: a clear flame, burning without smoke or sound, was regarded as a good omen. Vegetable offerings to the gods, such as pounded peas and barley flour, were supposed to indicate good fortune if they blazed up immediately they were cast into the fire.

Capnomancy – divination by smoke – was, of course, associated with pyromancy. The smoke from the burnt offerings could be interpreted, or the gods' intentions could be discovered from the smoke produced by burning incense. The appearance and behavior of the smoke were considered important, as was its smell.

PYROMANTIC VARIATIONS
Botanomancy Divination by the burning of leaves and branches.
Causinomancy Divination from objects cast into a fire.
Daphnomancy Divination by the burning of laurel leaves. The louder the sound made by the leaves burning, the better the omen.
Halomancy Divination by casting salt into a fire.
Pyroscopy Divination by burning a sheet of paper on a white surface, and examining the resulting stains.
Sideromancy Divination by casting an odd number of straws onto iron brought to red heat in a fire and reading the omens in the patterns formed by the straws, their movements as they burn, and the nature of the flames and smoke.

STONES IN THE FIRE
On Halloween, each person present should scratch an identifying mark onto a white stone, and then cast it into a blazing bonfire. The next day, they should search for their stone among the cold ashes. If the stone is there and is undamaged, it is a good omen for the next 12 months; a missing, cracked, or otherwise damaged stone is a bad omen.

PICTURES IN THE FIRE

Sit quietly in front of a fire that has died down to a bed of glowing coals, and scatter a handful of salt over them. When the flames and crackling have died down, gaze into the fire and carefully study any pictures that you see there. The more clearly the fire glows, the better the omen is said to be.

Continue concentrating, in silence, for 10–15 minutes. If by then you have seen nothing of importance, it is said that the flames have no message for you and that you should abandon your effort for at least 24 hours.

For a shape to have meaning, it must stand out clearly from among the coals. Here we list the interpretations of some of the shapes you may see.

Building Happiness.

Building collapsing Change in residence or in place of work.

Castle Someone is thinking of you.

Cat Happiness at work.

Clover Great prosperity.

Cow Someone is thinking of you.

Dog (1) Friendship.

Eagle A warning.

Face (2) If bright, happiness caused by the person whose face is seen; if dull, unhappiness caused by that person.

Flowers (3) Disappointment.

Fountain Happiness.

Fruit If the fruit seems to have been picked – an unhappy love affair; if the fruit is still hanging from the tree – trouble that will pass and be followed by happiness.

Hand (4) If outstretched, someone close to you needs help; if clenched, a surprise.

Hatchet Disaster.

Horse A journey.

Lion, tiger, or other wild animal News from a distance.

Mountain Success.

Pillars A love affair. Bright pillars indicate the return of a former lover.

Ring One large ring – a wedding; two rings – a hasty wedding that might prove unfortunate.

Sea If calm, a peaceful life; if troubled, a troubled life.

Sheep Good luck.

Ship A journey.

Shoes Good news.

Stairs or steps A wish will be granted, quickly if they are bright, slowly if they are dull and dark.

Sword Danger.

Tree Great success in love or business.

Windmill If bright, change for the better; if dull, change for the worse.

Wings Travel.

EMBERS

The shape of any embers or cinders flying from the fire is also held to be significant. If several people are consulting the flames at the same time, the omen relates to the person nearest to the cinder.

Cradle A baby or a proposal.

Purse Money coming.

Bird Letter coming.

Dagger Quarrel coming.

Heart Someone is thinking about you.

Coffin Bad news.

WISHES IN THE FIRE

Write your wish on a piece of paper, and cast it onto a blazing fire. If the paper flies up the chimney, your wish will come true; if it is burned, your wish will not be granted.

If you do not have access to an open fire, place the paper face down on a fireproof dish, and light the paper with a match. If the paper burns away completely, your wish will come true; if it is only partly burned before the flames go out, your wish will not be granted.

Geomancy

Although geomancy properly means divination by the earth, the "earth" in question is usually sand, dust, or dry soil. Arab geomancers have interpreted the patterns made when a handful of sand or dust was cast onto a smooth surface; Navaho wise men have allowed the sand to trickle through their fingers into prophetic patterns on the ground; and some African witch doctors have read the marks made by a crab scrambling around in a bowl of wet sand. Newer methods involve the interpretation of random marks made in the sand with a pointer – a process similar to automatic writing.

Paper geomancy
In the absence of sand, marks can be made on paper with a pen or pencil. In paper geomancy, the diviner exerts the minimum of control over his pencil while it makes four groups of four rows of random points. The points in each row are then counted: an even number in a row is represented by two dots, an odd number by one dot. This converts each group of four rows into one of 16 possible shapes made out of dots (shown *above right*) whose Latin names (translated *right*) probably date from the thirteenth century. Some diviners choose to interpret these shapes as they stand. Others prefer to manipulate them according to a complex set of rules, translating some shapes into others, and interpreting the resulting patterns in the light of their relationship with the 12 astrological houses.

DOTS ON PAPER
1 **Fortuna major** Great good fortune.
2 **Fortuna minor** Less good fortune.
3 **Via** Way.
4 **Populus** People, nation.
5 **Acquisitio** To seek, to gain.
6 **Laetitia** Happiness.
7 **Amissio** Loss.
8 **Puella** Girl.
9 **Puer** Boy.
10 **Conjunctio** Joining, meeting.
11 **Albus** White.
12 **Rubeus** Red.
13 **Carcer** Prison.
14 **Tristitia** Sadness.
15 **Caput draconis** Dragon's head.
16 **Cauda draconis** Dragon's tail.

Reading the sand

Spread out some fine, dry sand or soil in a tray, or on a flat space on the ground. You will need some form of pointer to make marks on the sand – a sharp stick, perhaps, or even a pencil. Sit in silence, either in complete darkness, or with a blindfold around your eyes. The querant should sit next to you, concentrating on the question to be answered.

Rest your wrist on the edge of the tray, with the tip of the pointer just touching the sand. Clear your mind of all thoughts, and allow the pointer to move of its own accord. Only inspect the omens on the tray when you are sure that the pointer has finished moving.

Letters, parts of words, or complete words may have been formed, or you may see a series of symbols. A rough timescale can be established by considering the whole width of the sand as one year, and dividing it into sections for the months.

M, m (a) Maybe.
N, n No.
P, p Perhaps.
Y, y Yes.
Short, separated lines Lack of purpose.
Short, deep line A visitor.
Long, deep line A journey.
Small, scattered crosses (b) Dissension and conflict.
Large cross Love affair (happy if distinct, unhappy if indistinct).
Small circle Coming marriage.
Large circle (c) Misfortune at hand.
Triangle Successful career.
Square Protection.
Birds News, travel.
Mountain Fame, a move or change.
House Stability.
Sword (d) Success and peace if pointing upward; failure or illness if pointing downward.

Aeromancy and hydromancy

All the elements had an important part to play in the divination arts of the ancient world. But many of the details of aeromancy (divination by atmospheric conditions) and hydromancy (divination by water) have become obscure, leaving us with few ways of using these arts in foretelling our future today.

Winds, storms, clouds, rainbows – almost anything occurring in the sky – could be interpreted in aeromancy. The Etruscans and Babylonians were especially concerned with thunder and lightning; the Hindus interpreted the castles in the air formed by the shapes of clouds. It is possible that one or two of these omens now form part of our weather lore; echoes persist in the European superstitions that thunder in the east foretells bloodshed, and that high wind at Christmas or Epiphany foretells the death of a king. Some societies considered the effect of the wind on other objects – bells hung in a tree, for example, whose ringing could be interpreted. Or the ripples formed when a breeze blew over a bowl of water – a link with hydromancy, where ripples played an important role. Ripples were usually formed by dropping pebbles into a sacred pool, but precious stones could be used instead. The size, speed, and number of ripples were taken into account, and the system became very elaborate. Later societies also took account of the shape of the pebbles used: the seer would first use a round stone, then a triangular one, and finally a stone cube.

Hydromancy could also involve drinking the water from sacred springs, which were said both to induce prophetic visions and to cause madness. And other forms involved still water – gazing into pools or bowls of water in search of prophetic visions. But this is more properly a form of scrying, of which the most popular form today is crystal-gazing.

GODS OF AEROMANCY AND HYDROMANCY

1 Adad The Babylonian god of thunder and lightning, who was also the god of prophecy.
2 Ea The Babylonian god of fresh water, who was all-seeing and all-knowing, and was also the god of magic incantations.
3 Hapi The Egyptian god of the deified Nile, who was sometimes worshipped in the form of the bull-god Apis.
4 Tin One of the principal Etruscan gods, sometimes known as Tinia, and later associated with the Roman god Jupiter. Like Jupiter, Tin was the god of thunder and lightning. He had three thunderbolts – the first two were hurled as a warning, the third as a punishment.

FORMS OF AEROMANCY

Austromancy Divination by the study of winds.
Ceraunoscopy Divination from thunder and lightning.
Chaomancy Divination from aerial visions.
Meteormancy Divination from meteors and shooting stars.

ANSWERS FROM THE AIR
Using a window Take two pieces of paper that are the same size, shape, and weight. Color one black. Concentrate on your question, and drop both pieces from an upstairs window. If the white piece of paper lands first, the answer to your question is yes.
Using an electric fan Write the possible answers to your question on separate pieces of paper, which should all be of the same size, shape, and weight. Place them face down on a table, and turn on an electric fan (**a**). The first piece of paper to be blown face up onto the floor gives you the answer to your query.

ANSWERS FROM WATER
For an answer to a question Write 13 questions on separate sheets of paper, and drop them all into a bowl of water. The answer to the question that first floats to the top is yes.
For an answer from the ripples Concentrate on your question as you drop a pebble into a bowl of water (**b**). Count the number of ripples on the surface of the water: an odd number means that the answer to your question is yes, an even number that it is no.
To know the name of your future partner Write down as many first names of persons of the appropriate sex as you can remember, each on a separate piece of paper. Roll each into a small ball, hold them all in the air above your head as high as you can reach, and let them all fall together into a bowl of water. The first piece of paper to float to the top will carry the name of your future partner.

Scrying 1

Scrying is divination by gazing into a reflecting surface. No-one knows when or where it began, but it has a long history in nearly all the world's cultures. Almost any reflecting surface can and has been used at one time or another – water, glass, polished metal, precious stones, blood, even soap bubbles.

Scrying has links with hydromancy, because at first water and other liquids were the most important and the most easily available reflectors. The water could be a sacred pool or spring (a form of divination called pegomancy), or a liquid could be held in a special container. The Babylonians gazed into liquids in sacred bowls; the Egyptians into a pool of ink in the hand; the Hindus into bowls of molasses; and the Greeks lowered mirrors into sacred fountains and springs.

Mirror-gazing (catoptromancy) is another form of scrying. The earliest mirrors were of polished metal, and were often decorated on the non-reflecting side. The ancient Chinese, for example, had polished bronze mirrors decorated with cosmological and astrological symbols, and looked in them for the reflections of demons. Witches in the fourteenth century were said to use mirrors of polished onyx to speak to spirits. But by the late Middle Ages, when mirror-gazing was at the height of its popularity, many of the mirrors would have been of the silvered glass with which we are familiar today; catoptromancers were recommended to expose their mirrors to the lunar rays before staring at the reflection of the moonlight in the glass. (Even today we have superstitions that involve gazing into a mirror by moonlight in the hope of seeing your future marriage partner.)

But the most widespread and popular form of scrying is crystallomancy – crystal-gazing. Crystal balls have been known in Europe since about the fifth century, but they were also used by the Mayans and Incas, by North American Indians and Australian aborigines, and by tribes in Borneo, New Guinea, and Madagascar.

SIMPLE CATOPTROMANCY
To know how long it will be until you marry Look at the reflection of a full moon in a hand mirror, preferably one that is silver-backed. The years to your wedding can be estimated from the length of time that passes before you see a cloud obscuring the moon or a bird flying across it.

To see your future partner Look into a mirror at midnight on Halloween while holding a lighted candle, and you should see the reflection of your future partner looking over your left shoulder.

Nostradamus
Michel de Notredame (1503–1566), known as Nostradamus, is probably the most famous seer of all time. His prophecies – all published during his lifetime – included the Great Fire of London in 1666, the French Revolution, Napoleon's defeat at Waterloo, Hitler's rise to power and its consequences, the atom bomb attacks on Hiroshima and Nagasaki, and much more.

Although Nostradamus was a noted astrologer, most of his published prophecies were obtained by scrying. His preferred method seems to have been to gaze into a brass bowl of water resting on a brass tripod, but he is also known to have used a looking glass to see the futures of specific individuals. He wrote his prophecies in quatrains (four-line verses) in a mixture of French, Latin, and words of his own invention, decorated them with puns and anagrams, and employed initials, abbreviations, and nicknames when referring to people.

The lamen

Some crystallomancers believe that the crystal should
be supported on an ornate circular table called the
lamen, which stands within a magic circle. Both the top
of the lamen (**A**) and the magic circle on the floor (**B**)
are engraved with mystic names. The pedestal
supporting the crystal bears the name SADAY, and is
flanked by two candlesticks engraved ELOHIM and
ELOHE respectively.

Other crystallomancers feel that this ritual is
unnecessary, and that a simple black cloth to prevent
any reflections in the crystal is all that is required.

A

B

Scrying 2

Using the crystal

The experts recommend the use of a sphere about 4in (10cm) in diameter, made of beryl or quartz crystal. You may prefer to use a glass sphere instead, but you should ensure that it is free of any blemishes or bubbles that might distract you.

You are the only person who should handle your crystal ball. Wash it in vinegar and water, polish it with a velvet cloth or a chamois leather, and keep it wrapped up when you are not using it. Always keep it away from extremes of heat and cold, and do not allow the direct light of the sun to fall on it, as this is said to ruin the susceptibility of the crystal. Moonlight, however, is said to be beneficial.

Sit in a north-facing room: there should be just enough light to read by. Not more than two other people should be in the room with you, and they must sit quietly, at least an arm's length away. Hold the crystal in your hand, or place it on a small stand on a table.

A black background – a cloth on the table and a curtain behind the crystal – will aid your concentration, and act as a background for your images. Or, if you prefer, you can support the crystal on the traditional lamen within its mystic circle of names (as shown *left*). Sit still, empty your mind, and gaze into the crystal.

The crystal should fill with a milky hue which then changes through a range of colors until it becomes black. This blackness will then roll away and reveal the images. You may see symbolic shapes and colored clouds, which you will need to interpret. Or you may see moving, sequential images – as if you were watching a film – in which case you need only report what you see.

Do not worry if at first you are unable to see anything in the crystal. Scrying is said to come easily to only about one person in 20 – people who are psychically sensitive and receptive, with powers of perfect concentration. Other people will need practice and perseverance to develop any latent powers. Remember that you can practice scrying with very simple materials – a mirror, perhaps, or a glass of water.

Mental attitude

Whichever your preferred form of scrying – a crystal ball (**a**), a mirror (**b**), or a bowl of liquid (**c**) – the correct mental attitude will be an important factor. In the past, crystallomancers and catoptromancers have adopted elaborate rituals to prepare themselves and to create the right atmosphere of inner tranquillity and calm. Your own personal rituals will evolve in time – you may, for example, find that some form of meditation helps to clear your mind before you begin scrying.

CLOUDS IN THE CRYSTAL

White clouds Good fortune.
Black clouds Ill fortune.
Violet, green, or blue clouds Joy.
Red, orange, or yellow clouds Danger, trouble, difficulty.
Ascending clouds An affirmative reply to your question.
Descending clouds A negative reply to your question.
Clouds moving to the right Spirits present.
Clouds moving to the left Spirits have departed.

SYMBOLS IN THE CRYSTAL

Anchor Safety, hope.
Beetle Long life.
Bird A message.
Crown Glory, responsibility.
Eye Good fortune, forethought, but can be a symbol of evil.
Frog Fertility, something beneficial but hidden.
Fruit Children.
Globe Travel.
Heart pierced by a dagger Suffering.
Lighthouse Danger ahead, but there is hope.
Mask Deceit, tragedy.
Scales Justice, even-handedness – or the reverse.
Skull Death, wisdom.
Snake Health, knowledge, temptation.
Star Success, but be careful.
Swords A quarrel.
Water-lily Creativity.

EVENTS OCCURRING IN THE CRYSTAL

If at front of crystal Events relate to the present or the immediate future.
If at back of crystal Events relate to the remote past or the distant future.
If to your left Events are real.
If to your right Events are symbolic.

Tasseography 1

Reading the teacups (tasseography) probably began with the ancient Chinese. They were accustomed to taking omens from the appearance of the inside of bells – and their handleless teacups, when inverted, looked very like small bells. So the teacups became associated with the bell omens, and the patterns formed by the tea-leaves inside the cups came to have a divinatory significance.

Of course, if you dislike tea you can always read the grounds left in the bottom of your coffee cup, or the residue left by any other drink – the Romans, for example, read the lees of their wine. Because it results from both personal and random factors, the pattern made by the sediment left at the bottom of any drinking cup has always been considered of great importance in predicting the drinker's future, no matter what the original contents.

Molybdomancy and ceromancy

Other societies have used other methods to produce symbols similar to those found in the tea-leaves. In medieval times, molten tin or lead was dripped into cold water to produce the characteristic shapes. This method, called molybdomancy, was a by-product of the alchemists' attempts to transmute these base metals into gold, as shown *right*.

A safer alternative to lead is wax. In ceromancy, melted wax is allowed to drip into a shallow dish of cold water, and the resulting shapes are interpreted. Ceromancy was very popular in the eighteenth century, when correspondence was normally fastened with sealing wax . And it is still important to Voodoo priests , who conduct ceromantic readings that can last from dusk to dawn.

Reading coffee grounds *right*
You can prepare coffee grounds for a reading in the same way as you prepare tea leaves – drinking nearly all of a cup of unstrained coffee, swirling the cup, and inverting it into the saucer. Alternatively, you can pour the dregs from your coffee cup onto a clean white plate, swirling the plate clockwise so that the liquid runs off the edge and the grounds disperse over the surface in a scattering of symbols. The recognition and interpretation of the symbols is as for tea-leaves.

Reading the teacups

Teacups used for tasseography should have a wide mouth and sloping sides. The inner surface should be smooth and undecorated, and be either white or a plain pastel color. The tea should have a fairly large leaf and very little dust, and the cup should be filled without using a strainer.

It is thought to be important that the querant (the person whose fortune is to be told) actually drinks the cup of tea, leaving just enough liquid at the bottom of the cup to allow the leaves to be swirled. Traditionally, the querant then takes the handle of the cup in the left hand, and swirls the leaves clockwise, three times, making sure that the liquid remaining in the cup reaches right up to the rim. The querant then inverts the cup in the saucer, and allows the liquid to drain away for a count of seven.

You can now turn the cup the right way up, hold it with the handle facing you, and begin the reading. You should first consider the overall appearance of the cup: a great many leaves imply a rich, full life; a small scattering of a few leaves imply a tidy, disciplined mind. Consider also the type of symbol that predominates so that you can make an overall assessment of good or ill fortune. Then continue with a detailed reading of the symbols themselves.

The handle of the cup represents the querant: symbols occurring close to the handle suggest something occurring close to the querant's home. Symbols pointing toward the handle imply something approaching; those pointing away imply departure. Some readers consider that events in the past are shown by symbols on the left of the handle, while those in the future are shown on the right. But more commonly the vertical position in the cup is taken as an indication of time, with events occurring in the present or in the near future being shown near the rim of the cup, and those occurring at a more distant time appearing near the bottom. The actual bottom of the cup is considered unlucky and indicates ill fortune.

Remember to take into account the sizes, proportions, positions, and clarity of the symbols relative to one another. It is the overall combination of the signs that is important: signs should not be considered in isolation. As with so many other forms of fortune telling, your reading must interpret the whole picture, not just its separate sections.

Do not worry if at first you find the symbols indistinct, and have difficulty identifying them. It is said that if you allow your mind to range freely, and let your instincts and imagination take over, you will find that practice and experience soon increase your levels of perception.

Positions in the cup
a Present or near future.
b More distant time.
c Unlucky area.
d The querant.
e Something departing.
f Something approaching.

© DIAGRAM

155

Tasseography 2

A

Abbey Freedom from worry.
Ace of clubs A letter.
Ace of diamonds A present.
Ace of hearts Happiness.
Ace of spades Large building.
Acorn Success. At top of cup – financial success; near middle of cup – good health; near bottom of cup – improvement in health or finances.
Aircraft Sudden journey, not without risk. Can imply disappointment. If broken – an accident.
Alligator Treachery, an accident.
Anchor At top of cup – success in business and romance; middle of cup – prosperous voyage; bottom of cup – social success; obscured – anticipate difficulties.
Angel Good news.
Ankle Instability.
Ant Success through perseverence.
Anvil Conscientious effort.
Apple Business achievement.
Apron A new friend.
Arc Ill health, accidents.
Arch Journey abroad, a wedding.
Arrow Bad news.
Ax Difficulties and troubles that will be overcome.

B

Baby A series of small worries.
Bag A trap ahead. If open – you can escape; if closed – you will be trapped.
Bagpipes Disappointment.
Ball A person connected with sport, or variable fortunes in your life.
Balloon Short-term troubles.
Barrel A party.
Basin Trouble at home. If broken – serious trouble.
Basket If empty – money worries; if full – a present; near handle of cup – a baby; near top of cup – possessions; full of flowers – social success; surrounded by dots – unexpected money coming your way.
Bat False friends, a journey ending in disappointment.
Bath Disappointment.
Bayonet A minor accident, a spiteful remark.
Beans Poverty.
Bear Facing handle – irrational decisions cause difficulties; facing away from handle – a journey.
Bed Inertia.
Bee Social success, good news. Near handle of cup – friends gathering; swarm of bees – success with an audience.
Beehive Prosperity.
Beetle Scandal, a difficult undertaking.
Bell Unexpected news. Near top of cup – promotion; near bottom of cup – sad news; two bells – joy; several bells – a wedding.

Tea leaf symbols

1	Aircraft.	7	Candle.
2	Anchor.	8	Chair.
3	Ant.	9	Claw.
4	Baby.	10	Dagger.
5	Bee.	11	Devil.
6	Bull.	12	Dog.

Bellows Plans will meet with setbacks.
Bird Good news.
Birdcage Obstacles, quarrels.
Bird's nest Domestic harmony, love.
Bishop Good luck coming.
Boat Visit from a friend, a safe refuge.
Book Open – expect legal actions, future success; closed – delay, difficult studies.
Boomerang Treachery, envy.
Boot Achievement, protection from pain. Pointing away from handle – dismissal; broken – failure.
Bottle One bottle – pleasure; several bottles – illness.
Bouquet Love and happiness.
Bow, bow and arrow Scandal, gossip.
Box Open – romantic troubles solved; closed – the lost will be found.
Bracelet Impending marriage.
Branch With leaves – a birth; without leaves – a disappointment.
Bread Avoid waste.
Bridge An opportunity for success.
Broom Small worries disappear, a false friend.
Buckle Disappointments ahead.
Bugle Hard work necessary.
Building A move.
Bull Quarrels, enmity.
Buoy Keep hoping.
Bush New friends, fresh opportunities.
Butterfly Frivolity, fickleness. Surrounded by dots – frittering away money.

Cab A disappointment.
Cabbage Jealousy causes complications at work.
Cage A proposal.
Camel Useful news.
Candle Help from others, pursuit of knowledge.
Cannon News of a soldier or a government employee.
Cap Trouble ahead – be careful.
Car Good fortune.
Cart Success in business.
Castle Financial gain through marriage, a strong character rising to prominence.
Cat A quarrel, treachery, a false friend.
Cattle Prosperity.
Chain An engagement or wedding.
Chair An unexpected guest. Surrounded by dots – financial improvements.
Cherries A happy love affair.
Chessmen Difficulties ahead.
Chimney Hidden risks.
Church Ceremony, unexpected money.
Cigar New friends.
Circle Success, a wedding. With a dot – a baby; with small lines nearby – efforts hampered.
Claw A hidden enemy.
Clock Avoid delay, think of the future, a recovery from illness.

Clouds Trouble ahead. Surrounded by dots – money trouble ahead.
Clover Prosperity.
Coat A parting, end of a friendship.
Cockatoo Trouble among friends.
Coffeepot Slight illness.
Coffin Bad news.
Coin Repayment of debts.
Collar Dependence on others for success and happiness.
Column Promotion, success, arrogance.
Comb Deceit, a false friend.
Comet An unexpected visitor.
Compass Travel, a change of job.
Corkscrew Curiosity causing trouble.
Crab An enemy.
Crescent A journey.
Cross Sacrifice, trouble, ill health. Within a square – trouble averted; two crosses – long life; three crosses – great achievement.
Crown Honor, success, a wish coming true, a legacy.
Crutches Help from a friend.
Cup Reward for effort.
Curtain A secret.
Cymbal Insincere love.

Daffodil Great happiness.
Dagger Impetuousness, danger ahead, enemies plotting.
Daisy Happiness in love.
Dancer Disappointment.
Deer A dispute or quarrel.
Desk Letter containing good news.
Devil Evil influences.
Dish Quarrel at home.
Dog Good friends. If running – good news, happy meetings; at bottom of cup – friend in trouble.
Donkey Be patient and optimistic.
Door Strange occurrence.
Dot This emphasizes the importance of the nearest symbol. Several dots – money.
Dove Good fortune.
Dragon Unforeseen changes, trouble.
Drum Scandal, gossip, a new job, arguments.
Duck Money coming in.
Dustpan Strange news about a friend.

Eagle A change for the better.
Ear Unexpected news.
Earrings Misunderstanding.
Easel Artistic success.
Egg Prosperity, success – the more eggs the better.
Eggcup Danger is passing.
Elephant Wisdom, strength, lasting success, a trustworthy friend.

Tasseography 3

Engine News on its way fast.
Envelope Good news.
Eye Overcoming difficulties, take care.

F

Face One face – a change, a setback; several faces – a party.
Fairy Joy and enchantment.
Fan Flirtation, indiscretion.
Feather Instability, inconsistency, lack of concentration.
Feet An important decision.
Fence Limitation to activities, minor setbacks, future success.
Fender Beware of a person you dislike.
Fern Disloyalty, an unfaithful lover.
Finger Emphasizes the symbol at which it points.
Fir Artistic success. The higher the tree, the better.
Fire Achievement, avoid over-hasty reactions.
Fireplace Matters related to your home.
Fish Good fortune in all things, health, wealth, and happiness.
Fist An argument.
Flag Danger ahead.
Flower Wish coming true.
Fly Domestic irritations. The more flies, the more petty problems.
Font A birth.
Fork A false friend, flattery.
Forked line Decisions to be made.
Fountain Future success and happiness.
Fox A deceitful friend.
Frog Success through a change of home or job, avoid self-importance.
Fruit Prosperity.

G

Gallows Social failure, enemies confounded.
Garden roller Difficulties ahead.
Garland Success, great honor.
Gate Opportunity, future happiness.
Geese Invitations, unexpected visitors.
Giraffe Think before you speak.
Glass Integrity.
Glove A challenge.
Goat Enemies threaten, news from a sailor.
Gondola Romance, travel.
Gramophone Pleasure.
Grapes Happiness.
Grasshopper News of a much-traveled friend.
Greyhound Good fortune.
Guitar Happiness in love.
Gun Trouble, quarrels.

H

Hammer Overcoming obstacles, ruthlessness, work

that is uncongenial.
Hand Friendship.
Handcuffs Trouble ahead.
Hare Timidity, news of a friend.
Harp Harmony in love.
Hat A new occupation, a change. Bent and broken – failure likely; in bottom of cup – a rival; on side of cup – diplomacy.
Hawk Sudden danger, jealousy.
Hayrick Think before you act.
Head New opportunities.
Heart Love and marriage, a trustworthy friend.
Heather Good fortune.
Hen Domestic bliss.
Hill Obstacles, setbacks.
Hoe Hard work leading to success.
Holly An important occurrence in the winter.
Horn Abundance.
Horse Galloping – good news from a lover; head only – romance.
Horseshoe Good luck.
Hourglass A decision that must be made.
House Security.

Iceberg Danger.
Initials Usually those of people known to you. If next to a triangle, the initials of strangers.
Inkpot A letter.
Insect Minor problems soon overcome.
Ivy leaf Reliable friend.

Jester Party or social gathering. Alternatively – avoid frivolity, be serious.
Jewelry A present.
Jockey Speculation.
Jug Gaining in importance, good health.

Kangaroo Domestic harmony.
Kettle Minor illness. Near handle of cup – domestic bliss; near or at bottom of cup – domestic strife.
Key New opportunities, doors opening. Crossed keys – success; two keys near bottom of cup – robbery.
Keyhole Beware of idle curiosity.
King A powerful ally.
Kite Wishes coming true, do not take chances, scandal.
Knife Broken relationships. Near handle of cup – divorce; on bottom of cup – lawsuits; crossed knives – arguments.

Ladder Promotion.
Lamp Near handle of cup – money; near rim of cup –

celebration; on side of cup – personal loss; on bottom of cup – postponed social event; two lamps – two marriages.
Leaf Prosperity, good fortune.
Leopard News of a journey.
Letter News. Near dots – news about money.
Lighthouse Trouble threatening, but averted. Success through a friend.
Lines Straight and clear – progress, journeys; wavy – uncertainty, disappointment; slanting – business failure.
Lion Influential friends.
Lock Obstacles in your path.
Loop Impulsive actions could bring trouble.

Man Near handle of cup – a visitor; clear and distinct – dark-haired visitor; not well-defined – a fair-haired visitor; with arm outstretched – bringing gifts.
Mask Deception.
Medal A reward.
Mermaid Temptation, an offer that is not what it seems.
Miter Honors.
Monkey A flattering mischief-maker.
Monster Terror.
Monument Lasting happiness.
Moon Full – a love affair; first quarter – new projects; last quarter – fortune declining; obscured – depression; surrounded by dots – marriage for money.
Mountain Obstacle, high ambition.
Mouse Theft.
Mushroom Growth, setbacks. Near handle of cup – a home in the country.
Music Good fortune.

Nail Malice, injustice, sharp pain.
Necklace Complete – admirers; broken – the end of a relationship.
Needle Admiration.
Net Traps for the unwary.
Numbers Indicate a timescale, the number of days before an event occurs.
Nun Quarantine.
Nurse Illness.
Nutcrackers Difficulty is passing.

O

Oak Good fortune.
Oar A small worry, help in difficulties.
Octopus Danger.
Opera glasses A quarrel, loss of a friend.
Ostrich Travel.

Tasseography 4

Owl Gossip, scandal, failure. At bottom of cup – financial failure; near handle – domestic failure.
Oyster Courtship, acquired riches.

P

Padlock Open – a surprise; closed – a warning.
Palm tree Success, honor, happiness in love.
Parachute Escape from danger.
Parasol A new lover.
Parcel A surprise.
Parrot A scandal, a journey.
Peacock With tail spread – riches, land; surrounded by dots – a life of luxury; next to a ring – a rich marriage.
Pear Comfort, financial ease.
Pentagon Intellectual balance.
Pepperpot A troublesome secret.
Pig Material success begins emotional problems.
Pigeon Sitting – an improvement in trade; flying – important news.
Pillar Supportive friends.
Pipe Thoughts, solution to a problem, keep an open mind.
Pistol Danger.
Pitchfork Quarrels.
Policeman Secret enemy.
Pot Service to society.
Profile New friend.
Pump Generosity.
Purse Profit. At bottom of cup – loss.
Pyramid Solid success.

Q

Question mark Hesitancy, caution.

R

Rabbit Timidity, be brave.
Railway Long journey.
Rainbow Happiness, prosperity.
Rake Be organized.
Rat Treachery.
Raven Bad news.
Razor Quarrels, partings.
Reptiles Treacherous friend.
Rider Hasty news.
Ring Completion. Near top of cup – marriage; near middle of cup – proposal; near bottom of cup – long engagement; complete ring – happy marriage; broken ring, or ring with cross next to it – broken engagement; two rings – plans working out.
Rocks Difficulties.
Rose Popularity.

S

Saucepan Anxieties.
Saw Interfering outsider.

Scales A lawsuit. Balanced scales – justice; unbalanced scales – injustice.
Scepter Power, authority.
Scissors Domestic arguments, separation.
Scythe Danger.
Shamrock Good luck, wish coming true.
Sheep Good fortune.
Shell Good news.
Ship Successful journey.
Shoe A change for the better.
Sickle Disappointment in love.
Signpost Draws attention to the symbol at which it points.
Skeleton Loss of money, ill health.
Snake Hatred, an enemy.
Spade Hard work leads to success, or avoid taking sides.
Spider Determined and persistent, secretive, money coming.
Spoon Generosity.
Square A symbol of protection, comfort, peace. Alternatively – restrictions, setbacks.
Squirrel Prosperity after a hard time.
Star Good health, happiness. Five-pointed star – good fortune; eight-pointed star – accidents, reverses; five stars together – success without happiness; seven stars together – grief.
Steeple Slight delay, bad luck.
Steps An improvement in life.
Sun Happiness, success, power.
Swallow Decisiveness, unexpected journeys.
Swan Smooth progress, contented life.
Sword Disappointments, quarrels.

T

Table Social gathering. Surrounded by dots – financial conference.
Teapot Committee meeting.
Telephone Forgetfulness causes trouble.
Telescope Adventure.
Tent Travel.
Thimble Domestic changes.
Toad Beware of flattery.
Torch A turn for the better.
Tortoise Criticism.
Tower Opportunity, disappointment.
Tree Changes for the better, ambitions fulfilled. Surrounded by dots – your fortune lies in the country.
Triangle Something unexpected. Point upward – brings success; point downward – brings failure.
Trident Success at sea.
Trunk A long journey, fateful decisions.

U

Umbrella Annoyances, a need for shelter. If open – shelter found; if shut – shelter refused.
Unicorn A secret wedding.
Urn Wealth, happiness.

Vase A friend in need.
Vegetables Unhappiness followed by contentment.
Violin Egotism.
Volcano Emotions out of control.
Vulture Loss, theft, an enemy in authority.

Wagon A wedding.
Walking stick A visitor.
Wasp Trouble in love.
Waterfall Prosperity.
Weather vane A difficulty, indecisiveness.
Whale Business success.
Wheel Complete – good fortune, earned success; broken – disappointment; near rim of cup – unexpected money.
Wheelbarrow A meeting with an old friend.
Windmill Business success through hard work rather than brilliance.
Window Open – good luck through a friend; closed – disappointment through a friend.
Wings Messages.
Wishbone A wish granted.
Wolf Jealousy, selfishness.
Woman Pleasure.
Worms Scandal.
Wreath Happiness ahead.

Yacht Pleasure.
Yoke Being dominated.

Zebra Adventures overseas, an unsettled life.

Astrology 1

1

Astrology explores the effect of the sun, moon, and eight of the planets of the solar system upon the earth and its inhabitants. It is a convention in astrology to refer to the sun and the moon as planets, and to view the universe as if the earth were at its center. Thus there are ten astrological planets that appear to move around the earth – planet comes from the Greek *planetes,* meaning wanderer.

Each of these planets is reputed to influence our lives. How this happens is said to be determined by the signs of the zodiac – twelve constellations of stars beyond our solar system that became associated with ancient legends and myth. It was against the background of these zodiac constellations that the planetary positions were charted to determine the nature of events on earth. The horoscope or birth chart is a symbolic map of the sky made to show the potential and characteristics of a person born at a particular time and place on earth. A modern birth chart is very similar in shape and form to the charts drawn by the Greeks during the first and second centuries AD – the word horoscope comes from two Greek words, *horos* meaning time, and *skopos*

2

3

4

5

meaning observer. The Greeks were also responsible for the introduction of astrology into India and, later, into the Arab world.

Although the Greeks did much to further the spread of astrology, people had begun to look to the stars for guidance very much earlier, as long ago as 8000BC. Believing that their fates were determined from the sky, the Assyrians, Babylonians, Egyptians, and Mayans all employed astrologers to observe, record, and predict the positions of the stars and the timing of events important to their survival and prosperity. The first known textbook on astrology was written by the mathematician Ptolemy, who was working in Egypt between 150 and 180AD. The Greeks constructed the earliest known ephemeris (a table that shows the positions of all the planets for each day of the year). An ephemeris is similar to the nautical almanacs used by sailors to chart their positions at sea.

Until the seventeenth century astrology, the understanding of the significance of the stars, was considered synonymous with astronomy, the study of the movements and positions of the stars. Research into astrology declined in the eighteenth and nineteenth centuries but has attracted interest again more recently, with some studies seeming to support astrological theories and others to condemn them.

Modern astrology deals with the effects that the planets are believed to have on individual lives and events, and is more often used to assess character and potential than to predict specific future events. The aim of a chart interpretation is to describe clearly the personality that is revealed in the birth chart; the traditional body of knowledge used by astrologers to do this comes from ancient mythology, centuries of observation and adaptation, and now includes ideas from analytical psychology. The calculations that are needed to make a chart of the positions of the planets for any specific time are based on astronomical information. Several methods of calculation are practiced by astrologers: here tropical astrology is used, giving the position of planets by zodiac sign.

Celestial pictures
1 Mayan calendar stone.
2 The celestial sphere according to Ptolemy's astrology, as shown in a sixteenth-century woodcut.
3 Early Arab zodiac.
4 Cabalistic map of the heavens, showing the stars as Hebrew letters. The Cabalists combined these letters into statements that predicted the future.
5 Seventeenth-century zodiac combining Roman, Greek, and Egyptian astrology.

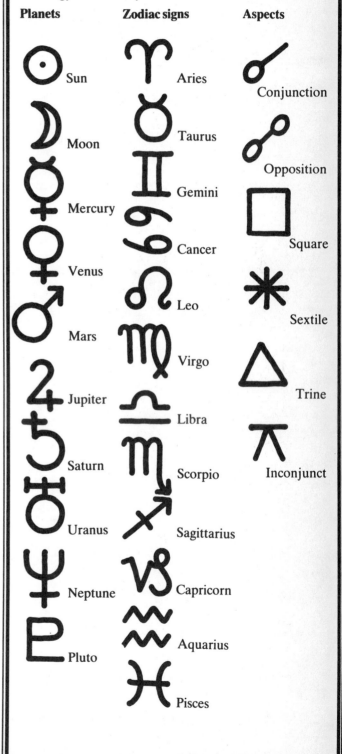

ASTROLOGICAL SYMBOLS

Each of the ten planets and 12 signs of the zodiac has its own identifying symbol (sometimes called a glyph) used to show its position on a birth chart. Some specific angles between planets (called "aspects") are also identified by a symbol. These symbols are among the conventions of astrology with which you will need to become familiar.

Planets	Zodiac signs	Aspects
Sun	Aries	Conjunction
Moon	Taurus	Opposition
Mercury	Gemini	Square
Venus	Cancer	Sextile
Mars	Leo	Trine
Jupiter	Virgo	Inconjunct
Saturn	Libra	
Uranus	Scorpio	
Neptune	Sagittarius	
Pluto	Capricorn	
	Aquarius	
	Pisces	

©DIAGRAM

163

Astrology 2

A birth chart and its interpretation contain a great many features. Here we take an overall look at the parts of a sample chart, and at the terms in which astrologers refer to them, before going on to consider each separate feature in detail.

Parts of the chart

The complete chart shows the relative positions of 10 planets, 12 houses, and 12 zodiac signs. The circle in the center represents the earth, surrounded by the houses numbered 1 to 12. This chart has been erected by the equal house system, with each house occupying 30° of the full circle of 360°.

The horizontal line across the left of the chart is called the cusp (beginning) of the first house. The cusp of the first house is always in the ascendant position (ASC). This was the position of the sun as it rose on the eastern horizon on the date of birth. On this chart Virgo is the ascending sign, sometimes called the rising sign. The 12 signs of the zodiac are always arranged in the same order around the outer wheel but the placing of the wheel is determined by the sign of the ascendant. Each zodiac sign occupies 30° of the outer wheel.

The positions of the planets are marked on the inner edge of the zodiac wheel and are identified by their symbols. MC stands for the Latin *medium coeli* meaning midheaven. The midheaven is on the cusp of the tenth house indicating the position of the sun at noon on the date of birth. If the clock time of birth is not known, the sun can be placed in the midheaven position and the houses omitted.

Unlike geographical maps, south is always placed at the top of a birth chart. Consequently the sun-sign of a person born during the day will be in the upper half of the chart; for a person born during the night, the sun-sign will be in the lower half of the chart. Ms S was born in the early afternoon, so her sun-sign Gemini is in the upper half.

A sample birth chart *above*

This is the birth chart of Ms S, who was born on May 25, 1931: her date of birth is used to find the positions of the planets when it is noon at Greenwich, England on that date.

Ms S was born at 2.30pm BST. As the time given is British Summer Time (BST) it must be corrected to Greenwich Mean Time (GMT) in order to calculate the chart. The corrected time is 1.30pm GMT.

The latitude and longitude of the place of birth are also used in the calculations. Ms S was born near Preston in England, located 53°46′ north of the equator and 2°41′ west of the Greenwich meridian.

Position of planet										
3° 22′ ♊	☉	Sun								
13° 11′ ♍		☽	Moon							
8° 52′ ♉		△	☿	Mercury						
5° 22′ ♉		△	♂	♀	Venus					
21° 45′ ♌					♂	Mars				
18° 59′ ♋	✳					♃	Jupiter			
22° 54′ ♑			✳	♂			♄	Saturn		
17° 56′ ♈			△	□	□			⛢	Uranus	
3° 2′ ♍	□		△	△					♆	Neptune
19° 15′ ♋				♂	♂	□				♇ Pluto

ASC	24° 30′ ♍
MC	24° 30′ ♊

Table of major aspects *left*

This table, containing information extracted from the birth chart, shows the precise positions of the planets in degrees and minutes. Measurements around the zodiac wheel are made counterclockwise, so it can be seen, for example, that the sun on the chart is only 3°22′ into Gemini, while the moon is 13°11′ into Virgo.

The planets are said to be in aspect with each other when the angle between them is one that traditionally emphasizes harmony or tension. For example, an angle of 90° is called a square aspect; one of 120° a trine aspect; and one of 60° a sextile aspect. The sun's aspects with other planets on this chart can be read from the column headed by the sun on the aspect table. Each aspect has its own symbol. The sun is square Neptune: an aspect of tension. The moon, however, is trine Mercury and Venus, and sextile Jupiter: these are harmonious aspects.

1

	Elements			
Qualities	Fire	Earth	Air	Water
Cardinal	♅	♄		♇ ♃
Fixed	♂	☿ ♀		
Mutable		☽ ♆	☉	

2

	Areas of interest			
Qualities	Life	Purpose	Relationship	Endings
Angular		♇ ♃	♅	♄
Succedent			♂	☿ ♀
Cadent	☉			☽ ♆

3

a Mutual reception	None
b Dignity	♄ in ♑ ♀ in ♉
c Detriment	♆ in ♍
d Exaltation	♃ in ♋
e Fall	None
f Ascendant ruler	☿
g Dispositor	♀
h Rising planets	None
i Chart shape	Bucket

1 Qualities and elements associated with zodiac signs

This table shows the three qualities, sometimes called the triplicities, and the four elements, sometimes known as the quadruplicities, which combined together represent the 12 zodiac signs. The planets are placed in the box appropriate to the zodiac sign in which they are situated on the chart.

It can be seen that there are five planets in earth signs on this chart, and that the planets are fairly evenly distributed among the three qualities. Thus the astrological signature of this chart is balanced earth.

2 Qualities and areas of interest associated with houses

This table relates to the houses in which the planets are situated. Three qualities, similar to those associated with the zodiac signs but with different names, are combined with four areas of interest to produce 12 houses.

It can be seen that five planets are in houses of completion on this chart and that the planets are once more fairly evenly spread across the three house qualities, indicating that Ms S's main interest in life is in making balanced endings.

3 Other features of the chart

An astrologer may also extract a number of other significant features from a chart: some of these are shown in the table *above right*.

a When two planets are placed in each other's sign, they are said to be in mutual reception. Each planet traditionally rules one or two of the zodiac signs. For example, the sun is the natural ruler of Leo and the moon of Cancer, so if the sun is in Cancer and the moon in Leo, the sun and moon would be in mutual reception, a very harmonious arrangement. There are no planets in mutual reception in this chart.

b Planets are in dignity when they are in the sign of which they are the natural ruler. Saturn rules Capricorn and Venus rules Taurus, so Saturn and Venus are both in dignity in this chart; powerful and fortunate positions.

c Detriment is the opposite to dignity and happens when a planet is in the sign opposite to the one it would naturally rule. Neptune is the natural ruler of Pisces, but in this chart Neptune is placed in the opposite sign of Virgo; Neptune in Virgo is in a detrimental position.

d Planets are exalted when they are in the sign from which they draw the source of their power. Jupiter in this chart is exalted in Cancer.

e Other signs are said to restrict a planet's power: the planet is then said to be in fall. For example, if Jupiter were in Capricorn, the sign of law and limitations, Jupiter's expansive power would be restricted. There are no planets in fall on this chart.

f The planet that is the natural ruler of the sign on the ascendant is called the ascendant ruler; in this chart it is Mercury, because Mercury rules Virgo. Mercury also rules Gemini (the sun-sign on this chart), which makes Mercury doubly important.

g A planet is said to be the dispositor when it disposes of or takes over the rulership of the whole chart. Taking each planet on the chart in turn, the rulership of the sign in which it is placed is followed through to conclusion. The sun is in Gemini. Gemini is ruled by Mercury. Mercury on the chart is in Taurus. Taurus is ruled by Venus. Venus on the chart is in Taurus, and Venus rules Taurus, so Venus is said to dispose of Mercury, rather like a takeover bid.

The same conclusion is reached for all the planets, making Venus the dispositor of all other rulers on this chart. Since Venus is already in dignity in Taurus, this makes Venus very important.

h Rising planets are those that are placed on or very close to the ascendant. No planet is close enough to the ascendant in this chart to be called a rising planet and thus gain the extra importance such a planet is given.

i The shape of a chart is determined from the pattern made by the planets. This is a bucket chart, with the planets in the upper half forming the base of the bucket and the single planet, Saturn, alone in the lower half forming the handle. As Saturn is also in dignity in Capricorn, Saturn would be given special attention in the interpretation of this chart.

©DIAGRAM

Astrology 3

Before a birth chart can be fully comprehended, the characteristics of the planets, zodiac signs, and houses must first be understood. As their separate meanings become clear, so the links between them will fall into place.

The tables for the zodiac signs and the houses can be read together, as the order given links the signs across the table with their natural houses. For example, the first house has many Arien characteristics, the second house

many Taurean characteristics, and so on. There is also a natural progression downward through the table of houses.

As it is a convention of astrology to call the sun and moon planets, ten planets appear on a birth chart. Each zodiac sign is ruled by the planet that is most in harmony with it temperamentally. Venus, for example, is in harmony with Taurean loyalty and a Libran need to be fair-minded: thus Venus rules both Taurus and Libra.

Cusps

The cusp of a sign or a house marks its starting point. The cusps of the signs and houses do not usually coincide, as can be seen in Ms S's chart *right*. The cusps of the first, fourth, seventh, and tenth houses – the angular houses – are particularly important, and are indicated on the chart by double lines.

Planets on the cusp of a sign are just entering the named sign, and so the personality may retain some of the characteristics of the previous sign.

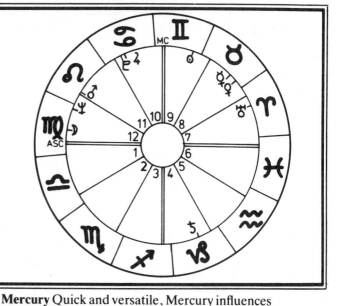

THE PLANETS
What?

This is the question answered by the position of a planet in a chart. For example, you would find out what changes might be likely by locating the position of Uranus on the chart.

Planet	Symbolism	Area of Influence
☉ Sun	Source of life	Personality
☽ Moon	Mirror of life	Moods
☿ Mercury	Messenger	Thoughts
♀ Venus	Goddess of love	Feelings and values
♂ Mars	Warrior	Action and drive
♃ Jupiter	Prophet	Expansion
♄ Saturn	Lawgiver	Responsibilities
♅ Uranus	Awakener	Changes
♆ Neptune	Mystic	Imagination
♇ Pluto	Dark lord	Transformation

A brief interpretation of the planets

The sun Energizing and fortifying, the sun is the masculine principle in everyone's makeup. Associated with dignity, health, leadership, ego, and the capacity for experience.

The moon Nurturing and receptive, the moon is the feminine principle in everyone's makeup. Associated with fluctuations, cycles, habits, reflex actions, desires, fertility, and the need to touch.

Mercury Quick and versatile, Mercury influences reason, thought, the capacity for emotion, local travel and activities, dexterity, words and the intellect, and everything associated with communication.

Venus Gentle and sensuous, Venus influences love, the arts, affections, pleasures, possessions, morality, marriage, sociability, and whatever is most valued.

Mars Active and competitive, Mars is linked with power, physical movement, construction, sexual energy, courage, self-assertion, strength, and initiative.

Jupiter Broadminded Jupiter aspires to philosophy, benevolence, prosperity, optimism, growth, and long-distance travel. He likes to have plenty of space.

Saturn Persistent and wise, Saturn is associated with truth, aging, ambition, responsibility, the capacity for a career, and with all the great lessons life can teach us. Saturn's placing in the chart may indicate restrictive overcompensation against feelings of insecurity.

Uranus Original and humanitarian Uranus is the breaker of traditions, associated with science, invention, magic, electricity, psychology, the will, and the unexpected.

Neptune Subtle and mysterious, Neptune rules the sea, all liquids, illusions, dreams, deceptions, ideals, religions, and thus rules drama, films, anesthetics, drugs, prisons, hospitals, and all institutions.

Pluto Ruler of the underworld, Pluto reveals what has been hidden including the subconscious self. Pluto rules atomic power, birth and death, group processes, and problem areas we have to solve alone and unaided.

THE SIGNS OF THE ZODIAC
How?
This is the question answered by the signs of the zodiac. For example, you can discover how a person thinks by locating the sign in which Mercury is placed. (Mercury's area of influence is the thoughts.)

THE HOUSES
Where?
This is the question answered by the houses. For example, you can discover where most energy will be expended by locating the house in which Mars is placed. (Mars' area of interest is action and drive.)

Zodiac sign	Name	Quality	Element	Ruler
♈ Aries	Ram	Cardinal	Fire	Mars
♉ Taurus	Bull	Fixed	Earth	Venus
♊ Gemini	Twins	Mutable	Air	Mercury
♋ Cancer	Crab	Cardinal	Water	Moon
♌ Leo	Lion	Fixed	Fire	Sun
♍ Virgo	Virgin	Mutable	Earth	Mercury
♎ Libra	Scales	Cardinal	Air	Venus
♏ Scorpio	Scorpion	Fixed	Water	Pluto
♐ Sagittarius	Archer	Mutable	Fire	Jupiter
♑ Capricorn	Goat	Cardinal	Earth	Saturn
♒ Aquarius	Waterman	Fixed	Air	Uranus
♓ Pisces	Fishes	Mutable	Water	Neptune

	Quality	Element	Areas of everyday life
1	Angular	Life	Identity and outlook
2	Succedent	Purpose	Values and freedom
3	Cadent	Relationships	Awareness and contact
4	Angular	Endings	Security and home
5	Succedent	Life	Creativity and children
6	Cadent	Purpose	Work and service
7	Angular	Relationships	Marriage and partnership
8	Succedent	Endings	Regeneration and sex
9	Cadent	Life	Aspiration and beliefs
10	Angular	Purpose	Honor and status
11	Succedent	Relationships	Friends and hopes
12	Cadent	Endings	Subconscious secrets

The three qualities of the signs
Cardinal signs use their abilities to achieve ambitions.
Fixed signs hold on to what they have and resist change.
Mutable signs are always searching and often changing.

The four elements
Fire Glowing or volcanic, fire is not easy to contain and is a process, not a substance. Once burning, fire will use up air and may boil water or scorch earth.

Earth Solid or sandy, earth can be used for building or planting; it can channel water, make a fire-place, and coexist with air.

Air Windy or balmy, air is always on the move and quite invisible; it rises above earth, makes bubbles in water, and is transformed by fire to which it is essential.

Water Clear or muddy, water seeks its own level and can evaporate, freeze, and reflect rainbows; it can put out a fire, flood the earth, and dampen air.

By further considering how fire, earth, air, and water behave you can extend your interpretation of the signs.

The duality of the zodiac qualities and elements
Combining the qualities and elements of the signs gives an indication of characteristic behavior. As we all choose how to behave, these characteristics can be positive – or negative.

Aries Independent, dynamic – arrogant, hasty.
Taurus Loyal, stable – possessive, stubborn.
Gemini Adaptable, communicative – scheming, gossipy.
Cancer Sympathetic, sensitive – manipulative, touchy.
Leo Self-assured, generous – pompous, pretentious.
Virgo Discriminating, humane – petty, insular.
Libra Refined, diplomatic – apathetic, fickle.
Scorpio Probing, passionate – suspicious, jealous.
Sagittarius Enthusiastic, honest – big-headed, blunt.
Capricorn Responsible, economical – inhibited, mean.
Aquarius Altruisitic, just – vague, two-faced.
Pisces Sacrificing, intuitive – lazy, unreliable.

The three qualities of the houses
Angular houses are where action is initiated.
Succedent houses are where action is stabilized.
Cadent houses are where we learn from actions and adapt.

The four house elements
The houses of life People with several planets in these houses have boundless energy, enthusiasm, and conviction. *First house:* physical energy. *Fifth house:* creative energy. *Ninth house:* spiritual energy.

The houses of purpose People with several planets in these houses are stable, reliable, and practical. *Second house:* possessions and finances. *Sixth house:* occupation. *Tenth house:* recognition.

The houses of relationships People with several planets in these houses need other people. *Third house:* chance relationships. *Seventh house:* close relationships. *Eleventh house:* social relationships.

The houses of endings People with several planets in these houses are sensitive to the way in which we may attain freedom. *Fourth house:* letting go of physical security. *Eighth house:* enlightenment of the mind. *Twelfth house:* release from secret fears.

The cusps of the angular houses
These are particularly important points on a chart.

Cusp of the first house of life This is the ascendant; your appearance in the world and how other people often see you on first acquaintance.

Cusp of the fourth house of endings. This is the point of origin; your family roots and psychological foundation.

Cusp of the seventh house of relationships This is the descendant (where the sun set on the day of your birth); here you relate with another and begin to lose yourself.

Cusp of the tenth house of purpose This is the MC or midheaven; the high point of achievement and what has been learned from life.

Astrology 4

The shape of the chart
Understanding a chart can be compared to getting to know a new piece of music. You first gain a general impression; then, as the chart is read in detail, the main themes emerge to be followed by the more subtle connections.

The first impression is made by the shape of the chart – the general pattern made by the arrangement of the planets. Seven major shapes can be distinguished, and these are said to coincide with the seven major personality types. The shapes can be a useful guide when you are interpreting a chart, and may also give extra emphasis to a characteristic that appears in your more detailed interpretation.

As it is the placing of the planets in the zodiac signs that is significant in deciding the shape of a chart, here we show the seven major types on charts without house divisions. Similarly, the individual names of the planets are not needed when forming this general impression, and so their positions are indicated by dots.

THE SEVEN MAJOR CHART SHAPES
1 Splash In this type of chart the planets occupy as many signs as possible, and may be spread fairly evenly around the wheel. At their best, splash people have wide interests – but at their worst may spread themselves too thinly.

2 Bundle Here the planets are grouped closely together in four or five consecutive signs. This is the rarest of the major chart shapes, and indicates a personality with a driving specialist interest.

3 Locomotive The planets in this type of chart are generally arranged fairly evenly around nine consecutive signs, leaving an empty group of three signs. The name locomotive is used because in engineering a driving wheel has an extra weight of metal to create a balance against the driving rod. Locomotive people have exceptional drive and application to the task in hand. The leading planet moving clockwise around the wheel is important, as it may indicate which area of the personality is a prime motivating force.

Semicircles and quarters
The line extending from the ascendant across the center of a chart (**I**) is called the horizon or equator. Planets appearing in houses 1–6 below this line are in the northern half of the chart and are called the night planets. Planets placed in houses 7–12 above the horizon are in the southern half of the chart and are called the day planets.

The line extending vertically down the middle of a chart from the MC (**II**) is called the meridian. Planets placed to the left of the meridian are called eastern planets; those placed to the right are called western planets.

The four major semicircles of a chart are thus: day, representing objectivity and an outgoing nature; night, representing subjectivity and privacy; east, indicating free will and independence; and west, indicating

flexibility and dependence.

Combining the meridian with the horizon (**III**) gives the four major quarters of a chart. Planets in houses 1–3 occupy the eastern night quarter (**A**); planets in houses 4–6 occupy the western night quarter (**B**); planets in houses 7–9 occupy the western day quarter (**C**); planets in houses 10–12 occupy the eastern day quarter (**D**). Each quarter represents a combination of the characteristics of the contributing semicircles. The eastern night quarter indicates a love of privacy and dislike of compromise; the western night quarter indicates imagination and a reserved nature; the western day quarter indicates ambition combined with a somewhat indecisive nature; and the eastern day quarter indicates a rebellious independence.

4 Bowl This shape is easy to recognize because all the planets fall in approximately half the chart. Bowl people scoop up experience and are very self-contained; the leading planet of the bowl could be said to lead them into various experiences. The bowl has particular importance if all the planets fall above or below the horizontal line of the ascendant, or if they all fall in the eastern or western halves of the chart.

5 Bucket Here nine of the planets fall in one half of the chart, while the tenth (called the singleton) is placed opposite them, forming the handle of the bucket. Bucket people direct their energies toward the achievement of one objective, and the singleton often indicates the nature of this purpose. They are not usually very concerned with self-preservation.

6 Seesaw To form this shape of chart two groups of planets must appear opposite each other, and there must be two or more empty signs in the two empty sections. The number of planets in each group may vary, but ideally there should be five planets on each side of the chart. Seesaw people always see both sides of an issue and may view life itself from two points of view. They may need to balance their interests and activities.

7 Splay This arrangement of planets is not always easy to define, but there must be at least one group of two or three planets placed closely together while the rest are distributed around the chart. Empty signs are usually distributed evenly as well. Splay people are individualists who do not like being classified or regimented. A splay chart may have planets in all three of one of the elements. For example, planets in all three earth signs would indicate an individualist in practical affairs, while planets in all three air signs would suggest intellectual independence.

BOWL CHARTS

Bowl shape charts in which all the planets are placed exclusively in one major half of the chart are not common, but when they occur they add extra emphasis to the bowl characteristics. They present a challenge that can be met by scooping up experience and using it to advantage. Bowl charts are named from the semicircle in which the planets fall: a day bowl chart, for example, is one in which all the planets are in the day half.·

Day bowl A person with this chart is likely to be ambitious (and even somewhat calculating and self-centered), with many acquaintances and a small number of very close friends. England's Queen Victoria (**a**) and the American author Henry James both had day bowl charts.

Night bowl A person with this chart is probably a natural loner who is shy, but who may have unusual insights and a natural artistic talent. Night bowl charts include those of the English poets Elizabeth Barrett Browning (**b**) and John Milton, and of the Flemish painter Rubens.

East bowl A person with this chart is often very individualistic, dislikes taking orders or making compromises, and may have difficulty with personal relationships. East bowl charts include those of the author Franz Kafka (**c**), the composer Stravinsky, and the artist Marc Chagall.

West bowl A person with this chart can develop good human relations, is socially diplomatic, but may be strongly influenced by the opinions of others and so find self-assertion difficult. US President Woodrow Wilson (**d**) and the deaf and blind Helen Keller both had west bowl charts.

©DIAGRAM

169

Astrology 5

Before interpreting a chart an astrologer will read the positions of the planets in order, noting them down so that there are no omissions. The positions of the sun, moon, and ascendant are usually noted at the top of a reading, because these are the three most important placements.

A table of dignities gives more information about the rulership of the planets. Information from this table is also noted down as it is essential for a complete reading.

TABLE OF DIGNITIES *below*

Dignity If you have a planet in dignity, you control the conditions in that part of your chart.

Detriment If you have a planet in detriment, you must accept the conditions in that part of your chart.

Exaltation If you have a planet in exaltation, you feel very positive and happy in that part of your chart.

Fall A planet in fall indicates an area of your chart where you may not feel at ease. For example, the sun is in fall in Libra. This does not mean that one-twelfth of the world's population is uncomfortable! It means that people with the Libran sun sign are always trying to improve their circumstances, and have an urge to try and keep everything around them harmonious.

Conventions of rulership Before the discovery of Uranus, Neptune, and Pluto – the planets that now rule Aquarius, Pisces, and Scorpio respectively – these three zodiac signs had other ruling planets, often called the old rulers. The old ruler of Scorpio was Mars, the old ruler of Aquarius was Saturn, and the old ruler of Pisces was Jupiter. The table of dignities takes account of the old rulership.

When the idea of rulership was first developed, Mars, Saturn, and Jupiter were given dual characteristics that now match the modern interpretations given to Pluto, Uranus, and Neptune. It is thought by some astrologers that there are still two more planets to be discovered in our solar system, and that these will become the rulers of Virgo and Libra. Meanwhile, Virgo is ruled by Mercury and Libra by Venus.

Planets in mutual reception

Mutual reception occurs when two planets are in one another's sign of the zodiac. For example, on Mr A's chart *right*, Venus (the ruler of Taurus) is in Gemini, while Mercury (the ruler of Gemini) is in Taurus: Venus and Mercury are thus in mutual reception.

Mutual reception emphasizes the energies of both planets as they work together.

Planet	Dignity		Detriment		Exaltation		Fall
☉ Sun	♌		♒		♈		♎
☽ Moon	♋		♑		♉		♏
☿ Mercury	♊	♍	♐	♓	♍	♒	♓
♀ Venus	♉	♎	♏	♈	♓		♍
♂ Mars	♈	♏	♎	♉	♑		♋
♃ Jupiter	♐	♓	♊	♍	♋		♑
♄ Saturn	♑	♒	♋	♌	♎		♈
♅ Uranus	♒		♌		♏		♉
♆ Neptune	♓		♍		♋		♑
♇ Pluto	♏		♉		♓		♍

MR A's CHART *right*

If the sun and the ascendant are in the same sign of the zodiac on a chart, it emphasizes the effect of that sign on the personality. In Mr A's chart, for example, both the sun and the ascendant are in Aries: his personality can thus be described as double Aries.

Reading of the chart for Mr A

Sun sign Aries **Moon sign** Virgo **Ascendant** Aries
Special feature Double Aries
Shape A bucket in the night half with some splay features.

Planet	Reading
☉	Sun rising exalted in Aries in the first house.
☽	Moon in Virgo in the sixth house.
☿	Mercury in Taurus in the first house.
♀	Venus in Gemini in the second house.
♂	Mars on the cusp of Pisces in the eleventh house.
♃	Jupiter exalted in Cancer in the third house.
♄	Saturn in Gemini in the second house.
♅	Uranus in Gemini in the second house.
♆	Neptune on the cusp of Libra in the sixth house.
♇	Pluto in Leo in the fourth house.
MC	Midheaven in Capricorn.
ASC	Ascendant in Aries.

Mercury and Venus are in mutual reception.

Information from the table of dignities

From the table of dignities we can see that Mr A has the sun in his chart exalted in Aries, indicating that he will feel very comfortable with his basic personality. As he is also a double Aries and his sun is rising in the first house of self, he will always project himself in a positive way. It may also mean that he may be over-enthusiastic about himself sometimes, giving the impression that he is arrogant and self-centered.

Mr A has Jupiter exalted in Cancer in the third house of chance relationships. This means that he will be very comfortable and happy meeting neighbors and relatives, having chance conversations, and generally taking any opportunity to learn something new. As Jupiter in Cancer is very generous, sympathetic, and enjoys

contact with all kinds of people, Mr A is likely to make a lot of people feel very happy and well looked after.

Mutual reception

Mr A has Venus and Mercury in mutual reception with each other. This means that his thoughts and affections are in harmony, and he will reflect his values in the way he communicates, especially about the affairs of the first and second houses.

Sun sign tables *below*

This diagram (**A**) will allow most people to find their sun sign easily. However, the sun does enter and leave signs on slightly different dates in some years. So anyone born on or near the cusp of a sign will need to check further in a detailed table of sun sign changes – one of the reference works you will need when you begin to draw up detailed charts. For example, an extract (**B**) from such a table for 1953 shows that the sun entered Aquarius on January 20 at 8.22 hours GMT, entered Pisces on February 18 at 22.41 hours GMT, and so on.

A

Aries
March 22 – April 20

Taurus
April 21 – May 21

Gemini
May 22 – June 22

Cancer
June 23 – July 23

Leo
July 24 – August 23

Virgo
August 24 – September 23

Libra
September 24 – October 23

Scorpio
October 24 – November 22

Sagittarius
November 23 – December 22

Capricorn
December 23 – January 19

Aquarius
January 20 – February 19

Pisces
February 20 – March 21

B	**1953**	20 ♒ 8.22	18 ♓ 22.41	20 ♈ 22.01	20 ♉ 9.26	21 ♊ 8.53	21 ♋ 17.00	23 ♌ 3.53	23 ♍ 10.46	23 ♎ 8.07	23 ♏ 17.07	22 ♐ 14.23	22 ♑ 3.32
		1	2	3	4	5	6	7	8	9	10	11	12

Astrology 6

An astrologer who has prepared a complete reading from a client's birth chart then goes on to consider the interpretations of the ten planets in the different zodiac signs and houses. Here we consider them in their traditional order of importance, beginning with the sun. The positions of the sun, the moon, and the ascendant symbolize a person's essential nature, and are often related to the past, present, and future parts of a life cycle. The sun expresses personality in the present, the moon reflects moods to which we have become conditioned in the past, and the ascendant represents the future outlook. The ascendant in a sign shares the same potentials as the sun in that sign, and so the same interpretations apply.

During the earlier part of life the sun and moon are said to dominate the chart as the sun seeks to express itself and come to terms with the moon's influence. Yet underlying the whole chart is the subtle influence of the ascendant that symbolizes the leader of the succession of signs and houses around the chart, and orients them in time and space.

The ascendant is always on the cusp of the first house of self, but may be in any one of the zodiac signs. It symbolizes the outlook of the person, and influences physical appearance. In astrological terms, maturity is said to be reached when the person has begun to express the nature of the outlook represented by the ascendant sign. The mature self is said to emerge as the parts of the personality (in particular those represented by the sun and the moon) are integrated and the individual achieves full expression.

The sun, the moon, Mercury, Venus, and Mars are regarded as the personal planets, symbolizing individual resources. They move quite quickly through the signs, ranging from the moon, which stays in a sign for only about two days before moving on, to Mars, which may stay for about two months. Although slower-moving, Jupiter and Saturn also modify the personality. Jupiter takes about a year to move through a sign, and Saturn about 2½ years.

The planets that move very slowly – Uranus, Neptune, and Pluto – are regarded as the generation planets, representing collective resources. The signs in which these planets are placed on a chart show how people born within a few years of each other are likely to respond to the larger social issues. The aspects made by these planets and their house positions are more important in a chart than their sign position. Uranus takes about seven years to move through a sign; Neptune takes about 14 years; and Pluto takes 13–32 years.

The separate interpretations for the positions of the planets in the signs and houses should never stand alone – they should always be considered in relation to each other. The aspects between the planets should also be taken into account, as should the natural house positions and planetary rulers of the signs. No single feature of a birth chart should be considered in isolation: seeing the whole picture is the real art of interpretation.

Traditional planets
Until the eighteenth century, astrological treatises described and illustrated the influence of only seven planets, as shown in the woodcut *above*. The seven "traditional" planets – the sun, the moon, Mercury, Venus, Mars, Jupiter, and Saturn – are all visible to the naked eye, and have probably been known since prehistoric times. The so-called "modern" planets can only be seen with a telescope: Uranus was discovered in 1781, Neptune in 1846, and Pluto in 1930.

SUN
Symbolism Source of life.
Area of influence Personality.
Associated with dignity, health, ego, and leadership; the sun's place in the chart shows how and where you want to shine.

The sun in the zodiac signs
Aries Headstrong, enterprising, you like to do your own thing and have your own way; may be opinionated.
Taurus Persistent, steadfast, you like luxury and security; a faithful friend but an implacable enemy.
Gemini Sensitive, restless, eloquent, you love variety and change and like to socialize; may be vague.
Cancer Cautious, broody, imaginative, you like to feel secure. Home is important; defensive when shy.
Leo Confident, proud, generous, you stand up for yourself; you like attention and can be patronizing.
Virgo Modest, cool-headed, thoughtful, you have a strong sense of duty; may be fussy about rules.
Libra Charming, sociable, diplomatic, you are always able to compromise with others; may be indecisive.
Scorpio Determined, shrewd, secretive, you like to know all that is going on; can be jealous and sharp.
Sagittarius Friendly, enthusiastic, tolerant, you love freedom and adventure; may be extravagant and blunt.
Capricorn Self-disciplined, loyal, serious, practical, you work hard to achieve; sometimes slow to trust others.
Aquarius Unpredictable, full of new ideas, you like to express your ideas freely; can be rebellious and distant.
Pisces Versatile, sensitive, kind to others, you love to dream but may sometimes find it hard to be practical.

The sun in the houses
1 Here the sun acquires some Arien characteristics and is strongly placed. Personal affairs need much time.
2 Here the sun acts like a Taurean sun. Ambition for material gains and effective at acquiring things.
3 The sun here has many of the communicative qualities of Gemini. A lively mind, friendly to neighbors.
4 Often conservative and strongly influenced by home. Here the sun shows Cancerian qualities.
5 Here the sun behaves like Leo, the sign it rules. A strong place for creativity, success, and enjoyment.
6 Dedicated to good work habits and health, keen to help others. The sun here acts like the sun in Virgo.
7 Friends and enemies are the key to the personality with the sun here, behaving much like a Libran sun.
8 Here the sun has many Scorpionic qualities. Has a deep interest in the nature of things.
9 Here the sun has some Sagittarian characteristics. High ideals, broad interests, perhaps foreign travel.
10 Here the sun takes on some qualities of Capricorn and gains purpose and a desire for status and success.
11 Social ambition and cooperative ventures appeal to the sun placed here, behaving much like an Aquarian.
12 Here the sun may have difficulty expressing itself fully, acquiring the dreaminess of a Piscean sun.

MOON
Symbolism Mirror of life.
Area of influence Moods.
Associated with emotions, devotion, and the nurturing instinct; the moon's place in the chart reflects your moods.

The moon in the zodiac signs
Aries Emotionally dominating but can blow hot or cold. Sincere, enthusiastic, but nervous at asking for help.
Taurus Emotionally steady, can be loyal or stubborn. Faithful, sentimental, affectionate, but may be timid.
Gemini Emotionally versatile, perceptive, often able to be dispassionate; may need to do several things at once.
Cancer Emotionally possessive but can be totally devoted and trusting. Thrifty, intuitive, easily hurt.
Leo Emotionally bountiful but can be fiery and self-concerned. Magnetic, romantic, honest, and loving.
Virgo Emotionally appreciative but can seem very shy. Generous but emotionally demanding and insecure.
Libra Emotionally gracious but needs to be approved of by others. Sociable, affectionate but indecisive.
Scorpio Emotionally intense but often very controlled. Can be jealous, proud, sacrificial, but deeply hurt.
Sagittarius Emotionally idealistic, acute judgment, but a happy-go-lucky naïvety and a need for total freedom.
Capricorn Emotionally inhibited but supersensitive and dignified. Can be melancholic or have rare great passions.
Aquarius Emotionally detached, a preference for cool friendship. Very idealistic but needs outlets for tension.
Pisces Emotionally subjective with an instinctive feeling for others. Sometimes sentimental and self-pitying.

The moon in the houses
1 Very imaginative and sensitive to feelings within the self. Moody and changeable, perhaps shy.
2 Capable of being very persuasive, has a great need for material security. Can be generous or mean.
3 Restless, expressive, dramatic. A lack of long-term concentration, but a good memory and avid curiosity.
4 A very strong feeling for home, family, parents, or family history, although there may be many changes.
5 Strong romantic emotions and a love of theatrical effects. Creative in cycles. Often fond of children.
6 A strong desire to serve or look after people. Rather nervous, changeable in habits. Has vague illnesses.
7 Responsive to others' needs and generally popular, but indecisive. Subject to changes in friendships.
8 A great need for security and thus an interest in love, sex, and affection. Can sometimes be rather morbid.
9 Very philosophical with a natural ability to teach others. Likes to study the meaning of life at any level.
10 Sometimes this position is like living on constant view to the public. May be many changes of occupation.
11 An objective view of organizations and clubs. Often many helpful friends; sometimes some false friends.
12 Rather retiring and uncomfortable in strange surroundings. Often likes seclusion or working alone.

©DIAGRAM

Astrology 7

MERCURY
Symbolism The messenger.
Area of influence Thoughts, mind.
Associated with reasoning ability, words, travel, and dexterity; Mercury's place in the chart shows how you best communicate.

Mercury in the zodiac signs

Aries An impulsive mind, quick, direct, witty, inventive. Looks ahead, can improvise, but may be impatient.
Taurus A mind that values facts and weighs the evidence. May have mental inertia.
Gemini A very quick, communicative, logical, witty, and perceptive mind. Many thoughts, may not be thorough.
Cancer A receptive, impressionable, retentive mind. Arguments make you adamant. Very subjective.
Leo Broadminded, able to solve problems and speak with authority, may ignore details or be quick-tempered.
Virgo An analytical, practical, methodical, sensible mind. Able to be impersonal, sometimes critical.
Libra An active, diplomatic, and just mind, looking for the perfect compromise. Dislikes losing arguments.
Scorpio An acute, shrewd, probing mind. Opinions rarely change and can be forcefully stated.
Sagittarius An independent, progressive, honest mind. May be scatterbrained, often very direct or even blunt.
Capricorn A serious, cautious, ambitious mind with a memory for detail. Dry-witted or even satirical.
Aquarius A resourceful, original, observant mind with an interest in abstract ideas. Can be stubborn or eccentric.
Pisces A very receptive, osmotic mind capable of exact insight; can be woolly-minded and sometimes morbid.

Mercury in the houses

1 Self-conscious, you may find it hard to understand the feelings of others. Point of view starts from the self.
2 Value-conscious with a rational, commercial sensitivity. Point of view starts from "What can I gain?"
3 Communication-conscious and restless, you may say "What can I learn, where can I go, who can I meet?"
4 Family-conscious and thrifty, your point of view begins from home, family, history, or a need to collect.
5 Pleasure-conscious and full of bright ideas you are on the lookout for novelty, chance, fun, and lots of affairs.
6 Conscious of duty you apply thought systematically – a need to have back-up plans and many irons in the fire.
7 People-conscious, your outlook starts from "What can we do together?" Partnerships are important.
8 Conscious of hidden motives and intuitive, your point of view starts from "What's really going on here?"
9 Conscious there is always something new to be learned, your outlook is free-ranging and philosophical.
10 Conscious of status, your point of view begins from "How can these facts be used to my best advantage?"
11 Socially conscious, your thoughts are concerned with what is best for a group of people.
12 Conscious of inner feelings on which you base decisions, you may be guarded or insecure.

VENUS
Symbolism Goddess of love.
Area of influence Feelings, values.
Associated with affections, sensuality, and pleasure; the position of Venus in the chart shows where your values lie.

Venus in the zodiac signs

Aries Magnetic, ardent, demonstrative, outgoing, you like to present yourself well. May be overwhelming.
Taurus Faithful, steadfast, sensual, artistic, you love luxury and touching things. May be possessive.
Gemini Generous, friendly, bright, you love to roam around freely. May be fickle in romance or affection.
Cancer Idealistic, gentle, devoted, caring, you have an instinct to nurture. May become too clinging.
Leo Warm-hearted, lavish, romantic, you love life and love to be noticed. Can be very jealous.
Virgo Undemonstrative, shy, inhibited, your sensuality is hidden. Can behave in exactly the opposite way.
Libra Attractive, gracious, appreciative, you may be more in love with love than with your partner.
Scorpio Passionate, magnetic, loyal, you can feel desolate or become cruel if rejected sexually.
Sagittarius Adventurous, humorous, idealistic, you deal out affection freely but may hate commitments.
Capricorn Dedicated, proud, reserved on the surface, you may hide a fear of your sensuality being rejected.
Aquarius Detached, cool, friendly, you do not like to be tied down and may prefer platonic relationships.
Pisces Gentle, compassionate, tender, you may be very self-sacrificing or much too hypersensitive.

Venus in the houses

1 You value yourself, and are often happy, balanced, and kind. You enjoy luxury and may like to be spoiled.
2 You value your possessions and talents, and like your work to be pleasant in luxurious surroundings.
3 You value pleasant friendships and a charming family. You dislike arguments and prefer persuasion to force.
4 You value a comfortable, organized home, which you may create yourself. Your ethical values are strong.
5 You value affection, pleasure and giving pleasure to others, children, love affairs, and creative ventures.
6 You value service both given and received. You may be a "Good Samaritan," if sometimes indulgently.
7 You value harmony, the law, and social graces. You may be happy in marriage, business, or in public life.
8 You value sensuality and life itself. Spiritual peace may be important. You may benefit greatly from others.
9 You value enthusiasm and zeal, whether you have it yourself or not, and you enjoy travel.
10 You value status and diplomacy and may be very popular with associates who are willing to help you.
11 You value a variety of friendships and affiliations, but sometimes you may be too idealistic in a group.
12 You value seclusion and privacy, from which position you may feel an urge to serve others.

MARS

Symbolism The warrior.
Area of influence Action, drive.
Associated with power, sex, and competition; Mars' position in the chart shows how and where energy is used.

Mars in the zodiac signs

Aries Energy used for self-willed vigorous action; a dislike of routine or timidity. Sexually dynamic.
Taurus Energy used to plow through all obstacles; likes to be the boss. Sexually earthy but may be jealous.
Gemini Energy used to put ideas into action quickly; can sell anyone anything. Sexually prefers variety.
Cancer Energy used acquisitively and protectively; may smolder emotionally. Sexually sensitive.
Leo Energy used to act generously and courageously. Great sex appeal – winner or loser but never also-ran.
Virgo Energy used to develop strategies for perfection; may be more ardent in work than in love. Sexually shy.
Libra Energy used paradoxically to fight for peace. Sexually, likes the soft lights and sweet music approach.
Scorpio Energy from vast hidden sources tends to explode into action. Sexually demands all or nothing.
Sagittarius Energy used for a perpetual love affair with life; sometimes burns the candle at both ends.
Capricorn Energy used to sustain effort; may speak softly and carry a big stick. Sexually persistent.
Aquarius Energy used galvanically for break-ups, break-downs, and break-throughs. Sexually innovative.
Pisces Energy often remains inward under pressure; dislike of physical action. Romantic and sensual.

Mars in the houses

1 Self-assertive, practical, competitive, may be boisterous. Keen to prove self.
2 Resourceful, generous. Devotes energy to getting rich quickly but may lose the gains just as quickly.
3 Assertive with words, impatient, restless, may be tactless. Loves to get into arguments or debates.
4 Devotes much energy to fulfilling a need for security. May have to move from birthplace.
5 Impulsive, a born promoter, may be athletic, likes to be up and doing but may be a bad loser. Creative.
6 Puts energy into work and service and expects others to do so too. A passion for orderliness in any area.
7 Energy attracts strong reactions one way or another from other people. May be a controversial personality.
8 Much energy devoted to lusty matters such as love, sex, life, death. Money usually important.
9 Energy put into many, often wide-ranging, ventures. May include extended self-education and travel.
10 Energy devoted to the achievement of an ambition. Strong driving force to reach a top position.
11 Much energy devoted to exploring and improving social affairs, creative promotions, or group interests.
12 Here energy may be limited or used indirectly; may behave like a rebel or a passive pressure cooker.

JUPITER

Symbolism The prophet.
Area of influence Expansion and freedom.
Associated with optimism, growth, space, order; Jupiter's place in the chart shows where your opportunities for improvement lie.

Jupiter in the zodiac signs

Aries Likes to improve the self and use opportunities to the fullest extent. May become too egocentric.
Taurus Likes to improve the value of money and the luxury it can buy. Extravagance can lead to dissipation.
Gemini Likes to be the fun-loving ideas person who is original and alert. Can become temperamental.
Cancer Likes to improve relations with a wide public and to share generously. May get too sentimental.
Leo Likes to improve conditions by making the dream a reality for someone. Can be exuberant or arrogant.
Virgo Likes to improve standards by attention to detail. May make mountains out of molehills or become lazy.
Libra Hospitable, likes to improve leisure time and pleasures, especially with a partner. Hopeless alone.
Scorpio Likes to improve life by thinking big and doing the work to match. Shrewd but can be uncompromising.
Sagittarius Likes to take opportunities to make life brighter for others. Always optimistic, may be reckless.
Capricorn Likes to expand through dedication, hard work, economy. Can be too orthodox or a martyr.
Aquarius Inspired to help people whatever their race or religion. Can be revolutionary or unrealistic.
Pisces Likes to improve the lot of the underdog but quietly and unassumingly. Can be too self-sacrificing.

Jupiter in the houses

1 Broad-minded, breezy, optimistic, humorous, you are the executive type but could become self-indulgent.
2 Prosperous, likeable, with wide appeal, you are the business type but could be showy or spendthrift.
3 Witty, happy-go-lucky, you are the type to have good relations with relatives, students, or the local public.
4 Generous, loyal, outgoing, you are the head-of-the-family type. You like to entertain and to be in control.
5 Dramatic, with wide interests, the happy-family type who also gambles – and wins if not too reckless.
6 Cheerful, usually lucky, you are the type for whom something always turns up. You enjoy your work.
7 Often gaining from others, you are the type to have a happy life and to lavish affection on your partner.
8 Resourceful, discerning, you like to manage the affairs of others. A positive attitude to life and sex.
9 Tolerant, faithful, devoted, you are the type to get along with people from other cultures and religions.
10 Self-reliant, trustworthy, proud, ambitious, you are the leader type but could become overbearing.
11 Benevolent with high aspirations, you enjoy many social contacts and devote time to people.
12 Kind, resourceful in trouble, you like to give in secret, perhaps because you doubt yourself.

© DIAGRAM

Astrology 8

SATURN
Symbolism The lawgiver.
Area of influence Responsibility.
Associated with truth and learning; Saturn's position on the chart shows how and where you compensate against insecurity.

The influence of Saturn
Traditionally, Saturn is represented as the cold, barren planet that imposes major restrictions on our lives. Modern astrologers believe, however, that Saturn simply shows us our own limitations. It is up to us to learn the lessons that this planet can teach us, and so to balance our needs realistically. Saturn's position can tell us much about our unconscious feelings of insecurity. The house positions show the possible sources of these feelings; the sign positions indicate how particular talents are developed to try and compensate for them.

Saturn in the zodiac signs
Aries Capable of using ingenuity to develop strength of character. May need to learn tact and cooperation.
Taurus Capable of being trustworthy and patient in everyday affairs. May need to reassess values.
Gemini Capable of being adaptable and systematic in scientific pursuits. May need to learn spontaneity.
Cancer Capable of being shrewd, able, and loyal to family or firm. May need to control self-pity and show genuine emotions.
Leo Capable of self-assured leadership in almost any field. May have to learn to enjoy life and laugh.
Virgo Capable of being precise and prudent in detailed work. May need to learn what is important.
Libra Capable of being responsible for work requiring good planning and justice. May need to learn tolerance.
Scorpio Capable of using a subtle, strong willpower to achieve success. May need to learn to forgive and forget.
Sagittarius Capable of building a reputation for being morally outspoken. May need to be less self-righteous.
Capricorn Capable of good organization and a responsible use of power and prestige. May need to relax.
Aquarius Capable of original abstract thought in any organization. May need to learn to express gratitude.
Pisces Capable of humility and understanding when working with others. May need to keep track of reality.

Saturn in the houses
1 Sense of personal inadequacy may spur you on.
2 Anxiety due to possessions, money, or lack of money.
3 Fear of the unknown or of being lonely.
4 Anxiety about age or being a nobody.
5 Anxiety when trying to express yourself fully.
6 A worrier anxious to prove your worth.
7 Difficulties in one-to-one relationships.
8 Sex and love can be sources of anxiety.
9 New ideas or new places may cause anxiety.
10 Irresponsible power urges cause anxiety.
11 Being given or offered affection can cause anxiety.
12 Anxiousness about life can cause isolation.

URANUS
Symbolism The awakener.
Area of influence Change and freedom.
A generation planet associated with ideas and the unexpected. House position shows where you behave out of character.

Uranus in the zodiac signs
Aries, c.1928–1934 Impetuous, self-willed pioneers taking charge of their lives and altering destiny.
Taurus, c.1935–1942 Determined, practical builders of economic reforms but liable to unexpected trouble.
Gemini, c.1942–1949 Brilliant, inventive people with original ideas for innovative reforms. Often fickle.
Cancer, c.1949–1956 Emotionally restive people seeking freedom in the home, marriage, and for women.
Leo, c.1956–1962 New rhythms, unconventional outlooks. Determined to change what does not suit them.
Virgo, c.1962–1968 An inquiring, down-to-earth interest in ecology, health, and advanced technology.
Libra, c.1968–1975 Charming, magnetic people out to rectify injustices and give meaning to relationships.
Scorpio, c.1891–1898 and 1975–1981 Intense, daring, fascinating, decisive people seeking new approaches.
Sagittarius, c.1898–1904 and 1981–1988 Equable, optimistic people with progressive, open minds.
Capricorn, c.1905–1912 and 1988–1995 Responsible and resourceful people determined to reconcile conflicts.
Aquarius, c.1912–1919 and 1995–2002 Strong, inventive, humanitarian people, free thinkers, but sometimes impractical.
Pisces, c.1919–1927 Imaginative, visionary, and often self-sacrificing, sometimes impractical or escapist.

Uranus in the houses
1 Always out of character compared with your peers as you are often ahead of your time. A nonconformist.
2 Value systems are your specialty since you invent your own to match your need for independence.
3 You behave out of character, often with genius. Open-minded, you are unpredictable and inventive.
4 You may like frequent changes of residence and have a changeable home life. You may fear being alone.
5 You may act out of character with regard to established conventions: marriage, children, rules.
6 You are prone to sudden upsets and minor illnesses and need to work in your own way. Often highly strung.
7 You are likely to be unpredictable or to behave in unusual ways in personal relationships or partnerships.
8 You may experience unconventional or unexpected events concerning money or sex; you experiment.
9 Unorthodox and independent, you may enjoy the unexpected while traveling or in legal matters.
10 Altruistic, you are a great fighter but a bad follower. Career and work are where the unusual may happen.
11 You may have strange, nonconformist ideas but are most likely to make unusual friendships.
12 You may have unusual or secret love affairs or unconscious conflicts that may surface unexpectedly.

NEPTUNE
Symbolism The mystic.
Area of influence Imagination and intuition.
A generation planet associated with the spiritual or escapist urge. House position shows idealistic or self-deceptive trends.

Neptune in the zodiac signs
Aries, c.1861–1874 Radical missionaries with strong egos, pioneering new philosophical ideas.
Taurus, c.1874–1887 Artistic and experimental with an instinct for business, but sometimes led astray by others.
Gemini, c.1887–1901 Alert, inquiring, restless people with new ideas on trade, travel, and communications.
Cancer, c.1901–1915 Emotional, patriotic, and mystical with strong ties to home and family despite upheavals.
Leo, c.1915–1929 Speculative, romantic, powerful, bringing flair, idealization, and new developments.
Virgo, c.1929–1943 Humanitarian, divided between reason and emotion. Throws baby out with bathwater.
Libra, c.1943–1956 Compassionate, peace-loving but impractical; "doing your own thing" causes problems.
Scorpio, c.1956–1970 Investigative and emotional with interest in new approaches both good and bad.
Sagittarius, c.1970–1984 Frankness reveals things previously hidden and brings out new universal ideals.
Capricorn, c.1984–1998 Conventional, practical, and conscientious – a period of applied knowledge.
Aquarius, c.1998–2012 Detached attitudes with a truly philosophical outlook – the start of a peaceful period.
Pisces Neptune was last here in c.1847–1861, a period of new cultural concepts.

Neptune in the houses
1 You may idealize yourself because you do not see yourself clearly. Charismatic with strong imagination.
2 You are idealistic about possessions but may be very impractical about money. An intuitive sense of value.
3 You dream about your idealistic world but may be vague or feel misunderstood. Persuasive and intuitive.
4 You idealize family or home but may be uncertain about your own identity. Artistic and musical.
5 You idealize romance and the people you love but may need lots of romantic affairs. Very creative.
6 You are idealistic about whatever you do but may drift along or have vague illnesses. Poetic, lonely, sensitive.
7 You idealize others in your life but may need to face the realities. Often influenced by or serving others.
8 You idealize the search for truth but may lead yourself or others astray. Charismatic and intuitive.
9 You idealize social and educational reforms but may be impressionable. Tolerant and intellectual.
10 You idealize your public image but may have self-doubts. High aspirations and awareness of motives.
11 You idealize those who are odd or different but may be unreliable. Generous with an accurate intuition.
12 You idealize insight but may deceive yourself or be deceived. Wise and extremely sensitive. A loner.

PLUTO
Symbolism The dark lord.
Area of influence Transformation.
A generation planet associated with that which is hidden. House position shows the complexities you have to resolve alone.

Pluto in the zodiac signs
Aries, c.1823–1851 A desire for reform, power, or revenge. Great daring, initiative, imagination.
Taurus, c.1851–1883 The growth of materialism with a great need for wealth, security, and permanence.
Gemini, c.1883–1913 A time of major changes through new inventions. Impetuous, intellectual, critical.
Cancer, c.1913-1938 A period of great upheaval, pride, and patriotism. Social awareness and a need for security.
Leo, c.1938–1957 A period when power was sought and developed. Self-confidence, perversity, business skill.
Virgo, c.1957–1971 A period of intensive technical development. Analytical, inventive, perfecting.
Libra, c.1971–1983 A period of social changes inspired by a sense of justice. Adaptable, responsible, but fickle.
Scorpio, c.1983–1995 A period predicted as innovative and may be redemptive. Environmental sensitivity.
Sagittarius, c. 1995–? The period predicted to be very reformative with a return to fundamental laws.
Capricorn A predicted period of efficiency, ambition, and an emphasis on organization and management.
Aquarius Predicted as a period of revelation and a love of freedom. Unconventional, revolutionary, ingenious.
Pisces Predicted as the next period of enlightenment in human history, a period of compassion and sensitivity.

Pluto in the houses
1 An urge to resolve the complete expression of the many sides of your strong, creative personality.
2 An urge to turn liabilities into assets and to prevent assets ruining your happiness.
3 An urge to make yourself heard, resolve your shortcomings, and face changes in your life.
4 An urge to identify and resolve the complexities of your origins and to transform yourself.
5 An urge to take risks and resolve your strong erotic, creative, and emotional feelings.
6 An urge to resolve your mission in life in your own very individualistic way.
7 An urge to use your dynamic personality to resolve issues of interpersonal circumstances.
8 An urge to investigate and resolve all hidden desires, obsessions, or mysteries – your own or other people's.
9 An adventurous urge to resolve a dream by trying absolutely everything life has to offer.
10 An urge courageously to resolve a need to assert yourself and gain identity or acclaim.
11 An urge to resolve your intense desire to reform the world single-handed.
12 An urge to resolve inner fears and frustrations, or to change personal limitations.

Astrology 9

Aspects are the different angular relationships between the planets on a birth chart; they reveal connections between the areas of personality represented by the planets. Aspects may emphasize, challenge, or show where adjustments may have to be made between the different parts of the personality in action. They are neither good nor bad; something of everything is needed to make a whole human being. Too much ease can become boring; too much stress can result in bitterness. Depth of character comes from a balance between tension and relaxation.

An understanding of the natural aspects between the signs of the zodiac is the key to interpreting the aspects between planets in those signs. Here we look at the six major aspects and how to locate and interpret them on a chart.

THE SIX MAJOR ASPECTS

These are the six angular relationships that are consistently given importance by astrologers because they describe the relationships between all the elements and qualities of the zodiac signs. Some astrologers also use up to ten minor aspects to emphasize the finer points of the major aspects.

Each angle or aspect has a symbol, a name, an orb, and a specific meaning. The orb is the number of degrees of deviation allowed from the exact angle of the aspect.

1 Conjunction Planets in the same sign act in the same way and concentrate their energies.
2 Opposition Conflict between opposite signs produces a potential for self-awareness and perspective.
3 Square Tension between the elemental ways in which two planets operate offers a challenge.
4 Sextile Planets placed in compatible signs offer opportunities.
5 Trine A satisfying, easy combination of planets.
6 Inconjunct Planets in signs that have nothing in common suggest a need to reorganize or reconcile parts of the self.

	Symbol	Name	Angle	Orb	Meaning
1	☌	Conjunction	0°	7°	Concentration
2	☍	Opposition	180°	7°	Perspective
3	□	Square	90°	7°	Challenge
4	✳	Sextile	60°	5°	Opportunity
5	△	Trine	120°	7°	Satisfaction
6	⚻	Inconjunct*	150°	5°	Reorganization

*Sometimes known as the quincunx.

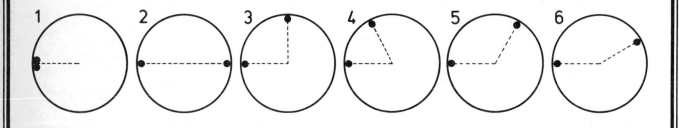

THREE OR MORE PLANETS IN THE SAME ASPECT

a) The stellium Three or more planets that lie within seven degrees of each other on the chart are called a stellium. Here the emphasis is even greater than a conjunction of two planets; individuality or a special interest are often indicated in this way. Conjunctions of this kind are often found on the splay-shaped charts.

b) T-Square When one planet is square to two others in opposition a T-square is formed.

c) Grand square Four planets in opposition are square to each other forming the most powerful aspect that can be found on any chart; sometimes this aspect is called a grand cross.

d) Grand trine Three planets in trine aspect form a grand trine, an aspect of ease, pleasure, and harmony.

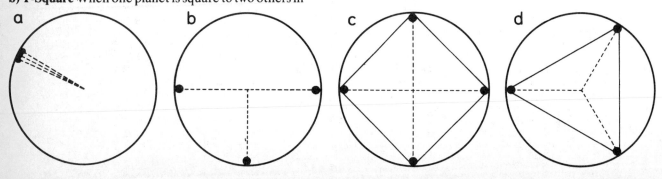

Squares and oppositions

These are always aspects between planets in cardinal (**A**), fixed (**B**), or mutable (**C**) signs.

Squares are the building blocks of a chart, indicating decisions and actions to be taken as a result of the challenges presented by life. They may indicate turning points, potential accomplishments, or disruptions. Oppositions can show areas where one polarity can compensate for something lacking in the other. They give perspective and can be areas of cooperation or conflict.

The quality of the aspects shows how decisions are made and action taken: cardinal aspects operate quickly and with the intention of solving the situation; fixed aspects are slow and deliberate and may show an acceptance of the situation; mutable aspects indicate variable actions that are often influenced by other people.

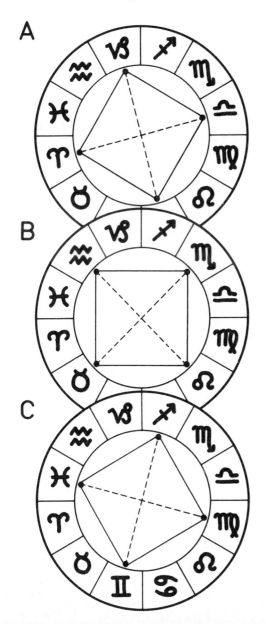

Polarities between the signs and the houses

The way in which identity is expressed by the different signs of the zodiac is a key to understanding the polarities between signs in opposition. The "good" and "bad" polarities that can exist within each identity are shown in the list *below*.

The house positions also have their opposites. Although houses as such are not regarded as being in opposition, the placing of the aspects in houses will show the area of life to which the aspect applies. Reading across the list the identity of the signs can be matched with their natural houses.

It is important to be aware that meanings should never be taken too literally; the art of good astrological interpretation lies in the ability to comprehend the wider, more symbolic meanings of the keywords. For example, investments are not necessarily financial: we may invest energy, time, and space.

SIGN	IDENTITY	SIGN	IDENTITY
Aries ♈	I exist Me first	**Libra** ♎	I cooperate I procrastinate
Taurus ♉	I have I indulge	**Scorpio** ♏	I desire I suspect
Gemini ♊	I think I scheme	**Sagittarius** ♐	I understand I exaggerate
Cancer ♋	I feel I brood	**Capricorn** ♑	I use I inhibit
Leo ♌	I will I pretend	**Aquarius** ♒	I know I'm unreliable
Virgo ♍	I study I worry	**Pisces** ♓	I believe I escape

HOUSE	AREAS	HOUSE	AREAS
1	Myself Outlook	**7**	Yourself Partnerships
2	What is mine Values	**8**	What is yours Investments
3	Life here and near Awareness	**9**	Life there and far Optimism and learning
4	Private life/source Security	**10**	Public life/image Status
5	What I give Creativity	**11**	What I receive Ideas
6	Physical health Service	**12**	Mental health Secrets

©DIAGRAM

Astrology 10

Sextiles and trines

These are always aspects between planets in harmonious signs of the zodiac.

Sextiles are aspects of 60° between a planet in a fire sign and a planet in an air sign (**1**), or between a planet in an earth sign and a planet in a water sign (**2**). These pairs of elements are compatible and offer a great deal of opportunity for self-expression.

Trine aspects of 120° are always between signs of one element, and indicate ease, stability, and a general feeling of joy and satisfaction. But several trines on a chart are not necessarily beneficial – too much of a good thing can lead to a very passive or indolent existence. Fire trines (**3**) are naturally energetic; air trines (**4**) are given to much thought and idealism; earth trines (**5**) are found in the charts of practical realists; water trines (**6**) experience every shade of feeling and may be quite intuitive.

Inconjuncts

These are always aspects between signs that have neither qualities nor elements in common. Consequently they may indicate areas where an adjustment or some reorganization has to take place. There is a strain between signs inconjunct, and this strain may be relieved by changing a habit or re-thinking a whole policy. As with all aspects, the more exact the angle the greater the importance of the aspect: an exact 150° angle indicates considerable strain between the two planets in the signs.

Inconjunct aspects between the signs are easy to locate: a sign is inconjunct with the sign each side of its opposite. For example, Aries can be inconjunct with both Scorpio and Virgo, or with either one of them (**A**): the cardinal fire sign of Aries has nothing in common with either the fixed water sign of Scorpio or the mutable earth sign of Virgo. Double aspects of inconjunction are doubly problematic.

Conjunctions

These aspects occur when planets are within 7° of each other: the planets may be in the same sign or in adjoining signs. Conjunctions concentrate energy, whose focus is determined by the sign and house position of the aspect. Shown on the chart are examples of an exact conjunction and a stellium.

a An exact conjunction of Neptune and the moon at 28° of Virgo. The moon conjunct Neptune is an extremely sensitive and impressionable combination making it difficult to tell illusion from reality. Virgo, however, ensures discrimination, but will add a strong pull between reason and emotion.

b A stellium of Uranus, Venus, and Saturn at 2°, 3°, and 9° respectively of Gemini. This indicates a self-willed, original, detached, fickle, sparkling stroke of genius, perhaps the result of a great need for security. Saturn's presence indicates that happiness and duty are seen as synonymous.

RECORDING THE ASPECTS

We can see how to construct an aspect table by considering a sample chart for January 2, 1999 (**1**). For simplicity the positions of the planets have been given to the nearest whole degree and the houses omitted.

A table showing the number of degrees between the planets (**2**) is needed before the aspect table can be constructed. Write down the degrees longitude of the planets (**a**). Then, beginning with the sun, work down the list counting the number of degrees between the planets, and record them in the table (**b**). Always remember that there are 30° in each zodiac sign, and that the degree of the planet is measured counterclockwise in each sign. Aspects between planets, however, can be measured either clockwise or counterclockwise. On this chart, for example, the angle between the sun and Mars is measured as shown in this calculation.

Sun 11° Capricorn	11°
Two signs (Sagittarius and Scorpio) 30° + 30°	60°
12° of Libra (remembering that Mars 18° Libra is measured counterclockwise)	12°
Total	83°

The sun and Mars are therefore 83° apart.

When the table is complete, ring all the angles between planets that form aspects. Remember that an orb is allowed, so that some aspects are not exact. For example, the sun and Mars at 83° apart are within the allowed 7° orb of a 90° square aspect.

It is now possible to construct the finished aspect table (**3**), inserting the correct symbol for each aspect. All the major aspects appear on this chart. Reading them column by column, beginning with the sun, they are:

Sun opposition moon, square Mars;
Moon square Mars, inconjunct Uranus and Pluto,
Mercury sextile Mars, square Jupiter, trine Saturn,
Venus sextile Jupiter, square Saturn, conjunct Neptune;
Mars inconjunct Jupiter.

In addition, it can be seen from both the chart and the aspect table that there is a T-square between the sun, the moon, and Mars.

INTERPRETING THE ASPECTS

Aspects are interpreted in order of their importance, always beginning with the sun. The aspects on our sample chart *above* give us the information below.

Sun opposition moon, square Mars Conflict between ego and emotions, challenged by cooperative Mars in Libra. Sun in Capricorn wants to use experience to fulfill ambitions, ignoring the feelings of the protective moon in Cancer. Perhaps a person of great ambition who could turn the conflict with inner feelings into devotion and use the challenge of Mars to act diplomatically and with decorum. This cardinal T-square indicates a person who gets things done to completion with a sense of self-worth and independence.

Moon inconjunct Uranus and Pluto Protective feelings are incompatible with an uncompromising desire to reform.

Mercury sextile Mars, square Jupiter, trine Saturn Independent thought compatible with energy and ingenuity produces a challenge to imagination.

Venus sextile Jupiter, square Saturn, conjunct Neptune Sense of dedication offers opportunity to exercise the imagination in ingenious new ways.

Mars inconjunct Jupiter A need to reconcile action and imagination – without letting imagination run riot.

Astrology 11

A birth chart must be constructed – "cast" – before it can be interpreted. Here we explain how to cast a sample chart. The method is slightly simplified from that used by professional astrologers, and gives ascendant and planetary positions accurate to the nearest degree, instead of to the nearest minute. If you would prefer the greater accuracy, or if you decide not to cast your own charts, it is possible to have charts cast ready for your interpretation. Advertisements from experienced astrologers or computer bureaux offering these services can usually be found in astrology magazines.

The equipment needed for drawing a chart is simple: pencil and paper, ballpoint pen, ruler, protractor, and a pair of compasses. You will also need a noon ephemeris for the year of birth and a table of houses for the latitude of birth (both available from shops supplying astrology books), and an atlas.

TIME AND TIME ZONES

Greenwich Mean Time (GMT) This is the clock time on the Greenwich meridian, longitude 0°.

Standard Time (ST) The 24 time zones of the world are all measured from the Greenwich meridian; each zone is 15° of longitude wide. The clock time in each time zone is called standard time, and is distinguished from all others by stating the longitude of the zone.

Moving east from the Greenwich meridian each zone is one hour ahead of the previous zone. For example, clock time in Sydney, Australia is at ST 150° E. This is ten zones east of 0°, and so ST 150° E is ten hours ahead of GMT.

Moving west from Greenwich meridian each zone is one hour behind the previous zone. For example, clock time in New York, USA is at ST 75° W. This is five zones west of 0°, and so ST 75° W is five hours behind GMT.

This basic pattern may be modified by national borders; each country chooses the standard time it finds most convenient.

Daylight Saving Time (DST) Some countries in higher latitudes advance their clocks during the summer, usually by one hour. This should be taken into account and the birth time corrected to standard time before a birth chart is constructed.

Sidereal time This is the actual time scale of the earth's rotation on its axis. One rotation takes 23h 56m 4.09s, and not the 24 hours we use for convenience on our clocks.

Local sidereal time (LST) This is sidereal time relative to a particular place.

Interval This is the difference between noon GMT and the time of birth GMT. For example, the interval for births at either 9am or 3pm GMT would be three hours.

Longitudinal equivalent This time adjustment (four minutes for each degree of longitude) takes account of the difference between the longitude of the actual place of birth and that of the Greenwich meridian, and is used in calculating the LST.

Noon ephemeris

These tables give sidereal times and planetary positions at noon at 0° longitude, and list them for every day of every year. As an example we show an extract from the ephemeris for April 1953 (**A**). The first column lists the date, the second the day of the week, and the third the sidereal time in hours, minutes, and seconds. Subsequent columns list the positions of the planets.

Tables of houses

These can be used to find the sign and degree of the ascendant that corresponds to the local sidereal time at different latitudes.

To use the tables of houses you should first find the table that is nearest in latitude to the place of birth. For Bristol, England, for example, at 51° 27′ N, the nearest house table (**B**) is that for London, England, at 51° 32′ N.

Calculations to find the position of the ascendant will give you a figure for the local sidereal time at birth. Locate the sidereal time nearest to this figure in the left-hand column of the appropriate table of houses. The position of the ascendant in degrees and minutes can now be read off from the column headed "Ascen"; the glyph at the top of the column will give the zodiac sign.

For a birth in Rome at a local sidereal time of 7h 28m 08s, for example, the nearest sidereal time shown in the appropriate table of houses (**C**) is 7h 30m 50s, giving the position of the ascendant as 17° 47′ Libra.

A

D M	D W	Sidereal Time. H. M. S.	⊙ Long. ° ′ ″	☽ Long. ° ′ ″	♆ Long. ° ′	♅ Long. ° ′	♄ Long. ° ′	♃ Long. ° ′	♂ Long. ° ′	♀ Long. ° ′	☿ Long. ° ′
1	W	0 38 12	11 ♈ 27 39	3 ♍ 25 32	22 ♎ 50	14 ♋ 28	24 ♎ 56	21 ♉ 30	8 ♉ 53	29 ♈ 32	19 ♓ 47
2	TH	0 42 8	12 26 48	15 50 16	22 R 48	14 29	24 R 51	21 43	9 36	29 R 9	19 D 52
3	F	0 46 5	13 25 55	28 25 41	22 46	14 30	24 47	21 55	10 19	28 42	20 2
4	S	0 50 2	14 25 1	11 ♐ 13 4	22 45	14 30	24 42	22 8	11 2	28 14	20 17
5	☉	0 53 58	15 24 4	24 14 6	22 43	14 31	24 38	22 20	11 46	27 44	20 37

CALCULATING THE POSITION OF THE ASCENDANT

In the table *below right* we show side by side the ascendant position calculations for two people – an English man and an Italian woman – born at the same moment in two different countries in the northern hemisphere. The following notes explain the method of calculation.

a, b Note the date and place of birth.

c, d Find the latitude and longitude of the place of birth from an atlas.

e Note the time zone in which the birth took place.

f Record the birth time in hours, minutes, and seconds, and note whether it occurred before or after noon.

g Note any difference in time between the time zone of birth and GMT.

h Correct the time of birth to GMT.

i Consult an ephemeris to find the sidereal time at Greenwich at noon on the day of birth.

j, k The interval is the difference in hours between noon and the GMT time of birth. For births occurring after noon the result is obtained by adding this interval to the sidereal time; for births occurring before noon the interval would be subtracted.

l, m Calculate the longitudinal equivalent by taking the degrees and minutes of longitude for which the adjustment is required and multiplying by four. Call the result minutes and seconds of time. For example, $2° 35' × 4 = 8m\ 140s = 10m\ 20s$. The longitudinal equivalent is subtracted for places west of Greenwich and added for those east of Greenwich to give the local sidereal time (LST).

n Use the local sidereal time to find the position of the ascendant in the appropriate table of houses.

For births south of the equator Work through the calculation to step **m**. Then add 12 hours to the LST you have calculated, which is for northern latitudes – moving due south to the same southerly latitude means moving halfway around the world in time. The corrected LST can then be used to locate the ascendant in a table of houses for southern latitudes. If these are not available, a northern table for the same latitude can be used, but the sign of the zodiac given for the ascendant must be replaced by its opposite – Scorpio would replace Taurus, Leo would replace Aquarius, and so on.

		English man	Italian woman
a	Date of birth	April 1, 1953	April 1, 1953
b	Place of birth	Bristol	Rome
c	Latitude	51° 27′ N	41° 54′ N
d	Longitude	2° 35′ W	12° 29′ E
e	Time zone	GMT	ST 15° E
f	Birth time	6h 00m 00s (pm)	7h 00m 00s (pm)
g	Zone correction	none	1h 00m 00s –
h	GMT	6h 00m 00s (pm)	6h 00m 00s (pm)
i	Sidereal time	0h 38m 12s	0h 38m 12s
j	Interval	6h 00m 00s +	6h 00m 00s +
k	Result	6h 38m 12s	6h 38m 12s
l	Longitudinal equivalent	10m 20s –	49m 56s +
m	LST	6h 27m 52s	7h 28m 08s
n	Ascendant	4° 37′ Libra	17° 47′ Libra

To the nearest whole degree, the ascendants are 5° Libra for the English man, and 18° Libra for the Italian woman. The difference is entirely due to geographical location.

Change of birthdate

When calculating the GMT of a birth time for births in places several time zones east or west of Greenwich, it is sometimes necessary to adjust the date of birth. The corrected date is then used when consulting the ephemeris.

For example, here is the first part of the ascendant position calculations for two people who appear to have been born at different times.

	English man	Australian woman
Date of birth	October 26, 1954	October 27, 1954
Place of birth	London	Sydney
Time zone	GMT	ST 150° E
Birth time	5h 40m 00s (pm)	3h 40m 00s (am)
Zone correction	none	10h 00m 00s –
GMT	5h 40m 00s (pm)	5h 40m 00s (pm)
GMT date	October 26, 1954	October 26, 1954

We can see that by deducting the ten hours that Sydney is ahead of GMT, midnight is passed and the time GMT is 5.40pm on the previous day. So these two people were in fact born at exactly the same moment.

B

TABLES OF HOUSES FOR LONDON

Sidereal Time.	10 ♈	11 ♌	12 ♍	Ascen ♎
H. M. S.	°	°	°	° ′
6 0 0	0	6	6	0 0
6 4 22	1	7	7	0 47
6 8 43	2	8	8	1 33
6 13 5	3	9	9	2 19
6 17 26	4	10	10	3 5
6 21 48	5	11	10	3 51
6 26 9	6	12	11	4 37
6 30 30	7	13	12	5 23
6 34 51	8	14	13	6 9
6 39 11	9	15	14	6 55
6 43 31	10	16	15	7 40
6 47 51	11	16	16	8 26
6 52 11	12	17	16	9 12
6 56 31	13	18	17	9 58
7 0 50	14	19	18	10 43
7 5 8	15	20	19	11 28
7 9 26	16	21	20	12 14
7 13 44	17	22	21	12 59
7 18 1	18	23	22	13 45
7 22 18	19	24	23	14 30
7 26 34	20	25	24	15 15
7 30 50	21	26	25	16 0
7 35 5	22	27	25	16 45
7 39 20	23	28	26	17 30
7 43 34	24	29	27	18 15
7 47 47	25 ♍	1	29	18 59
7 52 0	26	1	29	19 43
7 56 12	27	2	29	20 27
8 0 24	28	3 ♎	1	21 11
8 4 35	29	4	1	21 56
8 8 45	30	5	2	22 40

C

TABLES OF HOUSES FOR ROME

Sidereal Time.	10 ♈	11 ♌	12 ♍	Ascen ♎	2 ♎	3 ♏
H. M. S.	°	°	°	° ′	°	°
6 0 0	0	4	4	0 0	26	26
6 4 22	1	5	5	0 51	27	27
6 8 43	2	6	6	1 43	28	28
6 13 5	3	7	7	2 34	29	29
6 17 26	4	8	8	3 25	30	♏
6 21 48	5	9	9	4 16	♏	1
6 26 9	6	10	10	5 8	1	2
6 30 30	7	11	11	5 59	2	3
6 34 51	8	12	12	6 50	3	4
6 39 11	9	13	13	7 41	4	5
6 43 31	10	14	14	8 32	5	6
6 47 51	11	15	15	9 23	6	7
6 52 11	12	16	15	10 14	7	8
6 56 31	13	17	16	11 5	8	9
7 0 50	14	18	17	11 55	9	10
7 5 5	15	19	18	12 46	10	11
7 9 26	16	19	19	13 36	11	12
7 13 44	17	21	20	14 27	11	13
7 18 1	18	22	21	15 17	12	14
7 22 18	19	23	22	16 7	13	15
7 26 34	20	24	23	16 57	14	16
7 30 50	21	25	24	17 47	15	16
7 35 5	22	26	25	18 37	16	17
7 39 20	23	27	26	19 26	17	18
7 43 34	24	28	26	20 16	18	19

Astrology 12

PLANETARY POSITIONS

The ephemeris is used to find the positions of the planets at noon on the day of birth. The date of birth is found in the left-hand column of the ephemeris, and the degrees and minutes of longitude for each planet can then be read in order. The zodiac signs are shown between the figures on the ephemeris.

For April 1, 1953, for example, the appropriate ephemeris (**A**) gives the planetary positions shown in the table *right*. These readings are then corrected to the nearest whole degree. Take note of any planets near the cusp of a sign – Venus, for example, at 29° 32′ is almost but not quite on the cusp of Taurus, and so the degree reading is left in the correct sign of Aries.

Pluto The position of the planet Pluto is listed in a separate table in the ephemeris. The table for April 1, 1953 (**B**) shows that Pluto was at 21° 1′ Leo. The symbol R in the table under the glyph for Leo means retrograde, because at the time Pluto was apparently moving backward – a visual illusion when viewing the solar system from earth.

Correcting the moon's position The ephemeris gives the positions of the planets at noon. Unlike the other planets, the moon moves very quickly around its orbit, and its relative position in the zodiac signs can change by as much as 15° a day. The moon's position can be calculated very precisely, but it is also possible to use the following simplified method to make a close estimate. These calculations are for a person born on April 1, 1953, at 6.00pm GMT.

Use the appropriate ephemeris to find the position of the moon at noon on both April 1 and April 2. This shows that the moon was at 3° 25′ Scorpio on April 1, and at 15° 50′ Scorpio on April 2. To the nearest whole degree, this is a movement from 3° Scorpio to 16° Scorpio. This movement can then be matched with a 24-hour timescale running from 12 noon on April 1 to 12 noon on April 2.

Degrees 3 4 5 6 7 8 9 10 11 12 13 14 15 16
Hours 12   6pm   12   6am   12
From this scale we can see that at 6.00pm on April 1 the moon was at approximately 6° Scorpio.

Planet	Longitude	Nearest whole degree
☉ Sun	11° 27′	♈ 11° Aries
☽ Moon	3° 25′	♏ 3° Scorpio
☿ Mercury	19° 47′	♓ 20° Pisces
♀ Venus	29° 32′	♈ 29° Aries
♂ Mars	8° 53′	♉ 9° Taurus
♃ Jupiter	21° 30′	♉ 22° Taurus
♄ Saturn	24° 56′	♎ 25° Libra
♅ Uranus	14° 28′	♋ 15° Cancer
♆ Neptune	22° 50′	♎ 23° Libra

B
THE POSITION OF PLUTO (♇) IN 1953.

Date	Long.
	° ′
Jan. 1	22 ♌ 56
11	22 R 45
21	22 32
31	22 18
Feb. 10	22 4
20	21 49
Mar. 2	21 35
12	21 22
22	21 10
April 1	21 1
11	20 54
21	20 50
May 1	20 D 48

A

APRIL, 1953

D M	D W	Sidereal Time.	☉ Long.	☽ Long.	♆ Long.	♅ Long.	♄ Long.	♃ Long.	♂ Long.	♀ Long.	☿ Long.
		H. M. S.	° ′ ″	° ′ ″	° ′	° ′	° ′	° ′	° ′	° ′	° ′
1	W	0 38 12	11 ♈ 27 39	3 ♏ 25 32	22 ♎ 50	14 ♋ 28	24 ♎ 56	21 ♉ 30	8 ♉ 53	29 ♈ 32	19 ♓ 47
2	TH	0 42 8	12 26 48	15 50 16	22 R 48	14 29	24 R 51	21 43	9 36	29 R 9	19 D 52
3	F	0 46 5	13 25 55	28 25 41	22 46	14 30	24 47	21 55	10 19	28 42	20 2
4	S	0 50 2	14 25 1	11 ♐ 13 4	22 45	14 30	24 42	22 8	11 2	28 14	20 17
5	☉	0 53 58	15 24 4	24 14 6	22 43	14 31	24 38	22 20	11 46	27 44	20 37

Data sheet

When all the data required to cast a chart has been calculated and collected, it is collated on a data sheet in a sequence that is easy to transfer to a blank chart. Shown *right* is the data sheet for the woman born in Rome on April 1, 1953, at 7.00pm local time.

Birthdate April 1, 1953   **Place** Rome   **Time** 6.00pm GMT

Ascendant	18° Libra		
Sun	11° Aries	Jupiter	22° Taurus
Moon	6° Scorpio	Saturn	25° Libra
Mercury	20° Pisces	Uranus	15° Cancer
Venus	29° Aries	Neptune	23° Libra
Mars	9° Taurus	Pluto	21° Leo

Drawing the chart

Blank charts can be bought ready-printed, or they can be hand-drawn and photocopied to ensure a ready supply.

a) Make a blank chart by drawing two concentric circles. Divide the inner circle in half horizontally with a double line for the ascendant. Mark in the 12 house divisions at 30° intervals, and number them in a counterclockwise direction. The center of the chart can be a dot or a small circle, as shown.

b) Enter the ascendant on the blank chart. Using the data sheet for the Italian woman, we can see that her ascendant is 18° Libra. 18° Libra is above the eastern horizon: it can be measured upward from the horizontal ascendant line with a protractor. The rest of Libra, 12°, is below the eastern horizon and can be measured downward from the ascendant line. The 30° section of the wheel occupied by Libra can now be marked off, and its symbol entered, You should also mark the ascendant, its degree, and its sign.

Moving counterclockwise from Libra, divide the rest of the wheel into 30° sections.

c) Mark in the divisions for the 12 signs, and enter their symbols in order counterclockwise. The midheaven can now be marked in at the top of the chart.

d) Use the data sheet to enter the positions of the planets on the chart, beginning with the sun. Remember that all measurements are made counterclockwise around the wheel. For example, the Italian woman has her sun at 11° Aries. The measurement is made counterclockwise from the cusp of Aries, a mark is made, and the symbol for the sun drawn next to it.

e) Enter the positions of the other planets, marking them first in pencil so that any errors can be corrected. When complete, the shape of the chart can be seen: the Italian woman has a splay chart. The casting of the chart is now complete and it is ready for reading and interpretation.

Checking the chart

When the chart has been drawn it is a simple matter to check if the sun is in the correct part of the chart. The house divisions also divide the 24 hours of the day into two-hour periods (**f**). A birth at 11am would show the sun somewhere near the tenth house; a birth at 5am would show the sun just below the ascendant; and a birth at 5pm would show the sun just above the descendant. Slight differences will occur with different latitudes, but certainly a birth in the middle of the night should not show the sun above the horizon!

Astrology 13

By looking at a brief interpretation of the birth chart of Ms Y we can see how the individual interpretations of the planetary positions in the signs and houses can be summarized into an integrated picture.

DATA SHEET
Birthdate April 24, 1949 **Place** 50° 12′ N, 5° 17′ W
Time 12.20am British Summer Time (BST)*
Time zone GMT
Ascendant 16° Sagittarius

Sun	3° Taurus	Jupiter	1° Aquarius
Moon	16° Pisces	Saturn	29° Leo
Mercury	14° Taurus	Uranus	28° Gemini
Venus	5° Taurus	Neptune	13° Libra
Mars	25° Aries	Pluto	14° Leo

*Because one hour must be deducted to convert BST to GMT, Ms Y's birth time becomes 11.20pm GMT on the previous day. This corrected birthdate – April 23, 1949 – must be used when looking up the position of the planets in the ephemeris.

1

	Fire	Earth	Air	Water
Cardinal	♂		♆	
Fixed	♄ ♇	☉ ☿ ♀	♃	
Mutable	ASC		♅	☽

2

	Life	Purpose	Relationships	Endings
Angular	ASC	♆	♅	☽
Succedent	☉ ☿ ♀ ♂	♃		
Cadent	♄	♇		

INFORMATION READ FROM THE BIRTH CHART
Qualities and elements of the sign positions (1) Y's dominant behavior is fixed fire – Leo ruled by the sun in Taurus. This suggests that Y likes to transform things steadily in a practical way.
Qualities and areas of interest of the houses (2) Y's dominant areas of interest are succedent life, suggesting that she uses her material resources in a particularly creative way – four planets are in the fifth house of creativity, which is influenced by Aries, indicating flair and initiative.
Planets in dignity Venus in Taurus, Mars in Aries, both in the fifth house. These indicate that Y has control over her actions and her values in relation to her creative output.
Planet in detriment Saturn in Leo in the ninth house, indicating that Y must accept some restriction on her desire to expand her creative, fun-loving disposition.
Ascendant ruler Jupiter in Aquarius in the second house suggests that Y should have plenty of opportunity to expand her ideas and acquire material gains.

Dispositors The main dispositor is Venus in Taurus in the fifth house, showing that Y's standards and sense of values rule everything she does. There is also a single dispositor of Mars in Aries in the fifth house. This suggests that Y has a very dynamic, courageous, and pioneering drive, but that this part of her personality stands on its own and may need to be fully integrated into her system of values.
Chart shape There is no distinct shape, but some features of both the locomotive and splay types. The stellium of planets in the fifth house suggests strong individuality.

THE PLANETS IN THE SIGNS AND HOUSES
Sun in Taurus Persistent and steadfast, Y likes luxury and security. She is a faithful friend but an implacable enemy. *In the fifth house* the sun behaves like Leo – a strong position for creativity and success.
Moon in Pisces Emotionally subjective with an instinctive feeling for others, sometimes sentimental and sorry for herself. *In the fourth house* Y's home and origins will be important, although there may be many changes.
Mercury in Taurus A mind that values facts and weighs the evidence, rarely jumping to conclusions, perhaps somewhat inert. *In the fifth house* Y is pleasure-conscious and full of bright ideas.
Venus in Taurus Faithful, steadfast, sensual, artistic, Y loves luxury and touching things. She may be rather possessive. **In the fifth house** Y values affection, pleasure, and giving pleasure to others.
Mars in Aries Energy used for self-willed vigorous action, a dislike of routine or timidity. Sexually dynamic. *In the fifth house* Y is practical, competitive, and may be boisterous. She likes to prove herself.
Jupiter in Aquarius Inspired to help people whatever their race or religion, Y can be revolutionary or unrealistic. *In the second house* Y is prosperous and likeable. She has business sense but could be extravagant.

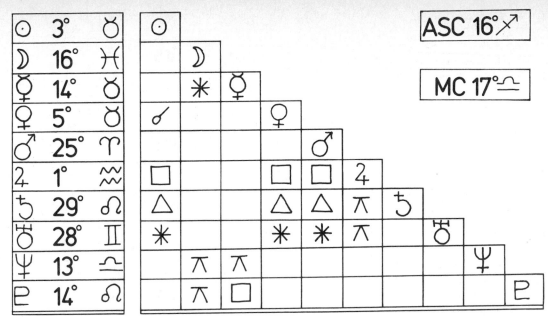

Planetary positions

Planet	Degree	Sign
☉	3°	♉
☽	16°	♓
☿	14°	♉
♀	5°	♉
♂	25°	♈
♃	1°	♒
♄	29°	♌
♅	28°	♊
♆	13°	♎
♇	14°	♌

ASC 16° ♐   MC 17° ♎

Aspect grid

	☉	☽	☿	♀	♂	♃	♄	♅	♆
☽									
☿		✶							
♀	☌								
♂									
♃	□			□	□				
♄	△			△	△	⚻			
♅	✶			✶	✶	⚻	✶		
♆		⚻	⚻						
♇		⚻	□						✶

Saturn in Leo Capable of self-assured leadership in any field, but may have to learn to enjoy life and laugh. *In the ninth house* Y may be anxious about being in new places or about new ideas.

Uranus in Gemini in the seventh house The brilliant but fickle generation. Y may be unpredictable or behave in unusual ways in her personal relationships.

Neptune in Libra in the tenth house The peace-loving generation. Y idealizes her public image, has high aspirations, is aware of her own motives, but may have doubts about herself.

Pluto in Leo in the eighth house The self-confident generation. Y has an urge to investigate and resolve all hidden desires, obsessions, or mysteries.

Ascendant in Sagittarius As she matures, Y is likely to express her ideas more freely and to become even more enthusiastic about life as she gains greater wisdom and tolerance from her personal experiences.

INTERPRETING THE MAJOR ASPECTS *above*
Sun conjunct Venus in Taurus in the fifth house will emphasize both of these planets.

Moon sextile Mercury, inconjunct Neptune and Pluto gives Y the opportunity to express her emotions but not her self-doubts or hidden desires. These remain quite separate from her main emotional makeup.

Mercury inconjunct Neptune, square Pluto means that her self-doubts are kept separate from her thoughts, but her hidden desires challenge her way of thinking.

Venus square Jupiter, trine Saturn, sextile Uranus Y's values and affections are challenged by her aspiring ascendant ruler Jupiter. She gains satisfaction from learning to enjoy life and laugh despite Saturn's restrictions. This enables her to be unpredictable in her personal relationships.

Mars square Jupiter, trine Saturn, sextile Uranus Y's drive and energy are involved in exactly the same way as her values (shown by the aspects of Venus).

Jupiter inconjunct Saturn and Uranus again shows a very separate part of Y's personality. Her Jupiterian optimism has no relationship with Saturn's restrictions or with her unpredictability.

Saturn sextile Uranus is a restriction that actually gives Y the opportunity to behave in unusual ways in her personal relationships, and may indeed be the cause of her behavior.

Neptune sextile Pluto means that Y is aware of her own hidden desires and is ambitious to resolve them.

SUMMARIZING THE CHART INTERPRETATION
Dynamic and courageous, Y is a strong individual steadily transforming almost everything she touches, even though she may burn herself out occasionally. She uses her resources creatively, with flair and initiative. There is some restriction or limitation connected with her creative desires, but she will expand her ideas and gain materially using her good business sense.

Y is sensual, imaginative, active, and enjoys luxury. Mars in Aries gives her considerable drive, which means she can be domineering at times. She would certainly make an implacable enemy, but her sense of values dominates all her behavior. She thinks sensibly, and enjoys giving to others. Although she is self-assertive, she does not like to be exposed to a large public.

The several inconjuncts, especially the double inconjunct between the moon, Neptune, and Pluto, are indicative of very separate parts of Y's personality that present problems. They show a limitation linked with a hidden creative desire that in some way affects intimate relationships. This seems to be something that she has difficulty in expressing emotionally but has had to learn to laugh about. There is an indication that she can find a way to resolve this problem, as she has a grand trine in fire signs linking Leo (where the problem planets Saturn and Pluto lie) with her ascendant (representing her mature personality) and her dynamic, individualistic Mars. Nothing is going to stop this attractive, creative woman from reorganizing her life conditions to solve these problems to her satisfaction.

©DIAGRAM

Oriental astrology 1

Just as in the west most people know the name of their astrological sun sign (Aries, Taurus, and so on), so in the east they know the name of the year of their birth – the year of the dog, the year of the goat, and so on. It is said that the Buddha invited all the animals to celebrate the New Year with him, but only 12 came. As a reward, the Buddha named a year after each of them. These years still run in the order in which the 12 arrived in his presence, with the rat first and the pig last. And so oriental astrology is based on a 12-year cycle. Each year of the cycle is a lunar year, based on the phases of the moon. Consequently, each year begins on a different date according to the western calendar, falling some time between January 21 and February 21. We are all supposed to inherit the characteristics of the animal that rules the year of our birth. And each animal is held to influence not only the people born in one of its years, but also the actual nature of the year itself. Obviously, as in western astrology, there are other factors in any individual horoscope – the date and time of birth, for example, with those born on New Year's Day showing the most marked characteristics of a sign. But detailed prediction in oriental astrology is extremely complex: at least two Chinese astrologers were executed by their Emperors for failing to predict the future correctly . . .

Lo-king plate *above*
The ancient Chinese consulted a horoscope disk, the lo-king, in order to predict the future. The 12 animals of their zodiac appear around the outside, and details of the stars and planets in the center.

The animals and their years
The 12-year cycle of the animals is shown in the list *right*. (In Vietnam, the year of the rabbit is known as the year of the cat.) A special year of the horse – the year of the fire horse – occurs every 60 years.

1925 BUFFALO (January 25, 1925 – February 13, 1926)
1926 TIGER (February 14, 1926 – February 2, 1927)
1927 RABBIT (February 3, 1927 – January 22, 1928)
1928 DRAGON (January 23, 1928 – February 10, 1929)
1929 SNAKE (February 11, 1929 – January 30, 1930)
1930 HORSE (January 31, 1930 – February 17, 1931)
1931 GOAT (February 18, 1931 – February 6, 1932)
1932 MONKEY (February 7, 1932 – January 25, 1933)
1933 ROOSTER (January 26, 1933 – February 13, 1934)
1934 DOG (February 14, 1934 – February 4, 1935)
1935 PIG (February 5, 1935 – January 23, 1936)
1936 RAT (January 24, 1936 – February 11, 1937)
1937 BUFFALO (February 12, 1937 – January 31, 1938)
1938 TIGER (February 1, 1938 – February 18, 1939)
1939 RABBIT (February 19, 1939 – February 7, 1940)
1940 DRAGON (February 8, 1940 – January 27, 1941)
1941 SNAKE (January 28, 1941 – February 15, 1942)
1942 HORSE (February 16, 1942 – February 4, 1943)
1943 GOAT (February 5, 1943 – January 25, 1944)
1944 MONKEY (January 26, 1944 – February 12, 1945)
1945 ROOSTER (February 13, 1945 – February 1, 1946)
1946 DOG (February 2, 1946 – January 21, 1947)
1947 PIG (January 22, 1947 – February 9, 1948)
1948 RAT (February 10, 1948 – January 29, 1949)
1949 BUFFALO (January 30, 1949 – February 17, 1950)
1950 TIGER (February 18, 1950 – February 6, 1951)
1951 RABBIT (February 7, 1951 – January 26, 1952)
1952 DRAGON (January 27, 1952 – February 14, 1953)
1953 SNAKE (February 15, 1953 – February 3, 1954)
1954 HORSE (February 4, 1954 – January 23, 1955)
1955 GOAT (January 24, 1955 – February 11, 1956)
1956 MONKEY (February 12, 1956 – January 30, 1957)
1957 ROOSTER (January 31, 1957 – February 18, 1958)
1958 DOG (February 19, 1958 – February 7, 1959)
1959 PIG (February 8, 1959 – January 27, 1960)
1960 RAT (January 28, 1960 – February 15, 1961)
1961 BUFFALO (February 16, 1961 – February 4, 1962)
1962 TIGER (February 5, 1962 – January 25, 1963)
1963 RABBIT (January 26, 1963 – February 13, 1964)
1964 DRAGON (February 14, 1964 – February 2, 1965)
1965 SNAKE (February 3, 1965 – January 21, 1966)
1966 FIRE HORSE (January 22, 1966 – February 8, 1967)
1967 GOAT (February 9, 1967 – January 29, 1968)
1968 MONKEY (January 30, 1968 – February 16, 1969)
1969 ROOSTER (February 17, 1969 – February 5, 1970)
1970 DOG (February 6, 1970 – January 26, 1971)
1971 PIG (January 27, 1971 – February 18, 1972)
1972 RAT (February 19, 1972 – February 2, 1973)
1973 BUFFALO (February 3, 1973 – January 23, 1974)
1974 TIGER (January 24, 1974 – February 10, 1975)
1975 RABBIT (February 11, 1975 – January 30, 1976)
1976 DRAGON (January 31, 1976 – February 17, 1977)
1977 SNAKE (February 18, 1977 – February 7, 1978)
1978 HORSE (February 8, 1978 – January 27, 1979)
1979 GOAT (January 28, 1979 – February 15, 1980)
1980 MONKEY (February 16, 1980 – February 4, 1981)
1981 ROOSTER (February 5, 1981 – January 24, 1982)
1982 DOG (January 25, 1982 – February 12, 1983)
1983 PIG (February 13, 1983 – February 1, 1984)
1984 RAT (February 2, 1984 – February 19, 1985)
1985 BUFFALO (February 20, 1985 – February 8, 1986)
1986 TIGER (February 9, 1986 – January 28, 1987)
1987 RABBIT (January 29, 1987 – February 16, 1988)
1988 DRAGON (February 17, 1988 – February 5, 1989)
1989 SNAKE (February 6, 1989 – January 26, 1990)

THE INFLUENCE OF THE YEARS

1 In the year of the rat Save up for the future, read the good books that will be published, and expect political surprises. A good year for rats, buffalo, dragons, monkeys, and pigs; a bad year for tigers, rabbits, horses, goats, and roosters; an indifferent year for snakes and dogs.

2 In the year of the buffalo Look after your garden, enjoy the good harvest, and take care not to be overworked. A good year for buffalo, horses, monkeys, and roosters; a bad year for tigers, snakes, goats, and dogs; an indifferent year for rats, rabbits, dragons, and pigs.

3 In the year of the tiger Try to find a little peace and quiet, but expect major changes in your life, and political upheavals (anything from snap elections to revolutions). A good year for tigers, dragons, horses, and dogs; a bad year for buffalo, rats, roosters, and goats; an indifferent year for rabbits, snakes, pigs, and monkeys.

4 In the year of the rabbit Take full advantage of a quiet year that allows you to rest, take holidays, and enjoy the company of friends. A good year for rabbits, dragons, snakes, horses, goats, and monkeys; a bad year for rats; an indifferent year for buffalo, tigers, roosters, dogs, and pigs.

5 In the year of the dragon Be ambitious and enterprising, and enjoy an exciting, successful, and exhausting year. A year that can set the world on fire – literally as well as figuratively. A good year for rats, tigers, dragons, monkeys, and roosters; a bad year for dogs; an indifferent year for buffalo, rabbits, snakes, pigs, horses, and goats.

6 In the year of the snake Be a lotus-eater, and enjoy a lazy, hedonistic year, as all your problems will appear to have been solved. A good year for rabbits, dragons, snakes, goats, monkeys, and dogs; a bad year for rats, buffalo, and tigers; an indifferent year for roosters, horses, and pigs.

7 In the year of the horse Get involved, but be tactful with the ruffled tempers around you; this irritability increases in the year of the fire horse. A good year for buffalo, dragons, goats, and roosters; a bad year for horses (especially the year of the fire horse), rats, snakes, and pigs; an indifferent year for tigers, rabbits, monkeys, and dogs.

8 In the year of the goat Be yourself, and try to find time for a little self-indulgence as you and the world muddle through a series of major and minor crises. A good year for goats, monkeys, and pigs; a bad year for buffalo, tigers, roosters, and dogs; an indifferent year for rats, rabbits, dragons, snakes, and horses.

9 In the year of the monkey Take some risks, launch some new ideas, and expect the unexpected. As no-one is thinking before they act, rebellions, revolutions, and insurrections are all possible. A good year for rats, tigers, horses, goats, dogs, pigs, monkeys, and roosters; a bad year for buffalo; an indifferent year for rabbits, dragons, and snakes.

10 In the year of the rooster Keep scratching around to make a living as unemployment rises, and watch your behavior while the forces of law and order are in full cry. A good year for rats, dragons, horses, roosters, and pigs; a bad year for tigers, rabbits, and snakes; an indifferent year for buffalo, goats, dogs, and monkeys.

11 In the year of the dog Although you feel very defensive, don't be too pessimistic as there is a great deal of idealism and generosity around. A good year for rats, dragons, dogs, and pigs; a bad year for buffalo, snakes, goats, and roosters; an indifferent year for tigers, rabbits, horses, and monkeys.

12 In the year of the pig Enjoy yourself, as there is enough of everything for everyone, and plenty to spare. Especially good for intellectuals and anyone setting out to make money. A good year for rats, tigers, rabbits, dragons, horses, monkeys, and pigs; a bad year for no-one; an indifferent year for buffalo, snakes, goats, roosters, and dogs.

Oriental astrology 2

Rat

A charming but aggressive opportunist. Clever, elegant, light-hearted, and sentimental. A gossip who needs company, a grumbler who can be a constructive critic. A bargain-hunter who hoards for the future and who is frightened of failure.
Compatible with the dragon, buffalo, and monkey; incompatible with the rabbit and horse.

Buffalo

A velvet hand in an iron glove – an affectionate, introspective idealist hiding behind a down-to-earth, authoritarian exterior. Placid and patient, but when roused the iron glove becomes a dangerous fist. A clever, original, and methodical mind hiding behind a conventional facade. A trustworthy, possessive conservative who can become prosperous only through hard work.
Compatible with the rooster, rat, and snake; incompatible with the monkey, goat, and tiger.

Tiger

A magnetic, respected leader whose stubbornness can lead to trouble. A rash, rebellious hothead who is also sensitive, introspective, and intensely emotional. Critical, quarrelsome, passionate, protective, lacking trust in others, and sometimes very indecisive. Capable of both petty meanness and grand, generous gestures.
Compatible with the horse, dragon, or dog; incompatible with the snake, monkey, buffalo, and rabbit.

Rabbit

A warm, affectionate friend who is clever, contented, and peace-loving. A bit of a show-off who enjoys company and entertains with traditional and generous hospitality. Sympathetic and sentimental, proud and condescending, cautious and industrious, apparently mysterious but sometimes superficial.
Compatible with the goat, dog, and pig; incompatible with the rat, tiger, and rooster.

Dragon

A gifted, generous, tactless, tenacious, demanding perfectionist who does everything (including the wrong things) very thoroughly. Honest, proud, enthusiastic, healthy, and energetic, an idealist who is always successful. A lover of show and spectacle whose apparent air of superiority hides a deep-down discontent.
Compatible with the rat, snake, rooster, and monkey; incompatible with the dog and buffalo.

Snake

An elegant, attractive, self-critical philosopher who can be a good-natured snob. An amusing, sentimental, romantic flirt who can be decisive and determined. Wise and intuitive, lazy and cautious, slow to anger but a bad loser when crossed. Possessive, lucky with money, and inclined to help in kind rather than in cash. A tendency to exaggeration and ostentation.
Compatible with the rooster, buffalo, dragon, and dog; incompatible with the tiger and pig.

Horse

A popular extrovert who can succeed at almost anything when at the center of attention. Quick-witted and cunning, attractive and healthy, loving crowds and flattery – a born politician. An impatient, intemperate egotist who lacks self-confidence, will never listen to advice, and who would give up everything for love. A fire horse carries these tendencies to extremes, and can burn out from excess.
Compatible with the goat, dog, tiger, and rooster; incompatible with the rat, monkey, buffalo, and pig.

Monkey

An intelligent, amusing, exuberant egotist, apparently friendly but in fact contemptuous. A vain, unscrupulous opportunist, inventive and curious, with a good memory. Independent, ambitious, successful, and good with money. Enthusiastic initially but easily bored, preferring infatuation to love.
Compatible with the dragon, rat, and goat; incompatible with the tiger, horse, and pig.

Dog

A shy, stubborn, introverted worrier, a cynical pessimist who becomes engrossed in details, ignoring the larger picture. A loyal, honest, reliable, courageous idealist with a strong sense of justice. Intelligent but inarticulate, antisocial but a good listener, discreet, dependable, and inspiring confidence. A hard worker, generous, but not good with money.
Compatible with the horse, tiger, and rabbit; incompatible with the dragon and goat.

Goat

A graceful, creative hedonist, happiest when supported by others who will bear all responsibility. A weak-willed duplicitous worrier who craves security, and is often the helpless center of attention. Lacks any sense of time, any self-control, and any respect for anyone else's property. Tends to assume that the grass must always be greener on the other side of every fence, and so is frequently discontented.
Compatible with the horse, pig, rabbit, and monkey; incompatible with the buffalo and dog.

Rooster

A popular, creative daydreamer who likes people but needs occasional solitude, who dislikes routine but works well under pressure. A frank advice-giver, leading a very up-and-down life, who loves and needs to be praised. Extravagant and self-satisfied, a boaster who undertakes too much but sometimes succeeds beyond all expectations.
Compatible with the buffalo, snake, horse, dragon, dog, and rat; incompatible with the rabbit and other roosters.

Pig

A transparently honest and trusting pacifist, innocent, gullible, and easily taken advantage of. Gallant and courteous, stubborn, scrupulous, and uncompromising, a loyal friend. Neither competitive nor good with money, but occasionally becoming rich. A sad and sensitive sensualist, an intellectual who reads indiscriminately.
Compatible with the rabbit and dragon; incompatible with the goat and snake.

METHODS OF PREDICTING

This list will enable you to find the main entries for all the methods of predicting your future described in this book. Each method is listed under its proper name; some are additionally listed under the agent used in the divinatory process.

NOTES

NOTES

NOTES

NOTES

NOTES

NOTES

NOTES

NOTES